Community Corrections

A Community
Field Approach

HV
9304
.C672
1990
West

David E. Duffee
State University of New York at Albany

Edmund F. McGarrell
Indiana University

anderson publishing co.
2035 reading road
cincinnati, ohio 45202
(513) 421-4142

COMMUNITY CORRECTIONS A Community Field Approach

Copyright © 1990 by Anderson Publishing Co., Cincinnati, OH

ISBN 0-87084-210-2
Library of Congress Catalog Number 89-80505

Kelly Humble *Managing Editor*

Cover Design by John H. Walker

Table of Contents

PREFACE

The initial ideas for this book were first outlined in 1976, while David Duffee was teaching in the Division of Community Development at the Pennsylvania State University. Duffee and several colleagues had been working on the theoretical aspects of an evaluation project for the Pennsylvania Bureau of Corrections. One of the most frustrating problems they encountered was that the community corrections literature of the time provided little guidance in their efforts to conceptualize the relationship of the halfway houses they were studying to the communities in which the houses were located. They turned up only a handful of research notes in which the variations among communities and the impacts of those variations on the correctional organizations were even acknowledged. Most of the literature provided a great deal of detail about the internal process of correctional programs, but little detail about how correctional programs fit or failed to fit into communities.

The textbook literature was even more disappointing and less useful than the research literature. Often the textbooks defined community corrections simply by providing a list of the types of correctional programs that the author was going to cover. The list in one text rarely matched the lists in the others, apparently because each author had his or her own favorite correctional programs. In these books the notion of community was never treated systematically. Students tended to accept the very simplistic and often misleading idea that community corrections programs were all correctional programs except those behind prison walls.

These deficiencies with the research and textbook literature in community corrections led Duffee and his colleagues, on several occasions, to outline a book that would integrate community theory with correctional research. Each attempt seemed to stall in mid-project, however. Then in 1986, Ed McGarrell completed his dissertation on the wavering policies in New York toward the imprisonment and deinstitutionalization of youths. A number of his ideas built on Duffee's earlier thoughts about the community-organizational connections important to corrections. The two of them finally egged each other into the completion of the volume.

Although the basic model presented in Chapter 1 of this book, and some of the other chapter notes, is several years old, the objectives in this volume are as topical now as when the ideas were initially outlined. The research literature in community corrections has improved, but the textbook coverage of the topic remains insufficient. We have sought to collect original community corrections research that deals with the integration of corrections and community, and present it in a form that would be useful to both researchers and students. Our chief concern is the systematic examination of the connections between various community settings and various community correctional programs. The general thesis is that community structure is comprised largely of interacting organizational forces and that the location of community correctional programs among those organizational forces will shape, to a large degree, the internal nature of the correctional program. However, we also see these community forces as dynamic, shifting forces, not static ones. Changes in those forces can make a long-struggling correctional program suddenly take off or can make a program with a long history of success suddenly have trouble. Moreover, under certain circumstances, the organizational forces of the correctional program itself can be responsible for significant change in communities.

We have examined these community/organization connections from three different but related perspectives. In Part One, we present three different views of correctional programs *as part* of community structure. A major objective here is to dispel the old idea that correctional programs and communities exist in some sort of "we-they" juxtaposition. Communities are sets of organizations in interaction. Correctional organizations are part of that community structure. But that structure varies, and the type of correctional organization varies. Those variations are patterned and have some predictable results. In Part Two, we present three studies of the internal technology of correctional organizations in different community settings. All three of these chapters demonstrate that correctional programs are shaped, in part, by their environment (e.g. budgetary constraints, cultural values, richness of human services in an area) and that the correctional program in turn tries different ways of connecting the correctional client to the community. Finally, in Part Three, we provide three research studies of community correctional programs undergoing change. One of the chapters studies policy change, the next examines program officials' perceptions of program characteristics, and the last compares officials' perceptions of effects to actual results. The three parts of the book are preceded by a conceptual overview of the community interaction approach in Chapter One.

Except for Chapter 1, each chapter is a case study or comparative case study of actual programs in operation. In some cases, the researchers were able to quantify some of their observations. In others, the authors have relied on qualitative approaches such as participant observation. All the cases are rich in descriptive detail, but each chapter also shares with the others a common conceptual scheme that seeks to blend community and organizational variables with correctional program issues. While this community interaction approach is not as yet developed enough to be a theoretical framework, we think that these chapters demonstrate its potential both as a means of developing systematic research and as a means of systematically studying the important community corrections issues in the classroom.

David E. Duffee
Edmund F. McGarrell

Chapter 1

Community Corrections: Its Presumed Characteristics and an Argument for a New Approach

David E. Duffee

The term "community corrections" would seem to imply that there is another form of criminal punishment that is not community corrections. But what is not community corrections? A newspaper editor once joked that the conservative mayor of an eastern city would have been happy to place an electric chair in the middle of the city football stadium and charge admission to Sunday afternoon executions. Would that have been community corrections? Was the public humiliation inflicted in Hawthorne's *The Scarlet Letter* an example of community corrections? Is a jail a community corrections facility? No, because it is an institution, or yes, because it is generally run by local government? For that matter, is not a state correctional institution located in *some* community, performing correctional functions for many communities, and paid for by all communities in a state? Why is it not considered a community correctional program?

The above questions should indicate the difficulty, and perhaps the meaninglessness, of fashioning a final definition of community corrections or of trying to decide what is or is not community corrections. One immediately apparent problem is that there are several different ways of conceptualizing the relationship between corrections and the community. We can talk about corrections *for* the community, as in taking a function away from a locality: a state prison is used by and paid for by communities but is operated by a state agency, usually in a locality far from the ones most often using it. We can talk about corrections *in* the community, as in placing an offender in a community: federal

1

probation supervises offenders in communities, although it is a federal organization making the placement and providing the supervision. We can talk about corrections *by* the community, as in a local community (or perhaps a county) making decisions about policy and financing of correctional programs. We can also talk about corrections *of* the community, as in altering job opportunities, initiating crime prevention programs, or making human services more accessible. Definitions of community corrections would vary considerably depending on which of these aspects are to be considered.

While it may be difficult to derive an authoritative definition of community corrections, it is important to understand that simple definitions are becoming increasingly more difficult to sustain. What is parole, if there is a frequent use of detention in the parole supervision process? Is the parolee in a community corrections program when on the streets and in an institutional program when detained, even if parole supervision continues? Is a jail sentence a non-community sentence if a portion of the jail time is served on work release? Is a probation term still a community sentence when the first six months of probation are to be served in jail? If there is a prison without walls in which all prisoners work in the city by day and return only to sleep at night; and, nearby, there is a half-way house for drug addicts in which none of the clients leave the premises for the first six months of their residency, which of these facilities is a community corrections effort? Changes in sentencing practice, changes in prison policy, and changes in probation and parole supervision have blurred considerably what may once have been a clear line between community and non-community corrections. If the institutional wall was once sufficient definitional clarity, it is no longer the case. Also, our understanding of community as a social and political entity has grown considerably in the last twenty years, to the point that talking about "the community" is no longer acceptable. Communities differ widely from each other on dimensions that are understandable and measurable. These differences can have significant impact on the likelihood that a correctional program can be established or on the quality of life that two parolees, living in different parts of the same town, will experience. Thus, our understanding and treatment of community corrections as a field of study and practice needs re-examination now.

The Characteristics of Community Corrections

Perhaps community corrections is such a fuzzy concept, suffering such accidental inclusions and exclusions, that it simply does not denote anything systematically or uniformly. Perhaps a probation chief in San Francisco and a probation chief in rural South Dakota simply share no common problems or practices. Consequently calling them both community correctional officials will not organize any body of knowledge helpful to both. Likewise, maybe communities vary so widely from one to another that one may indeed be galvanized to action while in another area the suggestion of collective, communal action is meaningless. While it may not be beneficial to seek a final definition of either *community* or *community corrections,* it may be quite helpful to become more specific with both of these terms in order to understand who may share problems in common with others.

One way to become more specific is to examine some of the characteristics of community corrections. This will, at least, more clearly define the separate concerns being expressed, why, perhaps, they do not fit together, and how they might be regrouped. Among the characteristics ascribed to community corrections, seven appear relatively common. It is often claimed that:

(1) Community corrections is innovative. Sometimes *innovative* simply seems to mean that community corrections is newer than the alternatives contrasted with it, but at other times people seem to mean that community programs are more adaptable, flexible or effective in solving problems.

(2) Service provision to offenders in community corrections programs will reduce crime. Sometimes "resources" are mentioned rather than services.

(3) Community corrections programs can or should change the relationship between the offender and the community, although the community remains undefined in this claim and thus no real study of a changing relationship seems to have been possible.

(4) Community corrections requires local effort and the development of a local constituency for corrections. Often this takes the form of exhortations to an apparently unwilling community to expend that effort. Alternatively, there is some mention of state and federal authorities manipulating local groups to act, but often with no attention to how this behavior can be viewed as local community action.

(5) Community corrections avoids the use of institutions, with a rare and uncomfortable acknowledgment that prisons are paid for by communities and seem to serve community functions, or that some communities appear to desire institutional rather than non-institutional correctional programs.

(6) More recently, community corrections endeavors have significant sanction value, or are compatible with the demand for retribution, and may be quite useful if we are concerned with restitution.

(7) Community corrections programs provide us with greater diversity in correctional options than is possible in "non-community" settings, and that part of this diversity is brought about by the increased competition observed in community corrections.

The Claim of Innovation

Except for the notion of community itself, *innovation* may be the most ambiguous characteristic of those claimed for community correction. It is simply not clear how to determine if an agency or program is innovative. However, a typology dealing with the degree of social change introduced by a program may enable us to make a preliminary assessment of the extent to which community correction represents anything new.

Roland Warren, Stephen Rose and Ann Bergunder (1974), in their analysis of community interorganizational structure, use three categories of change to assess the significance of innovations introduced by anti-poverty programs. Their first category is *gross change*, which is the most common and least significant. Gross change, to these authors, represents the daily, superficial changes that all organizations engage in, sometimes with much hoopla, but often without much thought or planning. Their examples include simple changes in nomenclature and minor improvements in upgrading facilities or manpower. In corrections, one might consider, as examples of gross change, setting standards for probation or parole caseload size, hiring a few ex-offenders, or altering the standard probation supervision conditions.

The second category of innovation identified by Warren, Rose, and Bergunder is one they call *secondary change*. This level of change includes no fundamental shifts in definitions of social problems, or in the agency means of addressing them, but does include significant shifts in access to or the quality of services. In Warren's words, secondary change is change in the existing system rather than change *of* the system. A couple of correctional innovations serve as illustrations.

In the process of implementing a new security/risk classification system called "performance screening," the Michigan Department of Corrections altered the proportion of inmates receiving community pre-release placements from 0 to 40 percent of all inmates released to parole (see Chapter 7). This shift has meant that about 2,000 persons a year are already in the community, in jobs or going to school, before parole commences. According to Warren and his colleagues, this program expansion could be seen as a secondary change, as it required no change in the correctional process or status of inmates, but it did drastically increase one resource for a client population within the existing system.

Another good example of secondary change in community corrections is the relatively new focus on community resources in probation and parole work. One form of this change, called "behavioral objectives" by Clear and O'Leary (1983), involves the specification of particular client problems, the development of planned actions to be completed by both the offender and the correctional supervisor, and the development of community resources better to achieve client objectives. Behavioral objectives has become a new form of probation and parole organization, coupled with a new information system, which makes probation and parole activity more accountable, if not more effective. Among its objectives are to evaluate officer behaviors and the community human resource supply. This change in organization does not alter the objectives of probation and parole supervision. One could argue that the same kinds of services are supplied as would be the case in traditional probation and parole organization. However, behavioral objectives aim to improve the quality and quantity of service rendered. As such, it may be a significant improvement in the existing system, or a secondary change.

The third level of innovation, according to Warren, Rose, and Bergunder, is *primary change*. By this, these researchers mean alterations in the paradigm by which social problems are defined and services are rendered. One could argue that there are three paradigms in regard to corrections. (1) The sickness paradigm argues that criminals are psychologically or socially inadequate to function in society and that crime is a symptom of individual pathology. Actions implied are usually some kind of therapy. The sinfulness paradigm argues that criminals and non-criminals alike are rational, but that criminals have chosen to be bad. The action taken is punishment, to make the criminal pay the consequences of the wicked choice. Leslie Wilkins (1965), among others, would argue that sickness/sinfulness are interchangeable paradigms because both have the consequence of prescribing control over the individual. (2) Another paradigm, arguably, sees crime as coping behavior. Persons commit crimes in order to solve problems. The action suggested is the provision of services or resources which make criminal behavior less attractive than the legal alternatives for solving problems. This action may require changing the situation or the groups around the offender, or altering the opportunities available, or altering the offender's skills and knowledge so that he can take advantage of the existing opportunities. (3) Finally, some would argue that much crime is evidence of class conflict. Laws are written to protect the property interests of the powerful and to defuse the political aspirations of the less powerful by describing their behavior as criminal. The action implied is revolution, to do away with the economic hierarchy of the present society. The action would, presumably, do away with the need for large correctional agencies.

If there were to be any primary changes in corrections, they would require, according to Warren and associates, shifts in paradigm for the justification and organization of correctional programs. If so, then primary change in community corrections would seem quite rare indeed. Perhaps the shift in Massachusetts from a training school to a group home and non-residential set of programs for handling juveniles, is the closest we can come to an example of paradigm shift in corrections. As described by Miller, Ohlin and Coates (1978), under the guidance of Jerome Miller, the Massachusetts system shifted from adherence to a sickness/ sinfulness paradigm to an inadequate opportunity, or crime-as-coping-behavior, paradigm. This change in philosophy, program, and staffing can therefore be seen as a primary change. Similarly, were one to implement Graeme Newman's corporal punishment scheme (1983) somewhere, it could be considered a primary change.

One could argue that simply clarifying correctional objectives, whatever they might be, could be considered primary change, because it would represent the development of a clear paradigm where no single paradigm has heretofore been controlling (see Gottfredson and Gottfredson, 1980). Such clarity, however, seems an unlikely development. It is probably accurate to describe most correctional programs as adhering to an admixture of the sickness/ sinfulness and coping behavior paradigms,in various and shifting degrees. Miller, Ohlin and Coates (1978) argue that the shifts are likely to continue, cyclicly, for years. If so, it is arguable that few changes in corrections could reach primary proportions, and while community corrections has often been billed as new, the degree of change involved is doubtful. While it is arguable that paradigm shifts in corrections have occurred in the past, equally significant shifts in the near future seem remote, unless it may be the shift back to a sinfulness paradigm, without any vestiges of the sickness or inadequate opportunity paradigms. Shifts towards an economically radical interpretation of crime would not be adopted without vast overhaul in the political system which the correctional apparatus supports (van den Haag, 1975:44-46).

Community corrections changes, then, can be expected to be gross or secondary in nature. But more importantly, for the assessment of community corrections, such changes in community corrections are inaccurately contrasted with the degree of innovation occurring in institutional corrections. For example, the important secondary change in pre-release program availability in the Michigan system was either a consequence of, or part of, innovation in classification procedures in the entire prison system. Likewise, the increases in equity of sentencing have affected prisons and parole alike, and in some states are also being built into probation decision-making and bail reform. In summary, it does not seem likely that community corrections is more innovative than non-community corrections, because degrees of custody, and shifts from liberal to conservative programming and back again, tend to occur throughout the correctional system in relatively synchronized fashion. Consequently, degree of innovation may be an important characteristic of any correctional program but probably does not enable us to distinguish community corrections from any other form corrections might take. Persons interested in innovation can probably learn as much from innovations in maximum security prisons as from innovation in parole or probation work, and may do well to study or practice both at the same time.

The Claim of Service Provision

There are only a few studies which examine whether community correctional programs actually provide more, or more effective, services than the offender would have received in prison, or on his own. There are also some studies of varying quality which attempt to investigate whether community correctional programs have an impact on recidivism. But it is rare indeed to find studies directly examining the claim that service provision reduces recidivism. However, that is precisely the claim made for many community programs.

Attention to the specification of services began relatively recently in corrections. Until the late 1960s, many correctional staff considered any sort of interaction with offenders to be helpful (probably because it was intended to be helpful), regardless of whether a problem requiring attention had actually been identified and without concern for how the service was presumably linked to the problem. Studt (1972) argued, for example, that California parole routines were relatively well developed when it came to surveillance, but sophomoric when it came to rendering assistance. Parole officers, she observed, were committed to a generalized, and often paternalistic, concern for care and nurturance of parolees, but spent little time considering how assistance was best rendered or when it was most willingly received. She argued that a true commitment to services required reference to particular conditions that needed changing or particular problems that needed remedy, coupled with specific actions designed to meet articulable objectives.

One of the earliest harbingers of correctional programming that would link problems with ameliorative actions was the work by Douglas T. Grant and Marguerite Grant (Warren). These two researchers strove to identify a client's interpersonal maturity level (problem/condition) and link it to particular intervention strategies (including type of program, or kind of service, and supervision style of staff). While the numerous correctional projects using Interpersonal Maturity Level have yielded mixed results (Grant and Grant, 1959; Warren, 1967; Lerman, 1975; Gottfredson, 1981), partly because the specified supervision strategies were not always adhered to (Lerman, 1975), this hard-nosed attention to specifying differential treatments, has, along with Studt's work, finally established the need to examine what services have what results with whom. Thus, it was not until the last dozen years that correctional research began to catalogue, systematically, specific problems encountered by offenders and particular actions taken by them or others to ameliorate the situation (Studt, 1972; Briggs, 1978; Clear and O'Leary, 1984; and Duffee and Duffee, 1981; Jester in this volume).

With our state of knowledge about services in its infancy, the claim that community corrections reduces recidivism by providing services can only be rhetoric or wishful thinking. The few existing studies which do focus on service provision and recidivism leave us with ambiguous information. Rossi, Berk, and Lenihan (1980) studied the relationships among provision of job-location service, provision of income maintenance payments, and ex-inmate return to crime. Their large samples in two different states and their sophisticated analytical design yielded results which would make any policymaker cringe: the employment service appeared ineffective, while provision of money had a direct negative effect on property crime but an indirect positive effect on property crime by increasing idleness.

An interesting study by Lichtman and Smock (1981) evaluated intensive supervision probation (ISP) caseloads to determine whether ISP increased the numbers of services received by probationers and whether the services rendered reduced probationer recidivism. Perhaps their most useful finding was that the ISP clients received only slightly more, and on occasion slightly different, services than regular caseload probationers, because the regular clients (controls) sought (on their own) the same types of services obtained by the ISP cases through probation officer referrals. Probationers may not need officer intervention in order to obtain available community services. These authors also found recidivism rates to be nearly identical for probationers under both kinds of supervision. Unfortunately, they could not tell us whether it was the persons receiving or not receiving services in either group that failed. Moreover, they provided no information about the effectiveness of the services received in solving the problems which generated the service attempt.

A couple of other studies are suggestive, if not exactly on point. A General Accounting Office (1976) evaluation of local probation in four widely dispersed counties in the United States found that probationers who received two or more referrals successfully completed their probation period more often than probationers who did not. However, there were no controls in this study for type of offender referred or not. Thus we do not know if it was the referral that was explanatory, or whether some other characteristic of offender (or staff) caused both the differential in referral rates and in success rates. In a Canadian study of parolees and mandatory releasees, Waller (1979) identified five situational or "dynamic" post-release variables which were significantly associated with success after prison release. These five variables were *fighting, seeing children or not, length of time employed in twelve months after release, undesirable associates,* and *regular drinking.* There is no indication, however, whether there are any services which can be linked to these conditions or problems so that parole officers could influence their occurrence.

In summary, it would seem that we simply do not know whether community corrections programs make available to their clients more, or more effective, services than they would receive without the program. Nor do we know whether rendering effective service has an impact on recidivism. Moreover, there are no data to indicate that prisoners receive less or different services than persons not in prison. A number of commentators would denigrate the amount of supervision, let alone service, that overworked, undersupported probation or parole officers can provide to anyone (e.g., Stanley, 1976). But there are the same complaints about prisons (Toch, 1977). There is some evidence that intensive programs, whether they occur in prison or in some other setting, provide the time and resources for more accurate problem identification, and thus occasionally for service provision (Toch, 1981; Duffee, Meyer and Warner, 1977, but see also the conflicts among services discussed by McEwen, 1978). But intense, high staff-to-offender ratios can occur in either residential or non-residential settings and thus do not allow us to characterize community corrections as something special. There is similar evidence that systematic assessments of needs or problems may be used better to identify problems, but this kind of information system can be instituted in either non-residential (Clear and O'Leary, 1983) or residential (Jenkins, et al., 1973; Wright, 1985) programs.

A concern for access to, and effectiveness of, services for offenders would certainly appear to be an appropriate priority for correctional staff, whether they run prisons, other residential programs, or non-residential correctional options. Again, there would appear to be no empirical support, to date, for the claim that community corrections provides more, or more effective, services than are available in prison. The objective of meeting offenders' needs would seem to cut across all kinds of correctional programs rather than serve as a basis for distinguishing one kind of program from another.

The claim that provision of services reduces recidivism would seem to be a premature and perhaps dangerous contention for any correctional program to make. The data simply do not exist. The claim, however, is remarkably close in its aspiration and its content to the broad recidivism reduction claims made in the name of rehabilitation. For those earlier claims, Martinson (1974) could find no support, helping to lead the return to a "get tough," punitive philosophy. To justify services on a similar promise to reduce criminal behavior, is, according to some people, an unethical position. Fogel (1975) argues that services should be provided only to those persons who want them and that offender status should never be used in determining eligibility for services.

The Claim for Changing the Relationship of the Offender and the Community

In a large measure, the emphasis on specific services and the concern for changing the relationship between the offender and the community are the same. The concern for increasing access to services and access to resources or opportunities arose with a change in ideologies in the 1960s. The sickness/sinfulness paradigm was partially replaced by one emphasizing alterations in situations rather than people. The reintegration policy arose as a new form of correctional supervision (O'Leary and Duffee, 1971; Studt, 1973; Hahn, 1975; but see Conrad, 1973).

Perhaps the best contrast between rehabilitation and reintegration, as it would apply to community supervision, was provided by Studt's study of parole supervision relationships (1972). Studt reported observing four kinds of relationship between parole officers and parolees in her study of California parole practices. One of these, the prosecutor/defendant relationship, was typically reserved for "escalation episodes" after the officer discovered the parolee was not being honest or consistent and sought to build a case for revocation. Another relationship, which Studt called the "superior/subordinate" relationship, involved little active supervision. Parolees in the relationship acted like subordinates requesting permission, advice, or information from their supervisors, the parole agents. Agents spent little time on the street and instead spent their time responding (bureaucratically) to requests and building a record about the behavior of their subordinates. Another relationship, the "guardian/ward" relationship, involved the parole officer acting as a concerned adult protecting and guiding the parolee who acted the role of less mature, less competent person in need of support. This, said Studt, was the relationship most often preferred by the officers, although not by the offender. Because of its paternalistic tone, with the assumptions of the offender's inferiority, this relationship was not structured to alter a parolee's access to resources. The officer was more likely to coach the client rather than actively intervene, and to stress attitude and commitment rather than specific behaviors.

Studt argues that only the fourth observed relationship, the "insider/outsider" relationship, was structured to alter access to services. In this relationship, the officer acts as gatekeeper to opportunities and uses his skills and knowledge to link the parolee to needed services. The parolee, in turn, acts as an outsider desiring membership in the community. It was this relationship, of the four, which the parolees preferred, because they saw it as the most helpful. However, Studt also noted several problems with the maintenance of this relationship as the basis for parole supervision. She commented that most often the officer and parolee did *not* belong to the same community, and very often the officer was not seen by service providers as a legitimate gatekeeper. Also, the officers were often unaware of the services and resources which they posed as providing access to.

Studt proposed that the insider/outsider relationship, shorn of its problems, would give substance to the policy of reintegration (1973). To some extent, these problems have been mitigated in the last dozen years, and the technology supportive of that relationship has been articulated (Dell'Apa et al., 1976; Clear and O'Leary, 1983). But research evaluating the implementation of this technology still indicates some problems, as well as some guidelines for continued refinement.

Perhaps the most interesting recent study on the implementation of a reintegration program is Alden Miller and Lloyd Ohlin's (1985) follow-up on the new, non-residential programs emerging in Massachusetts after closure of the training schools for juveniles. The first stage of their research focused on the opportunities perceived to be available by youths in school, youths adjudicated delinquent and participating in the new programs, and youths on the street. Miller and Ohlin discovered that while both delinquent and non-delinquent youths agreed on what kinds of activities were desirable, they disagreed markedly on their perception of what kinds of activities were actually available. The delinquents reported that many of the legitimate behaviors which they desired to engage in were not possible, while the non-delinquents reported lack of access to or lack of knowledge about the illegitimate activities which they found attractive. More important, these researchers discovered that the "social control" staff members in these communities were not sufficiently cognizant of the perceived opportunity structure. They preferred to supervise by "coaching" the youth about appropriate preferences, despite the fact that the attitudes of delinquents and non-delinquents were not very different.

In a related study, Duffee and Warner (1980) explored the correlations of the degree to which twelve halfway houses were able to solve the material and economic problems of their clients. They discovered significant variation in the extent to which the halfway house staff actively participated in the human service network of the community and that the houses with the more formalized and regularized links to service agencies had higher problem resolution rates. While it was the goal of all twelve houses to "reintegrate" the offender into a specific community, some house staff members spent much more time and effort providing access to services, or worked in more tolerant service agency environments, than did other house staff members. In the houses where the external service linkages were not so strong, more time was devoted to counseling, or to controlling the offender.

Finally, Jacobs, (1976) reported on the remarkable, and for community corrections proponents cautionary, success story of the relationship between the Vienna Correctional Center (VCC) and the town of Vienna, Illinois. Jacobs concluded that the success of VCC in developing and sustaining both a humane prison environment and a high degree of prison programming was due to the close and functional ties between the prison and the community. Almost all the community social functions were carried out with participation of, and dependence on, the prison staff and inmates. The town benefited economically, socially, and physically, while the reciprocal correctional benefit was the openness of the prison. Jacobs asserts that such relationships may be more feasible between prisons and small communities than between community correctional programs and large urban centers, which are less likely to be affected positively by any contributions the programs can make to the social ecology of the area. Jacobs seems to say that community correctional programs are simply neither large enough nor rich enough to provide to their clients that same access to services and resources that VCC can make available to its inmates. Gatekeeping requires clout, and many community programs do not have it.

These and similar studies (Stanley, 1976; McCleary 1978) would suggest that the claim for changing the relationship of the offender and the community is a relatively complex one, difficult to analyze or to assess. Most commentators, however, would agree that simply placing the offender in a community does not automatically imply that that person will enjoy a more supportive relationship with the community than before such placement. Some styles of supervision and some program objectives may, in fact, act to reduce an offender's access to opportunities (McEwen, 1978), while others are simply not relevant. Some communities simply have few resources for the offender, or anyone else to draw upon (Scull, 1977; Thomson, McAnany and Fogel, 1982). Other communities will not readily admit the offender or the correctional agency to the existing human service network. Coates, Miller and Ohlin (1978) suggest that many non-residential programs foster more normal human relationships than is true of closed institutions, but this assertion must be tempered by Miller and Ohlin's later finding that many non-residential programs do not provide greater access to services and resources, and Jacob's observations that some prisons, at least, may forge very favorable linkages with their surrounding communities.

In conclusion, the claim that community corrections changes the relationship of the offender to the community is an overgeneralization, or overly vague. We must know more about what aspects of the community vis-à-vis the offender are to be changed, and we also need to pay special attention to the kind of supervision technology which the correctional program employs before asserting that changes are taking place. Lastly, it is important to remember that not all parts of community have advantages, for offenders or other citizens.

The Claim of Avoiding Use of Institutions

The claim that use of community correctional programs avoids use of institutions is perhaps the most common and sensible claim made for such programs. After all, isn't a person on probation or in a halfway house *not* in an institution? But as with many other declarations of fact in criminal justice, this one, too, becomes more ambiguous as it is examined more closely. Most

community corrections programs are simply not designed specifically to avoid use of institutions. Since 1974, probation and parole,
among other community caseloads, have risen, but the rate of
incarceration has climbed even faster. Community programs do
not mean less use of incarceration unless there is some mechanism
by which to control prison population during the allocation of
community program resources. This would entail, among other
things, the utilization of guidelines for the placement of offenders
so that those possessing characteristics which would normally
imply incarceration are transferred to a non-institutional setting,
and the prison space set aside for those persons is not filled with
other offenders. Generally, this does not happen.

The complexity and ambiguity in determining whether the
development of a community program reduces incarceration rates
can perhaps best be seen through an example. One program which
is, according to some, specifically designed to reduce use of state
prisons, is the Minnesota Community Corrections Act (Blackmore,
1978). This legislation permits a county or collection of counties
which forms a Community Corrections Advisory Board to formulate a plan for dealing with offenders at the local level, and have
that plan approved by the State Department of Corrections, to
receive state funds for the operation of the local program. Funding
is based, in part, on a jurisdiction's baseline incarceration rate,
which is not to be exceeded. Costs of offenders sentenced to less
than five years, but sent to the state, are charged to the committing
county. Consequently, the fiscal soundness of the local correctional
program is tied to a county not exceeding its allotted number of
state commitments.

Richard Ku's (1980) analysis of the implementation of the Act
suggests that commitments to state prisons increased, but probably in spite of the Act rather than because of it. The Act was
instituted at precisely that time when incarcerative sentences
became more popular all over the country. He concludes that the
Act may have kept down the increase in incarceration.

However, in addition to Minnesota's state prison population
not dropping, the most frequently utilized option within the local
community corrections jurisdictions happened to be the local
jail. Persons have speculated that the increased funding to local
corrections has had the consequences of improving local jail facili-

ties and making judges more willing to use them (Blackmore, 1978). Another possibility is that judges are willing to cooperate with the plan to the extent of limiting state commitments, but are using local institutions rather than local non-institutional sentencing options.

Has this legislation actually been avoiding use of institutions? No one has a definitive answer, partly because many factors influencing incarceration rates changed, along with the Act, so that it is difficult to know the exact influence of the Act itself. Part of the answer depends on the cloudy definition of "community corrections" or "institution." While the Minnesota legislation is called a "Community Corrections" Act, the county or regional jail has played a central role in most of the participating counties. If one makes local/state distinctions, it appears that the Act has increased the attention to and coherence of local corrections (albeit with a financial prod from the state). However, one cannot claim unequivocally that emergence of this community program has reduced use of incarceration. It has, instead, shifted responsibilities for the carrying out of many punishments from state to local agencies.

Many other community programs do not even come as close as Minnesota's approach to reducing incarceration. Many programs billed as diversions from institutions suffer from the "net widening" phenomenon identified by Klein (1979) and Austin and Krisberg (1981). Diversion programs (pre or post adjudication) often turn out to supervise persons who, in Klein's words, are not eligible for diversion (meaning they were not facing, prior to the "diversion" placement, a more severe sanction than the diversion itself). In many cases, diversion programs seem to attract persons who otherwise would have been let off with no supervision at all.

Surveying what they consider this sorry state of affairs, Austin and Krisberg conclude that community corrections programs, as well as many pre-conviction reforms, have been transformed from the intended purpose of narrowing social control to one of widening, strengthening and building new nets for greater social control. More conservative observers (and doubtless many prosecutors) may not view this transformation as negatively as Austin and Krisberg. One possible reply is that programs which establish some form of supervision between all-or-nothing options is a useful, humane development. Return to the street without any supervision may not be the best situation even in those instances where prison is inappropriate. But whichever stance one takes toward this phenomenon, one must agree that "alternatives to institutions" are perhaps more often "alternatives to doing nothing." Moreover, one must accept the Sherman and Hawkins (1981) caveat that no program is an alternative to prison, unless its use includes direct limitations on the use of incarceration. In most American jurisdictions, all correctional resources are used as if they were limitless, and increases in one are not correlated with decreases in the use of another.

The Claim for Sanction Value

One recent influential criticism of community corrections in general is that it depreciates the value of the crime committed. One theme in this attack is that community sanctions have not provided a sufficient specific or general deterrent effect: because community sentences are perceived as easy time, more crimes are committed. The other theme heard in this criticism is that community norms are not adequately upheld by community sentences: punishment has not been meted out to the guilty, or justice has not been done. Both sub-arguments, although philosophically distinguishable, would appear to imply the same consequences; both deterrence and retribution require harsher sentences than can be implemented in the community.

These two criticisms both seem to suffer from some of the same illusions that apparently distort the vision of some community corrections proponents. "Community corrections" is not a single entity. It is not possible to lump all community sanctions together. Each possible punishment must be compared to every other one in terms of length, distastefulness, and visibility. Doing so, however, is obviously problematic. Who is responsible for determining, according to the length of the jail sentence, how much probation time should be served, or which kinds of probation conditions make that sentence more or less harsh than something else? (For one interesting attempt at such comparisons, see Barry and Greer, 1981).

Despite these problems, the criticism that many community sentences, and in particular probation, are too soft, has had recent influence on the redesign of community sanctions to make them appear harsher. These attempts may be heading up a strong current. Sherman and Hawkins (1981) argue that early during the penitentiary movement America came to equate prison and punishment. This cultural analysis is supported by some survey research which found that the public overwhelmingly agreed that punishments are too easy on convicted offenders (Duffee and Ritti, 1977). This survey discovered that the public appears to treat retribution and rehabilitation as separate dimensions. The majority of the survey respondents favored *both* punishment and provision of services. They were not opposed to treatment programs unless the means of providing services was perceived to reduce the degree of punishment received. Consequently, work release as a punishment met with considerable ambivalence, since the program required letting convicted felons out of prison.

In response to perceived lenience or laxness, a number of community programs have altered conditions of supervision, have asked new activities of offenders, or have attempted to present new public images of community supervision. Some probation departments, for example, are stressing their function as surveillance agencies and have sought to strengthen their ties with the police (Nelson and Harlow, 1980; and Harlow and Nelson in this volume). The Division of Parole in New York claims that its primary mission is the protection of the public, rather than treatment of or services to parolees. In many states, probation has been coupled with jail time, in order to give lesser offenders a "taste of the bars" before they are released to probation supervision. In addition, the utilization of community service sentences has increased, so that offenders not incarcerated are (very visibly) put to work to pay for their crimes (Gettinger, 1983).

Perhaps the most promising of these changes is "intensive supervision" (Gettinger, 1983; Petersilia et al., 1985 and Petersilia, Turner, and Peterson, 1986). The extent to which intensive supervision is really different than regular probation depends, of course, on a specific agency definition of "intensive." Gettinger reports that some agencies see intensive clients twice a day, while others contact ISP clients only two or four times a month. To the extent that probation or other community sanctions have suffered from perceived leniency, intensive supervision at least attempts to deal with the problem by redefining security and risk without resorting to institutions (unlike split sentences). This development, along with community service (see Pease, 1985), seeks to promote the view that probation is an onerous intrusion on liberty and therefore a punishment which exacts sufficient pain to achieve either or both retribution and deterrence.

A somewhat different defense of community sentences as a sanction occurs with the emergence of the demand for restitution. Restitution may be a sole sanction, or a condition of probation or parole supervision. Whether restitution is a punishment is a matter of philosophical debate (Harland, 1982). However, many persons in favor of restitution argue that, by requiring work or financial recompense for damages done, both the victim (if there is one) and the public are more satisfied that justice has been served.

While restitution research is meager, one recent study reports juveniles sentenced to restitution as a sole sanction were less likely to recidivate than juveniles sentenced to restitution and other conditions (Schneider, Griffith, and Schneider, 1982). And Harland's research suggests that restitution is unlikely to occur, even if ordered, when someone is sentenced to prison, since the offender will usually lose the ability to repay a victim when he is sent to prison. Consequently, in some cases, the demand for retribution and the demand for restitution may be at odds, with the judge choosing to punish the severity of the crime with a prison sentence or allowing restitution by placing the offender on probation.

Unless community corrections program designers successfully break the link in American culture between punishment and prison, the responses to the demand for increased sanctioning value are likely further to blur the lines between community and non-community punishments. At this point, the split sentence is replacing straight probation as the favorite punishment. The claim that increasing sanction value can be accommodated in community corrections is debatable, and whether sanction severity can be augmented without reducing services is questionable. (For a number of recent recommendations relative to the quandary, see McAnany, Thomson and Fogel, 1984).

The Claim for Diversity and Competition

The sixth characteristic often claimed as a benefit of community corrections is that these programs offer more diversity than is available in institutions and that they increase competition among the organizations providing services or implementing punishments. More specifically, it is often asserted that (1) the addition of community programs increases the sanctioning repertoire available to a judge; (2) community correctional programs increase the types of services available for offenders and increase their access to opportunities; (3) community correctional programs increase the involvement of private vendors in the public business of punishment; (4) increased competition for contracts and the utilization of performance criteria in letting contracts to private vendors increases the quality of supervision; and (5) community programs decrease the cost of corrections in public dollars by utilizing the greater variety, flexibility and lower pay scales often available in the private sector. While each of these claims can be separately investigated, they are lumped together here because it is assumed that competition and diversity are closely related.

Diversity in correctional options has not received appropriate attention in correctional research, the leading project to date probably being Robert Coates, Alden Miller and Lloyd Ohlin's *Diversity in a Youth Correctional System* (1978). These researchers followed 500 youths through the new Massachusetts Department of Youth Services from reception in a detention center through six months after release to community living. Their basic conclusions were that the deinstitutionalized system was a viable option to secure institutions for juveniles, provided greater options in placements, with more programs tailored to the specific needs of individuals, and yielded recidivism rates no higher than those found in the previous secure system. Some, but not all, of these conclusions are relevant to adult corrections as well. Most difficult, of course, would be the feasibility of a system for adults which did not utilize incarceration to a great extent. In addition to the Massachusetts research, Toch (1977) has investigated "activity" and "social stimulation" as aspects of prison environments, and Moos (1974) has included questions concerning variety in a number of his environmental scales for use in both institutional and non-institutional programs.

Comparing these very different research projects, we see one important distinction concerning diversity when discussing community corrections. We need to separate the issue of diversity at the "macro" or "system" level from the issue of diversity as experienced by an individual. It is perfectly possible for a system which contains many different smaller programs and options (and therefore is characterized as diverse) to channel any one of its clients so that the individual experiences no diversity in setting at all (see Klofas and Duffee, 1981). Consequently when one asserts that community corrections increases the diversity in the correctional system, it is important to ask whether our interest is in diversity of the system or in diversity for the individual, or both. In addition, one may wish to ask, at the individual level, whether we are concerned with diversity in one point in time, or in one program, or whether we are interested in diversity over time. (Does the individual want/ need lots of different things *now*, or does he want/need a number of different experiences over the course of his correctional sentence?)

While both levels of diversity are important, none of the above-mentioned research suggests that community corrections programs are necessarily more diverse than institutional programs. In fact, a number of persons would suggest that larger organizations probably allow for more diversity within themselves than smaller programs, but this finding applies to both institutional systems and non-institutional systems. Both Coates, Miller and Ohlin and Moos make a strong case that some prisons or some secure youth facilities are more diverse and considerably less onerous than some group homes or non-residential programs. These researchers and Toch (1977) would stress that diversity should be a goal of management at the macro level to allow as close a match as possible at the individual level between the program setting and an individual's needs or problems. At the individual level, some persons need variety in their environment and some do not. A diverse system can include some settings which can address many needs at once and other settings which allow for stability and constancy.

Some important questions concerning diversity have yet to be addressed adequately. One of the most important questions is of concern at the individual level. What are the effects of mixing different sanctions and/or treatments at the same time? The few relevant findings (Schneider, Griffiths and Schneider, 1982; McClintock, Walker, and Savill, 1961) suggest that multiple sanctions often do not mix. More is not always better. Another research question of importance is whether an increase in sanctioning options actually is utilized by decision-makers, or whether they simply gravitate from an older preference to a newer one. For example, popularity of the split sentence has made it the preferred sentence in some jurisdictions, and older options have fallen into disuse. A related question would be the extent to which the decision-makers are actually free to use apparent options. Does a judge, for example, have more room to maneuver now than ten years ago, or do plea bargaining negotiations or public sentiment limit sentencing options? Finally, the claim for diversity must be assessed against the possibility that correctional programs are merely duplicating services available elsewhere. As Lichtman and Smock (1981) point out, the diversity in services supposedly made available by intensive supervision was already available to many traditional caseload probationers.

Turning to competition, we can see that another supposed distinction between community corrections and institutional corrections probably breaks down. It is generally suggested that community corrections increases competition because it may utilize private contractors for the provision of services. But American prisons have been utilizing private contractors, particularly in relation to industry, since they opened (Beaumont and Toqueville, 1964 edition). A good deal of competition was removed from prison industries under state use laws, but competition of other sorts can be instituted without involving the private sector, while its involvement does not necessarily generate either competition or quality. Indeed, one problem with private vendors supervising prison industry was that contracts were often based on the political power of the vendor or simply on tradition, rather than on performance (See Williamson, 1981 for a general statement of the problem with such contracts.)

At the present time, private involvement in corrections is on the increase, both in community programs, and in prison construction and prison management (Logan and Rausch, 1985). One tempting argument for the increase is that the private sector can often perform the work less expensively and more efficiently than the government.

The extent to which these new arrangements actually provide superior performance is partly dependent on the skill of public agencies in managing and monitoring contracts. This skill requires public correctional agencies to make significant shifts in staffing patterns, staff skills and staff responsibilities. Until those changes occur, we may not be able to assess whether competition has increased and whether it has led to greater quality of services.

Whether private involvement decreases cost is also a tricky question. Only one study (Meyer and Wayson, 1976) has examined this issue in any detail for community programs. The basic finding was that private involvement reallocates costs more than it reduces them. Since many private programs require work from offenders and also operate with many volunteers, the true cost of these programs would include the value of this labor. However, by "cheaper," most community corrections proponents usually seem to mean only that direct governmental expenditures may go down, as various community groups, rather than the government agency, bear the brunt of service delivery. We should also not forget that some community programs on a per diem basis turn out to be considerably *more* expensive than the institutional programs they are compared with (Lerman, 1975; Minnesota Governor's Commission on Crime Prevention and Control, 1976). However, the cost of many institutional programs is often underestimated (Minnesota Citizen's Council on Criminal Justice, 1983).

In summary, the characteristics of diversity and competition would appear to be of concern across *all* correctional settings. Researchers and practitioners would do well to heed the advice that "gold is where you find it." The generalization that community corrections offers more diversity or more competition than other correctional programs not only begs the question of what is community corrections, but may also force us to overlook some of the negative qualities of the diverse collection of programs championed under that misleading label.

The Claim for Local Participation

Most proponents of community correction declare that one particular advantage of such programs is their involvement "of the community." The involvement is seen as a correctional benefit because it is assumed that crime is largely explained by variables associated with the community in which crime was committed and that, consequently, the best chance of correcting the behavior of the individual criminal is also in the community of residence. However, of all the characteristics associated with community correction, this one may have received the least attention. Very often correctional research, planning, and program design concentrate on the content of correctional programs rather than on the investigation of how the program was initiated or how political and interorganizational forces shaped program development and program outcomes. We are left with vague and often ambivalent evidence of community involvement in correctional programming. This state of knowledge is unfortunate, since it would seem that relative involvement of community in corrections would be at the heart of what community corrections might actually mean.

The claim that community is involved in community corrections often turns out upon closer inspection to be an urgent plea for communities to be supportive of probation, parole, work release, halfway houses and the like, when apparently they are not. And oddly enough, some of the best known examples of community corrections, such as the California Community Treatment Project (Lerman, 1975), were operated in several different areas by a state agency emphasizing a strong degree of control over client intake, staffing, and program content. At other times, the claim for community involvement takes an odd but generally unnoticed twist: state government, or even federal government, initiates a policy of subsidy or regulation or both in order to stimulate activity at the local level. In these instances, commentators often praise the local activity, without questioning the role played by the centralized government in instigating that activity. Community corrections proponents do not seem to deal directly with the apparently anomalous situation that many local correctional agencies, left to their own devices, often do not innovate with program settings and often seem to prefer the utilization of institutional to non-institutional correctional measures. Finally, many correctional experts do not deal systematically with the observed variations across various localities in program support, resource allocation, and program content. That one parole jurisdiction does things differently than another, or that one proposed halfway house meets with stiff resistance while another is welcomed with open arms is too often dealt with by hand-waving and resort to magical terms such as "turf squabbles" or "political differences."

Such differences can and should be explained empirically. In order to do so, observers must be cognizant of specific differences in such variables as locus of policy-making authority, mix of financial resource base, size and auspice of the correctional agency, and so on. A few studies, such as Vinter, Hall and Downs (1975) and Coates and Miller (1974) have taken such variables into consideration. But most correctional studies have not. Understanding the community nature of community corrections will not advance if we continue to advance faulty generalizations about the characteristics of community correction. Moreover, understanding is not likely to advance if arbitrary distinctions are made between community and non-community corrections. Prison A may have a high degree of interaction with a particular community while prison B does not. And probation department A may support reciprocal relationships with other departments of county government while department B does not. In this situation, we may learn more about community by lumping prison A and probation department A together and comparing them with prison B and probation department B than we would using the typical contrast of the two prisons against the two probation departments. It is to a more detailed, but still tentative, examination of the relationship between community and correctional program that we now turn.

The Dependence of Corrections on Community

Crucial to our thinking is the relationship between "community" and "corrections." Corrections is not something that happens *in* the community or something that is done *for* the community, and it certainly is not meant as something the community *should* do. Corrections is like business or education: it simply exists as one aspect or function of community.

Where there is no community, there can be no corrections. Without some minimal performance of a complex set of functions that provide a geographically based group of people the means to survive, there will be little correctional activity. The limiting case of this situation would be the completely anomic, disorganized area.

If there are no norms enforced, there can be no offenses, and no group response to correct the situation. There are indeed instances, such as that of Shakespearean London, or pre-revolutionary Paris, where social structure and cultural values were in such rapid flux that there was little systematic law enforcement or corrections (Chapman, 1970; Critchley, 1967). Similar conditions are occasionally observed today (Warren, 1978).

There may be, of course, some manner of law enforcement, or peacekeeping in areas where the sense of community is relatively lacking, and community response to crime quite ineffective and disorganized. We suggest that, in these instances of "relatively little community," we are dealing with relatively little corrections. What corrections exist in such settings will tend to be administered to the direct benefit of the actors concerned, rather than serving some abstract notion of community or state. The extreme instance of this process is the practice of individual revenge and retaliation which, in the absence of law or its administration, seems the only recourse for protection or satisfaction.

In order to distinguish between instances of little or no corrections, and retributively oriented corrections, we can apply van den Haag's (1975:10) distinction between revenge and retribution.

> Vengeance is self-serving since it is arbitrarily...taken by anyone who feels injured and wishes to retaliate ...Unlike vengeance, retribution is imposed by courts after a guilty plea or trial, in which the accused has been found guilty of committing a crime.

To restate the distinction in community terms, revenge is a simple response or the goal-seeking of an individual, uncontrolled by the organizational mechanisms of community. Our first true form of corrections is that which occurs when individual or group vengeance is replaced with the formation of a *community* response under the color of law, called retribution.

The more organized, and hence the more regulated, the individual response to a felt injustice, the more likely it is to approach our first notion of actual community correction. Vigilantism has been an informal, collective response to a certain notion of social disorder. This phenomenon still rests within the revenge category of behavior, but certain informal organizations with similar beginnings, such as the English Safety and Street Commission of the 1770's (Critchley; 1967:21-25), were the first signs of a new community response to the correction of social disorder. Thus the more extreme situations of "no community/no correction" may contain the seeds of order and organization and give rise to the implementation of criminal punishment.

Types of Community-Correctional Linkage

Roland Warren (1978) and Irving Spergel (1976) both insist that communities are not necessarily single social systems, as small groups or organizations are described. Instead, communities are fields of interaction in which a number of social systems intersect. The intersection can take a variety of forms and have a variety of results. Communities survive to the extent that the forms of interaction provide residents of a locality with access to the functions necessary for day-to-day living. These functions are (1) production, distribution and consumption, (2) socialization of values, beliefs, knowledge and skills, (3) social control, or the management of norms, (4) social participation, or identification with groups and belongingness to an area, and (5) mutual support, or activities which reduce deficiencies in times of trouble. Access to these social functions can be provided in a number of forms, with varying results for the quality of life in an area.

Warren and Spergel have concluded that two principal dimensions of community structure have much to do with the performance of those "locality relevant" functions. Some communities rely heavily on the activity of systems which are largely local in character, while other communities are heavily dependent on systems which are directed by and responsive to authority centers which are extra-local. In some communities, local actors are in constant communication with each other so that most local functions are carefully coordinated, while in other communities, local actors are fairly independent of each other.

Warren calls the former dimension the "vertical" axis of community structure. It refers to the extent that organizations and groups performing locality functions are either indigenous, or action units of extra-local systems. The latter dimension Warren calls the "horizontal" axis of community structure. It refers to the degree that organizations and groups at the local level interact in a planned, coordinated manner, or leave the relative contribution of each local unit to some market mechanism. Applying these dimensions to community corrections, three predominant variations can be commonly identified, as depicted in Figure 1.1.

Figure 1.1
Community Corrections Interactional Fields

Are local correctional units connected to extra local resource and policy making sources?		no	yes
	yes	community placed	community based
	no	no corrections	community run

Are local correctional units connected to other local units for resources and policy making?

Some community programs, such as the Bucks County (Pa.) Jail, are relatively autonomous of non-local sources for setting policy and obtaining and distributing resources. In the 1950s, Major John Case, then Superintendent of the Bucks County Jail, initiated a work release program with the support of local politicians and local employers. He eventually built an entirely separate work release center, several miles from the main jail facility. Such programs can be called "community-run" correctional programs. Their interactional field is relatively circumscribed, free of external directives but also lacking statewide sources of financial support and technical expertise.

Other community programs, such as the Pennsylvania state felony probation service, are financially supported and directed by a division of the Governor's Office, the Board of Probation and Parole. This kind of structure ties each probation office to each other office in the state through unified procedures, regulations, and employment standards. While relatively autonomous, on a formal level, from local political decisions and the relative wealth of any particular county, such organizations also have no direct linkages with local service agencies or local criminal justice agencies. These can be called "community-placed" correctional programs.

Finally, some programs exist in a matrix-like field with ties both to extra-local funding and policy-making centers and to other local action units. Perhaps the archetypal examples are the counties participating in the Minnesota Community Corrections Act. These county departments must meet certain state requirements to obtain their state funds, but the plan for utilizing these funds is devised by a local advisory board. Such community-based programs enjoy the benefits, but also operate under the constraints, of their connections to *both* local and non-local policy making and resource centers.

Community-Run Corrections

Our first type of community corrections, is, as the term suggests, almost totally controlled by the people in the locality where the offense was committed. The judgment is local and the disposition is locally administered, with reliance on local resources. Examples include the use of banishment, stocks and pillories, or whipping posts in Puritan New England, branding and maiming in Elizabethan England, or the thirty days/thirty dollars in the lower courts of 20th-century America.

Unlike the revenge motifs in every-man-for-himself situations, community-run corrections is not only organized, but legal. It involves the punishment for a duly demonstrated offense. Action is not taken on behalf of the victim, but on behalf of the formal community norms that have been violated. The principal emphasis or justification in such correction appears to be retribution, or the exacting of a physical or monetary (as well as social) payment for the commission of a wrongdoing.

There are several ways to explain the dynamics at work behind retribution. The most common one, that the punishment is exacted for a past wrongdoing, seems faulty. As is true in economics, sunk costs cannot be recouped. There is no way to "right" a past transgression. The more logical explanation involves the present consequences of the past act. Existing community norms are reaffirmed and, in most instances, presumably strengthened through the dramatization by the machinery of justice that crimes are not only disapproved but actively resisted. To state it another way, retribution prevents anomie, or supports the present normative order (New York Governor's Special Committee on Criminal Offenders, 1968). Consequently, there is not a great deal of concern in community-run correction for the condition or future behavior of the punished offender. The predominant concern is the function of punishment for the observing community: the conformist is symbolically rewarded for his behavior (van den Haag, 1975:21-22).

Community-run corrections is not necessarily harsh. Corrections, which is predominantly controlled by local norms and customs, will be harsh or lenient depending on community standards. A recent study by Van Buren (1984) examining the prosecutorial stages of criminal justice in five rural Wisconsin counties uncovered relatively unclogged courts, many guilty pleas without apparent negotiation, and relatively light sentences, with an emphasis on the use of fines. It was also found, however, that there were few serious crimes. Van Buren's counties could be characterized as relatively intolerant of minor transgressions, but also not severe in the means or outcomes of prosecution, relative to one urban comparison site. It should be remembered that some community-run programs, such as the Bucks County work-release program, are more liberal and more innovative than programs emerging in other kinds of community interactional fields.

Perhaps the greatest constraint on community-run programs is an inherent limitation on resources. If such programs lack ties to a central resource base for funding programs, they are unlikely to attract professionals who demand high salaries or to spend much money on programs or facilities. Community-run programs are therefore dependent on local cooperative efforts, which may in turn be dependent on the correctional administrator's ability to carve out a political coalition supportive of his organization. Such coalitions are often financially troubled, although there are exceptions.

Community-Placed Corrections

We use the term "community-placed" to refer to another set of community correctional strategies in which program impetus, policy formulation, and resource generation are primarily non-local, but the supervision of the offender occurs within distinct localities. For example, Federal Probation supervision occurs in many cities and towns across the country. The federal probationer utilizes various community resources, such as shelter, food, education, employment; and his placement in the community theoretically exposes the community to some risk. However, some Federal Probation policy is directed through regional offices from Washington, D.C., and the decision to place an offender on federal probation is made by a federal district judge, who may be considerably less attuned or sensitive to local matters than a county trial judge, most of whom are elected in one manner or another by local citizenry. (See Thomas Maher's chapter in this volume for an examination on the limits of centralization in the Federal Probation organization.)

Other examples of community-placed correction include state administered probation and/or parole operations, the community program operated by the California Youth Authority, the state-operated jail systems of Connecticut or Vermont, and the halfway houses operated by the Pennsylvania Bureau of Correction. In all these instances, there are marked distinctions between these programs and programs with similar nomenclature that are community-run or (our third type) community-based. The notion of "placement" is a fairly succinct denotation of their primary characteristics: these community-placed programs, while operating in communities, have authority and funding streams from higher levels of government. Sources of authority and revenue being what they are, these agencies generally tend to be more responsive to central authorities than they are to other community agencies. This is *not* to say that reciprocity and influence networks of significant size and strength are lacking between local agencies and groups and the community-placed agencies. But we do suggest that such agencies are considerably more isolated (or autonomous) from local policy and politics than correctional programs that are dependent upon local charity or tax dollars for their existence and upon county commissioners, mayors, or local community boards for their direction, operation and evaluation.

Because community-placed agencies are inevitably parts of larger systems, there is frequently found within them a different perspective on, understanding of, and utilization of community resources and values than would be true of other community correctional types. The local community in these instances is, in many respects, on the other side of a "we-they" boundary (see Duffee and Ritti, in Duffee, 1980:348-357). The community is approached as a significant but external environment rather than as the system of which the program is a component. From the administrative perspective, this perception is quite correct, but it frequently leads to conflicts on the local level between the field agency and the "environment." One problem, for example, is that community-placed organizations seem to have difficulty presenting themselves as community resources rather than as guests who partake in local supply, at some cost, to a frequently reluctant host. Given this problem, another emerges: there is frequent conflict between the local unit officials and their central headquarters superiors. While the chain-of-command may be unquestionable, local demands frequently necessitate discretion and organization flexibility for front-line operators. Front-line executives are often caught in the middle trying to balance the demands from headquarters for uniformity and consistency across the state with the demands from the informal influence network that exists on the local level.

The less-detailed perspective of community taken by executives in community-placed programs is generated by the nature of community-placed organizational structure. A local unit executive does not and cannot take his lead from other local program chiefs or local politicians. Instead, he remains connected to every other unit in the statewide program by way of policy and funding control from a central office. However, as we shall see in subsequent chapters, the relative responsiveness of a community-placed local unit to its headquarters as opposed to its local environment is variable, and may change significantly over time. The local Federal Probation offices, and the Pennsylvania Community Service Centers are less controlled by headquarters directives than one might expect, and instead are more responsive to conditions and norms in their particular localities. Other community-placed programs, such as the Michigan Department of Correction Community Treatment Centers, seem to remain closely tied to and controlled by their central offices (see the chapters by Maher and Duffee and Wright).

The goals of community-placed programs seem to contrast rather markedly with the orientation of community-run correctional programs. If community-run programs generally seem to emphasize maintenance of order in the local community, community-placed program objectives often seem future-directed and individually oriented. That is, they frequently emphasize reduction in future crime by addressing the needs, conditions or objectives of the individual offender. Furthermore, community-placed programs recruit (and attract) a different kind of staff: the professional human service worker whose ideology, training, and commitments usually reinforce the individualized aspects of these programs (Ohlin, Piven, and Pappenfort, 1956). The staffing differences are related to the funding differences. Centrally funded programs can usually meet the salary demands of credentialed professionals and technicians, while the staff's concern for maintaining local norms is viewed as less relevant to a centralized personnel office. The staff members tend to focus on what they see as commitment to their clients rather than focusing on the social order of a particular community.

Community-Based Corrections

Our last type of community corrections is perhaps the most complex and therefore the one for which ideal examples are most difficult to find. Community-based corrections, as we will use the term, refers to correctional programs which exist in a mixed community interactional field: relatively strong extra-local linkages and relatively strong local linkages for policymaking and resource generation. We suspect that many correctional programs are initiated in such a mixed field (the now defunct LEAA block grant process being one example of such initiation), but over time these mixed fields may shift towards community-run or community-placed fields. These shifts may be particularly likely when program initiators are unaware of the mixed structure they should be trying to maintain.

Our use of the term "community-based" may cause some confusion, since this term is used throughout much of the literature to indicate any non-institutional corrections operation. We will, however, rely on this term, albeit with our narrower meaning, since the concept seems the most appropriate descriptor of the type of correctional structure we have in mind. By "community-based" we shall denote all correctional supervision on the local level that combines local and extra-local resources but retains significant policy prerogatives at the local level.

Community-based structures are not simply compromises between the future/individual orientation found in community-placed and the present/group orientation found in community-run programs. Community-based corrections is not a mixed type, but a new type. Funding or portions of funding are extra-local, but policy is not prescribed by an extra-local central headquarters. Technical assistance may be provided by or through state or federal assistance, but personnel recruitment, training, orientation, and deployment are local affairs. Policy formulation and policy implementation are local decisions, but, of course, may be influenced by desires of outside resource providers.

Such programs are typically more active in other local community affairs than would be true of community-placed agencies. But these programs may be more autonomous than is true of community-run agencies, because they have some authority and access to resources which are not derived from other local organizations.

Examples of such programs might be the state-subsidy to county probation in California (Lerman, 1975) or county work-release programs subsidized on a contract basis by the Federal Bureau of Prisons. One of the best examples is the community-based program for juveniles operated in Massachusetts. When Jerome Miller closed the juvenile institutions in that state, some replacement centers were supported by state funds, but organized and operated by indigenous groups (Coates, Miller and Ohlin, 1978). The other good example is the Minnesota Community Corrections Act, described previously.

Perhaps the most significant difference between community-placed or community-run programs and community-based ones occurs on the dimension of functional consequence for the community. Neither community-run nor community-placed programs would seem to change community normative patterns or resource networks. Community-run activities, by definition, do not challenge the ideological or cultural justifications of retribution; indeed, they function to reinforce established normative judgments. Community-placed programs often emphasize helping individual offenders adjust to local community values and resource distribution patterns. These programs often do not have sufficient legitimacy to *change* local values.

Community-based programs, in contrast, involve the introduction of new resources into the community and often involve change in the local normative pattern by providing to disenfranchised (or underenfranchised) groups access to resources and technical competencies that previously had been denied them.

This tendency of community-based correction implies the last two points we wish to emphasize here. First, community-based programs, being diversified in structure and control, are also frequently diversified in types of clients served or problems addressed. Community-based programs are more likely to diversify than community-placed programs because there are fewer categorical limitations upon the nature of intake, and they are more likely to diversify than community-run programs, in which the predominant concern with the offender tends to be his symbolic utility for other people. Consequently, community-based programs may conceivably serve a variety of youth, whether adjudicated delinquents or not, and community-based halfway houses may invite walk-in clients as well as residents placed by state or local correctional authorities. Such programs, therefore, may be said to exhibit flexible and diverse service production processes or functions.

Secondly, as the discussion of the function of community-based centers implies, we are making no assumptions about the community as a unitary cultural and instrumental system. The community political structure may be very pluralistic, and there may be several, rather than one, clearly identifiable cultural value set. The introduction of a community-based system in such a community may increase or reduce community conflict, depending upon the program's size, mission, and the exact nature of its funding stream and authority lines. But in any case, the community-based program is likely to be an active agent in community change through means of conflict resolution, re-education, and advocacy. Community-based programs would appear the most likely of the three types to have the greatest impact on the communities in which they operate. Whether they also have greater impact on their clients remains unknown.

Discussion Questions

1. Why are the characteristics frequently used to describe community corrections generally unsatisfactory, upon closer inspection?

2. Is it possible to distinguish institutional from community corrections? In what ways are institutional and community corrections programs interrelated? What may happen if we ignore these relationships?

3. Why do we know so little about the relationship between correctional programs and communities?

4. Why might variations in the community interactional field produce different program characteristics?

PART ONE
CORRECTIONAL ORGANIZATIONS AS UNITS OF COMMUNITY STRUCTURE

In Chapter 1 we introduced three ideal types of community interactional fields in which correctional programs could be located. Community-run systems were described as correctional programs which were heavily dependent upon other local organizations for both policy decisions and resources. Community-placed systems were described as correctional programs which were heavily dependent upon extra-local (typically state or federal central offices) organizations for policymaking and resources. Finally, community-based systems were described as correctional programs which received policy and resource support from both local and non-local sources.

This typology, however, may create the misleading impression that these three combinations of local and non-local forces are enduring, static entities into which a correctional program must fit.[1] The static conception of the community fields would suggest there is only one kind of correctional policymaking and resource acquisition strategy that would work well in any given community. This is not true in the long run.

Communities, according to most recent theories, are not rigid, ordered systems. They are, instead, places in our political and social geography where many different organizational systems interact and, often, collide. Interaction patterns differ sufficiently from place to place so it is useful to compare the differences at one point in time. But we also need to remember that the interactional pattern in one place may differ significantly from one time to another. Communities embody a variety of forces and those forces shift direction and change their relative power. Moreover, many of the forces are organizational forces. Community structure is in large degree the patterned interaction of the different organizations which operate in that locality.

The three chapters in this section provide different analyses of the development of correctional programs within the context of these shifting forces within and among communities. The first two chapters focus on the interaction of particular correctional programs with local and extra-local community forces. The remaining chapter focuses on similar interaction patterns but within the context of two key issues that probation systems have traditionally faced—centralized versus local control and executive versus judicial control.

In Chapter 2, organizational sociologist David Duffee focuses on a more contemporary correctional enterprise, the development of a community halfway house. This case study provides a unique view of the planning, opening, transformation and stabilization of a halfway house initiated by a group of local citizens. Duffee chronicles the support for and conflicts engendered by what initially appeared to be a community-run halfway house and its ultimate transformation into more of a community-based program in which policy and resources were both locally *and* non-locally determined. This transformation is shown to be the result of the new organization's struggle for survival and its dependence on other organizations located on both the horizontal and vertical dimensions.

Chapter 3, by Robert Lilly and Richard Ball, chronicles the development of the contemporary community correctional movement involving house arrest and electronic monitoring programs. Lilly and Ball provide both an overview of the nationwide emergence of these programs and a more intensive analysis of the development of programs in Florida and Kentucky. These case study data highlight the interaction of local and extra-local forces on community corrections. Specifically, by contrasting these two states, Lilly and Ball are able to relate varied implementation responses to the responsiveness of local officials and to the nature and scope of state-level policymaking. In addition, the authors raise some more general issues concerning the extent to which these programs represent the further extension of social control into community life.

Thomas Maher, in Chapter 4, provides a thorough examination of the issues of centralized versus decentralized control in his study of the U.S. Probation Service. Maher's chapter is particularly insightful because it focuses attention on the relationship between these interaction patterns and organizational structure. Most researchers agree that one of the principal dimensions of organizational structure is the locus of decision-making, or the degree of centralization in an organization. This dimension is extremely important in human services such as probation, since the organization must both provide individual offices with sufficient flexibility to respond to local norms and local needs but also with sufficient uniformity in its policies and practices that systemwide goals can be met. The U.S. Probation System provides a rather unique context for examining these issues because of its centralized (Federal Court Administrative Office) and decentralized (Federal District Courts) management structure. Maher's study suggests that systems may get caught in the middle of these local and centralized demands and pressures, but that this dual authority structure may have short-range advantages for local office managers.

Notes

[1] This static view does, however, have some utility in the short run. It might help us, for example, to make systematic comparisons between certain urban and rural departments, or it might help us explain why certain communities must be approached cautiously and openly with a proposal for establishing a halfway house while in another community halfway house initiators cannot even identify actors who find the issue salient.

Chapter 2
The Birth of a Halfway House

David E. Duffee

This is the story of a new organization, a private halfway house for former prisoners. It is a tentative first step in correcting a deficiency in our community corrections literature: the lack of rich detail in accounts of organizational birth and infancy. The literature has numerous mentions of community resistence to new correctional organizations and some studies that compare and contrast reactions of different communities (e.g., Coates and Miller, 1974) or of different states (e.g. Vinter, Downs, and Hall, 1975). However, even the more detailed accounts generally paint their pictures with such a broad brush that the exciting and confusing variations of response within a single community get lost.

This is not an exemplary tale in the sense of being a model for how to proceed elsewhere. However, it may be an example of a relatively common set of dynamics that can be set into motion when:

(1) a small group of people wish to tackle a local problem;
(2) the initiating group must obtain cooperation from other autonomous groups in the community;
(3) but these other groups have other goals and operate under different constraints and therefore wish the initial project goals to be changed to meet their needs.

Phase I: Idea to Organization

The story takes place in a small eastern city, which I will call Capital City. In the late 1970s, a black man was released on parole

43

and decided not to return home to a large downstate metropolis. Instead, he settled in Capital City and enrolled as an undergraduate in a small, liberal arts college. There were a number of ties between the Equal Education Opportunity (EEO) program at this college and another EEO program at the Capital City Junior College, which had an active prison education program. The parolee became active in this group concerned with minority and ex-offender education. Upon his graduation, he was hired by the State Education Department, as an officer in its external degree program.

In about 1980, the parolee approached the Capital City Council of Churches with the observation that ex-offenders returning to Capital City had few social supports to assist in their transition to community living. His own personal experience in this regard was bolstered by his observation of the difficulties faced by other parolees as they attempted to finish their two-year degrees at the junior college. Frequently good students while in prison, they often failed to finish their educational programs when they transferred to campus.

The parolee's concerns converged with the those of the junior college EEO director. In his first few months as EEO director, two parolees, fresh from prison, showed up on his doorstep with no place to stay. He joined the parolee in proposing to the Council of Churches that something might be done for such parolees, particularly if they were interested in pursuing education at the junior college.

The Council of Churches, a federative body of protestant churches, was responsible for a number of church-related social service coordination efforts, but had committed itself to few direct service activities. The Council's board decided to form a task force to investigate the ex-offender problem and formulate a solution.

At about the same time, a minister in the predominantly black Northside neighborhood obtained of a small sum ($15,000) to start a halfway house. The extent of involvement of the Council Task Force is unclear. This minister's church was a member of the Council, and some initial planning papers for this halfway house indicate that some Task Force members were marginally involved. Within a year, the minister had absconded with both the halfway house funds and his congregation's money. Parole officers and police raided the house, confiscated a supply of weapons and drugs, and returned the house residents to prison.

While apparently no one on the Council of Churches Task Force was directly implicated in this fiasco, their fringe association probably reduced their credibility with the local parole office. Moreover, this incident certainly branded halfway houses as mistakes and church groups as naive do-gooders in the minds of both Capital City police and the district parole officers.

Despite this event, the Council Task Force pressed forward with its own plans for a support service for ex-offenders. In 1981, the project got a boost when a member church from the south side suggested that the Task Force could use its empty parsonage for the project for a nominal rent of $50 a month. When the parsonage was provided, it was uninhabitable. It had not been renovated since it had been built. The church was paying for its minister and his family to live in a nearby townhouse.

The parsonage was adopted by the Task Force for a residential program, called Help House. Members of the Task Force became active in the neighborhood of the parsonage. They sought neighbor support for the intended program in order to get zoning board approval for a variance that would permit them to use a single family dwelling for multiple occupancy.

This particular neighborhood was one of two predominantly black neighborhoods in Capital City, the other being the north side, where the previous halfway house mistake had occurred. The Council Task Force included several south-side residents, one of whom had been an inmate some ten years previously. He was friends with the parolee who had proposed Help House, but he was not an unqualified supporter of the project. He had a strong sense of identification with his neighborhood, and he was not convinced that parolees needed support (he pointed out that when he had come out, things were even worse and he made it on his own). Nevertheless, he agreed to join the Task Force and work with other members on a door-to-door canvassing of the immediate four-block area. Surprising itself, the group obtained over 200 signatures of neighbors in favor of the project.

Local opposition did arise, particularly from the south-side Neighborhood Association. The Association, while obstenibly representing neighborhood interests, was largely controlled by whites living in the extreme southern end of the area. Most of the immediate neighbors of the parsonage were black. Several of these neighbors had members of immediate or extended family who were either in prison or were the victims of serious crime. For example, an elderly woman immediately across the street from the parsonage was taking care of her granddaughter-in-law and her great-grandchild while her grandson was in prison. Her view was that the project was useful to both persons in prison and to their families.

While the neighborhood association managed to block the zoning application at the local level, the opposition dissipated at the appeal level upon the presentation of the 200 signatures of the persons most immediately affected. The mayor approved the variance. The Task Force agreement with the neighbors included the stipulation that the house would never admit either arsonists or sex offenders (the particular concern was child molesters). In addition, the Task Force made some verbal commitments to serve south-side residents before all other clients.

After the zoning approval, the Help House Task Force ran a story in a November, 1981, issue of the *Capital City News,* announcing the opening of its doors in the near future. This story caught the eye of two graduate students in the criminal justice program at the state university. They had both enrolled in a course for the Spring, 1982, semester that required field research in a local correctional program. After showing the story to their professor, they contacted the junior college EEO director, named as the chairman of the Task Force in the paper. He welcomed them both to the project, and they agreed to start work at the beginning of the spring semester in January, 1982. After the students made their first trip to Help House as their field research course began, they came back both frustrated and confused. They reported to their professor that, despite the news story, Help House at present:

(1) had no program funds;
(2) had no service plans;
(3) had no clients;
(4) was endowed with an uninhabitable building.

They were concerned that this situation would jeopardize their status in the field research course. The professor, while surprised at the news, told them that, on the contrary, the situation reported was rather welcome. It provided an opportunity to observe a project unfold from scratch. While the students accepted this, they both had difficulty negotiating a role in the project that met course requirements. At their urging, the professor met with the Task Force chairman to find out what kinds of roles they might be able to perform for the program. The chairman, in turn, asked the professor to attend the next Task Force meeting.

At this meeting, the Task Force members were just beginning to consider some crucial program issues. Questions included who would reside in the house, who would provide services, where funds would come from, and how cooperation with parole officials might be achieved. While the professor perceived that the group had a long way to go before it could possibly open its program, many Task Force members spoke as if opening was imminent. These differences in perception were attributable to the differing experiences of the persons who held them, on the one hand, and to their very different views on the nature of a halfway house program, on the other.

The professor had worked with a department of corrections in another state for several years as the evaluator of the department's pre-release facilities. The halfway houses, in his experience, were public organizations, well-endowed financially, and staffed by salaried professionals. Moreover, based on research reports from Minnesota (Minnesota Governor's Commission on Crime Prevention, 1975; 1976), he had reached the conclusion that private halfway houses run by inexperienced, non-professional staff were prone to over-counseling their clients rather than focusing on jobs and education, were likely to have poor relationships with the state prison and parole organizations upon which they depended for referrals, and were often poorly managed.

The Task Force members, on the other hand, appeared to hold very different views. They appeared to believe that the Task Force members themselves could provide residents with the necessary counseling, support services and referrals. Consequently, the budget they had prepared for the program was very small. It called for a director and a cook. It did not provide for 24-hour staff coverage, which was either considered unnecessary, or to be supplied by volunteers. The rest of the small budget was devoted to supplies and house maintenance. The type of program envisioned was a very informal one in which the residents were generally unsupervised—the house was a place to stay—and an array of concerned volunteers would provide a variety of services on an informal basis. While this version of the program gradually changed (and it is likely that the parole office would never have approved of such living arrangements), a few Task Force members clung very strongly to the notion that the program should be a very informal, self-help program, rather than an organization with a paid professional staff with responsibilities for resident supervision.

While the Task Force continued its planning, the local Council of Community Services finished its report of emergency shelter needs in the area. This report was based on a survey of persons seeking emergency shelter in November, 1981. The plight of the homeless was becoming evident throughout the country. The Council survey suggested that the homeless were no better off in Capital City than elsewhere. It reported that the City had 125 emergency shelter beds and that the demand for shelter reached as high as 300 requests per night. The Council reported that roughly 25% of the persons seeking shelter had recent correctional histories (were or had recently been on probation or parole, or had recently been in the county jail). It was this correctional subpopulation of the homeless that was reportedly most frequently turned down for emergency shelter admission. One reason for this was that the usual correctional client was a young male, while most shelter programs were set up for older, homeless men, the mentally ill, or homeless families. The homeless offender did not fit in.

The Council report had significant impact on a number of developments in the area, including Help House. First, the survey documented a general emergency shelter need in the area that was not being met. Second, the report provided support for the argument that the variety of shelter resources in the area should be coordinated. Third, relative to corrections, the report appeared to substantiate, in quantitative terms, the claim that there were inadequate residential services for ex-offenders in the area. Fourth, the Council became interested in Help House as a potential member of an emerging network of local shelters. On that basis, the Council assigned one of its senior officers to the Task Force as an advisor and permitted the Task Force to use Council communication and secretarial resources.

A Capital area Emergency Shelter Association (ESA) was formed, comprised of local shelter directors and interested others. Strong support was received from the Catholic Diocese and a number of local philanthropists. The ESA also formed a centralized shelter intake service, with a 24-hour hot line. The intake service, operated by Travelers Aid, conducted intake interviews and referred clients to the most appropriate shelter. Within this growing network of residential service providers, Help House was projected as the correctional link. If it got up and running, it could serve the emergency shelter clients with correctional backgrounds. The Capital City police department sent a representative to ESA, and the local probation department was actively involved. Parole, however, was not.

The chairman of the Task Force asked the professor if he would join the group on a regular basis. The professor had considerable reluctance to do this. However, he finally decided that a number of factors recommended his joining. First, the chairman had mentioned that the criminal justice faculty and their students were rarely involved in local projects. This report was repeated by a number of other local agency personnel. The professor decided that his department might, in fact, have had considerably less interest in local affairs than the educational or research opportunities, let alone the commitment to the community, might justify. Secondly, he became intrigued by the juxtaposition of his own "community corrections" experience and the one unfolding in front of him. In the pre-release system he had studied previously, the state bureaucracies developed the programs, and the communities either accommodated or resisted in varying degrees, but did not actively participate. Here, in contrast, was a community group initiating a proposal. Third, he decided that he had some experience with halfway house administration and program design, as well as considerable experience in dealing with state correctional officials, that could be useful to the Task Force. For these reasons, he agreed to join the group for the Spring, 1982 semester.

At the same time, he was concerned about pushing his version of halfway house program on the group. Consequently he decided to play a low-key role, at least for awhile. He spent most of his time in the Task Force meetings listening to the other members of the group, asking questions of clarification, and offering observations based on his past experience, when these seemed helpful.

By the middle of the semester, the professor thought he perceived a disjuncture between the stated goals of the program and the language the Task Force was using to describe the services to be offered to Help House residents. While the Task Force planners, and especially the parolee with the initial proposal, spoke of a program containing considerable resident self-determination, and of the need to provide an environment in which residents would become increasingly independent, their program design component continued to be couched in language of correctional rehabilitation. This language appeared to be borrowed from documents from other programs rather than represent the expression of Task Force intent. Toward the end of the semester, the professor submitted to the group an idea paper, based on the Task Force discussions and related to community correctional research in several other states. The paper argued for a program that did not prejudge the particular needs of residents, that would be prepared to meet the needs which research found to be most frequent, and that specialized services, such as counseling, should be obtained from other community agencies, including parole. In other words, Help House should operate as a residence rather than a treatment facility. Its staff would help identify residents' needs and goals and would act as broker for services available elsewhere in the community. This paper was accepted with some enthusiasm by the Task Force members. For example, the parolee said that the paper articulated the type of program the group had been struggling to express for some time. The Task Force adopted the concept paper as its statement of philosophy and basic program design. It served as the basis for a number of subsequent proposals and planning documents. The first of these was a ten-page proposal submitted to the state parole board in May, 1982. There was no immediate response to this proposal.

During the summer of 1982, the lawyer on the Task Force filed incorporation papers, and the Task Force became a not-for-profit organization independent of the Council of Churches.

Phase II: From Incorporation to Funding

In the autumn, an organizational meeting of the new corporation was called. A set of by-laws had been drafted, and a slate of first officers and board members was proposed. Many of these were people actively involved in the Task Force, although others were new. The chairman of the Task Force telephoned the professor to ask if he would join the board. He agreed to attend the meeting.

Just prior to the October meeting, at which the officers were to be elected, the parolee was arrested on a minor criminal charge and detained as a parole violator. While the charges were subsequently dropped, the parole officials stretched the detention on the parole violation warrant to a full 90 days before dropping the issue.

This event threw the election plans into disarray. The parolee, long the most active participant in the project, had been nominated as president of the board, while the Task Force chairman was to be chairman of the board. (It was not ever very clear why there would be both a chair and a president, as well as two vice-presidents, a secretary and a treasurer.) There was considerable confusion at the election about how to proceed under these circumstances. While a number of participants expressed strong support for the parolee and organized to his defense, other members seemed suddenly very uncomfortable with the thought of the parolee being elected an officer. Most of this group explained that their sole concern was how long he would be detained and therefore unable to perform presidential duties. The professor, however, thought that some of this group was getting its first real experience with its proximity to the the criminal process.

After a lengthy discussion, the director of the Council of Churches nominated the professor. He agreed to serve contingent on conferring with the parolee. This he did the following Sunday during visiting hours at the jail. The parolee expressed his desire to have the professor serve as president. He said that he did not know how long the parole violation would take to clear up, and that the organization had to go on in his absence.

Simultaneously, the professor was preparing to offer his field research course again in the Spring, 1983 semester. He announced this intention and suggested that interested students begin to seek an agency to work with during the fall. One of the new students in the department heard of the halfway house and came to the professor with a proposal. She suggested that there were a sufficient number of interested graduate students to staff the halfway house until funding for a salaried staff could be obtained.

The professor was doubtful of this but suggested that the student group put together a proposal and present it to the Help House directors. Subsequently, a group of eleven students drafted a proposal that they would work as volunteers in the program for a period of one year. Some of these students had considerable correctional experience, including a correctional officer of nine years, the student organizer, who had worked in a neighboring state department of correction for two years, a student who had worked with halfway houses in another state for two years, and a returning doctoral student, who had several years of counseling in juvenile institutions, and who had grown up in the Southside neighborhood. The proposal was quickly accepted by the board, under the condition that the professor would supervise this volunteer staff. It was agreed that they would begin work at the start of the Spring, 1983 term.

In the same fall, a new state assembly district had been created, carved out by the Democratic-controlled legislature. This new district included the parsonage within its boundaries. The assemblyman elected to the new seat in November was a member of a family who had long been powerful in the county Democratic Party. He won handily. His father had served as county sheriff, and, therefore, jail administrator from 1974 to 1979. His father had eventually resigned after a running battle with the county legislature about the budgeting of the jail. While the county had a long history of electing conservative judges, and had one of the highest incarceration rates in the state, the assemblyman's father had been a genuinely innovative correctional administrator. He had begun a work-release program with assistance from the state university, and had students from the school of social work active in the jail. These innovations had been squashed with his resignation, but his son had apparently inherited the commitment to correctional issues.

This propitious political change may never have led anywhere for Help House except for two additional events. Shortly after the turn of the new year, one of the state's major prisons rioted. A principal complaint of the inmates was overcrowding. The soaring prison population was hammered home to the newly elected governor and to the legislature in dramatic fashion.

Secondly, the Fall, 1982 semester also brought to the criminal justice department an unusual new Ph.D. student. An ex-inmate from California, he had worked since his release on correctional reform both in California and Hawaii. The professor, impressed with this student's experience, recommended that the Help House board elect him to an empty board seat. This student, in turn, suggested that Help House should seek funding directly from the state legislature.

No one else on the board of directors had even considered this possibility, nor knew how to proceed. However, the professor had a friend on the staff of a powerful black assemblyman from the western part of the state. He made an appointment to see the staffer and pled his ignorance of the entire proposal process. His friend outlined the lobbying process in detail, and made it clear that the first step was support of the new assemblyman, since Help House fell in his district. He also suggested that, as a project from a predominantly black neighborhood by a group largely controlled by blacks, the black legislators in the assembly would be quite supportive, if the local assemblyman wished to support the project.

As the new semester began, the student volunteers interviewed newly admitted students for any possible additions to their group. They found two, including a woman who had recently been the operations manager of a large pre-release center. This woman was elected by the students as their coordinator. This selection was surprising, since she was not part of the initiating group. It seemed based, in part, on her previous experience, and on the fact that she had no interest in more permanent connection with Help House. Some of the other students, looking toward the future, had decided that they would apply for staff positions if these became available. Since the new student was not a competitive threat, placing her at the helm of the volunteer project did not seem to hamper others chances of showing the board what they could do.

The new student coordinator, the ex-inmate from California, and the professor drafted a proposal for $90,000 funding from the legislature and delivered it in person to the assemblyman in February, 1983. His response was immediately positive. He promised that he would support the project if the local alderman supported it. The first vice-president of the board, a black woman from the south-side neighborhood, invited the alderman to her house to explain the program. Upon being shown that the proposal was not a diversion of funds already targeted for his community, and aware of the zoning petition signed by 200 of his constituents, his report to the assemblyman was very positive.

With this support assured, the California ex-inmate became an active lobbyist for Help House. He managed to dissolve objections from the executive branch—whose director of criminal justice programs claimed that the governor's correctional budget was already set—by getting the local district attorney to endorse the program. The D.A. and the director were personal friends from law school days. After some additional complaints that the idea was too late to fit the governor's plans, the criminal justice director admitted that it would be very nice to see a residential community correctional program in the capital.

Meanwhile, the students organized rapidly into three different committees, one for administration, one for community relations, and one for program planning. While each of the students had promised to work on the project for at least ten hours a week, the three committee chairs and the coordinator were devoting between thirty and forty hours a week to the project. Enthusiasm through March was very high, with a high point being a rock concert fund-raiser in which the students raised more than $1,000 for the program.

As the winter of 1982 began to melt, the energies of the persons working on Help House dissipated with it. There were a number of signs of trying to do too much with too little. The board of directors did not operate effectively. While this group was formally composed of between 20 and 30 people, few of them showed up at board meetings and fewer still were active in committees. Most of the work fell to the chairman, the president, the parolee (who upon his release from jail in February filled the position of second vice president), the advisor from the Council of Community services, and a few others.

The president met on several occasions with the state director of parole. The director was always friendly and personally supportive, but any overtures about a direct, formal relationship with parole were always deflected. The president began to surmise that the parole board might be happier if Help House simply disappeared.

Several issues separated Help House and the parole board. First, parole appeared uncomfortable with or even antagonistic to the Help House policy of serving the south-side neighborhood first. If there was ever to be a direct contractual relationship between Help House and parole, parole wanted control over selection of the parolees to be placed in the house. The decision of which parolees needed a residential placement would be made by the parole board at the time that the inmate was being considered for release from prison. The parole board did not perceive previous residence in the south side to be a prime consideration. Help House officials, in contrast, argued that the program would be most effective in providing residence to persons who already had ties to the particular community in which Help House was located. Moreover, Help House officials remained committed to their promise to the neighborhood that inmates from the south side would have first priority for admission. Secondly, there appeared to be considerable disagreement within the parole board about the value of contractual services. The personal support of the the director of parole seemed very sincere. However, he also admitted that the local district parole office, which would be directly responsible for working with Help House residents, was much less eager for this arrangement. There were at least two reasons for the negative feelings at the local level. One was a general concern among parole officers about the increasing encroachment of private corrections on their territory. Any proposal about the desirability of a program such as Help House seemed to be an implicit criticism of the services provided directly by parole officers. Second, the local district was still very aware of the previous halfway house failure in Capital City, and it became clear that the local district director felt that the Help House group was equally untrustworthy.

While the director of parole had the authority to order a contract, the central office officials were understandably loath to be heavy-handed. Moreover, the Help House president was firmly opposed to a coerced marriage—he knew that the district parole officers could scuttle Help House in short order, regardless of policy. It is possible that the president of Help House could have been effective in overcoming some resistance from the local district office. But relationships between the district office and Help House had been effectively severed before the president became involved. The director had, on several occasions, requested that the president make no direct contact with the district office, and the president felt that he should honor this request. Consequently, relationships between parole and Help House remained stagnant.

This frozen situation with parole had considerable negative effects on the student volunteers. When they had agreed to staff the house, they had been prepared for several months planning. But most of them had assumed that by the end of the Spring semester they might be operating an actual service agency. Continued planning became a stultifying, wheel-spinning exercise.

In addition, the president became exceedingly overtaxed. In addition to his full-time duties at the university, he was spending between 40 and 50 hours a week on Help House business. While he and the chairman had split up their duties so that the chairman ran the board and the president ran the volunteer operation, negotiated with parole, and engaged in other fund raising, this split did not work well. The president became less and less effective at working through other people and began doing more and more himself. His effectiveness in meetings plummeted and his patience with the slowness of other participants disappeared.

During the middle of this gradual deterioration in the internal dynamics of the Help House group, the state budget was settled. The assemblymen called the president on March 31, 1983, on the night before the official legislative vote, to inform him that Help House had been awarded $70,000. The next morning, this announcement was prominently displayed on the front page of the *Capital City News*.

Phase III: From Funding to Operation

The reactions to the announcement of the state funding were surprisingly mixed. The board of directors were elated—a long fought-for goal was becoming reality. But at the same time, there was something of a shock effect. The board, which had yet to mature as an organizational management group, now had to face the costs of accepting financial resources. It was not sure how to proceed, and many of the group, who had for years envisioned an informal program, were not necessarily pleased with the changes in program design that might follow the funding. Despite their many hours of work, the students had mixed reactions. Only one of them had had a direct hand in the legislative proposal. As a result, the announcement was not received as a group accomplishment. Additionally, the promise of salaried positions had immediate negative effects on the student group. The edge of individual competition for possible jobs fragmented the group.

Elsewhere in the city, reactions were mixed. The advisor from the Council of Community Services was very pleased. The criminal justice planner in city hall was upset that such a program was funded without his knowledge. Parole—at both levels—took the position that they had not had a hand in program design.

The immediate positive reactions faded quickly as it dawned on the board of directors that the process of receiving the money from the legislature was totally undefined. No one knew when the money would actually arrive, or what the next step was in order to receive it. The organization was still penniless, but a number of stakeholders did not perceive that. The church elders began to look across the yard at their parsonage in a new light. The students had renovated the entire building. It was now not only livable, but quite attractive. Since the church was pressed for money, it began to consider reclaiming the parsonage for its minister, or raising the rent charged to Help House. Shortly after the funding announcement, the church elders asked for $600 per month.

By summer, the student commitment to working for twelve months had disappeared. Most of them were bitter about lack of recognition from the Board, and lack of support and supervision from the president. Of the original group of 13, only four continued their commitment into the summer. However, the president saw little reason for them to continue.

The legislature eventually decided how to channel the appropriation to Help House. In June, it allocated the money to the Bureau of Crime Prevention in the state criminal justice planning agency, which in turn drafted a contract for $70,000. Contract staff in the planning office alerted Help House that the time lapse from contract to establishment of an account could take several months. Everything seemed to be on hold.

At the October, 1983 board meeting, Help House had a bank account of $40. It had $600 in back bills, and the heating season was approaching. The president estimated that the group needed to raise $10,000 simply to keep the house open until the state money was actually received. At the meeting, he outlined three alternatives to the board:

(1) simply quit, returning the appropriation to the state;
(2) seek a merger with another organization;
(3) find someone immediately to spend full time on fund raising and other organizational needs.

The president's preference was the second option, but the rest of the board rejected options 1 and 2 without much consideration. The general response was that the group had worked so long to build a separate organization that it could not give up now, just before the state money was available. However, when the president asked for suggestions on how to raise some carry-over funds, there was a long silence.

Finally, the one still-active student came up with a proposal. He would resign his job in the prison education program at the junior college and devote full-time to the program, if the board would appoint him director, meet some of his basic living expenses, and pay him the balance of his salary retroactively when the state funds eventually came through. The board agreed.

After a collective sigh of relief, the group turned to the problem of raising funds quickly. The president wrote a letter about the program to 400 alumni of the criminal justice department explaining the quandry and asking for donations. Sixteen alumni, many of them downstate police, contributed $600. The Council of Churches made an unscheduled donation of $1,000, and a number of member churches chipped in with smaller amounts. The short fall was still considerable. The president sought a loan from the university, but was turned down. Local banks refused on the basis that the organization had no history. However, a private research center associated with the criminal justice faculty agreed to a short-term, interest-free loan of $9,000. The crisis was over. On January 20, 1984, Help House received its first payment, of $20,000, from the state planning agency. The new director advertised for two staff positions and began interviewing applicants.

Phase IV: Growing Pains

The new executive director of Help House became the driving force in the organization, replacing the president as the key actor. His background, operating style, and personal view of Help House as a community project became important both to its growth and to its second crisis, in 1985. The director was a young black man who had grown up in the south side, not far from the parsonage. While he had participated in the student group, he was several years beyond the other participants in his educational program, and he had been working full-time at the junior college. Consequently, his direct participation in the student group had been limited. More importantly, his commitment to the project was based on his commitment to his childhood neighborhood rather than to his desire for practical correctional experience (which he already had). Unlike the other students, he knew the south side intimately. He was not seen as an outsider whose motivations were suspect, by either the neighbors or by the board of directors. Through his junior college position, he also knew many of the board members personally.

He was probably more committed to the neighborhood focus of Help House than anyone else. He saw the program as a means by which the neighborhood could assist itself, in terms of the types of services it provided, its basic policies, and its hiring decisions. In his view, it was not a program for offenders, but a program for people in the community, including some offenders. From this view emerged a series of informal but valuable connections with other neighborhood groups, both formal and informal. Some of these involved bending or ignoring rules, regulations, constraints, and objectives that were seen as important to state bureaucracy. On the other hand, the state bureaucracy were sufficiently inexperienced with monitoring this type of program that it was not immediately clear whether the state was supportive of the director's innovations, unaware of them, or simply unconcerned. In addition, the continual resistance from the state or district parole office to come to terms with the program placed Help House in an awkward position where innovation was required.

The director actually opened Help House to residents before state money arrived and before he hired staff. Shortly after his appointment, he simply announced to the emergency shelter intake unit that Help House was open for business. He was already housing two or three residents at a time when the staff was hired, and the program was serving between three and five residents on a regular basis by the spring of 1984 (the house had a capacity of seven). The director's decision to open despite lack of support or funds was a deliberate strategy. He decided that so much time had gone into planning at that point that the only way to make the program a reality was to force it into operation and pick up the loose ends as they appeared.

Inevitably, the loose ends began to appear. Help House entered a new phase in which it seemed to operate on two unconnected levels at once. Publically, the projected image was very positive. The program was up and running. Second year funding of $75,000 was obtained from the legislature through the same route: a proposal supported by the assemblyman. Since the program had actually just begun operation as the 1984 state fiscal year approached, there were few accomplishments to demonstrate, but nearly all the official actors were appreciative of this situation. Endorsements for a second year appropriation were obtained from the Catholic and Episcopal bishops, from the mayor, the county executive, and a number of service agencies. The governor also began a statewide program to build shelters for the homeless. Help House qualified for this program and submitted a proposal in the spring of 1985 to purchase and renovate an abandoned building around the corner from the parsonage. The Council of Community Services, the Emergency Shelter Association, and other necessary approvals for this application were obtained. In October, 1984, Help House was awarded $90,000 for this capital construction project.

While parole officially continued to ignore the program, state prisons were now so overcrowded that the parole board became much more liberal in its release decisions. Volume of new parolees was so high that real parole plans (a bona fide residence and job) were often non-existent. Parole officers were seeking support for their clients where ever they could get it. A number of officers resorted to referring their charges to the shelter intake service which, in turn, referred parolees to Help House. By this circuitous route, parole officers avoided their district supervisor's objections to working with Help House and still found shelter for their clients. In addition, since Help House was independently funded, it was open to probationers, ex-jail inmates and other ex-offenders. It had no trouble reaching capacity, and building a waiting list.

However, on another level, the program was not going well. The church became more and more demanding for increased payments and eventually demanded that Help House leave the parsonage in August, 1985. All the work that had gone into building south side support seemed lost, and efforts by board members, the director and his staff to find another suitable residence did not go well. The staff began playing musical rooms—renting a flat here and motel room there and borrowing space as it could from other shelter providers.

At the same time, the president prepared to take a leave of absence from the university to visit another university for a year. Since he was leaving the area, he resigned from the board. Later events suggested that this created a manpower vacuum, if not a leadership vacuum, at the board level. While the south-side woman who had been first vice-president stepped up to the presidency and led the group as well as she could, neither the staff nor the board had been aware of how much time the president had put into the program. Since the new president, and all the other board members, had far less flexible jobs than he (he had always perceived his Help House work as a legitimate university undertaking), his departure really created a gaping personnel shortage in the program. In effect, he had functioned as a fourth full-time staff member rather than as a part-time board member.

In January, 1985, the director temporarily stabilized the program location problem. A black women's social club, of which the new Help House president was a member, was operating out of a former city police precinct building in the north side. It was a large, dilapidated building and expensive to heat. The second floor was empty and contained the old police sleeping quarters—a kitchen, a shower and three large rooms. Help House moved in. The director agreed to pay utility charges for the social club in return for the space. This arrangement was immediately beneficial for both organizations, but it also violated a number of state rules and regulations. The old building was no longer up to code, and living conditions were poor. Additionally, the informal agreement between Help House and the social club turned out to be inappropriate in the eyes of contract monitors from the state planning agency. The agency formally audited the program and found a number of glaring procedural and accounting errors, although no evidence was found of misuse of funds. The accounting problems had begun well before the director's appointment. The first treasurer of the Board had never even balanced the checkbook. By the time the director had taken charge, bookkeeping was in a hopeless tangle.

The director, however, did not respond to the auditor's report appropriately. Whether he purposely ignored the seriousness of the problems or actually misunderstood their implications is not clear. However, he did seem to think that he had far more pressing priorities than pleasing the state planning agency—such as fixing up the living quarters, attempting to fill out a mass of technical papers for the renovation project, and most importantly, meeting the ever-present demands of the five to seven residents.

Under these pressures, relationships between the board and the director and between the director and his program coordinator began to deteriorate. The parolee who had initiated the program paid a surprise visit to the precinct house and came away incensed at the living conditions. The program coordinator began blaming the director for the program problems.

Despite these developments, the program applied for a third year of funding through the assemblyman and was awarded $46,000 in April, 1985. The assemblyman also made it clear that no further funding would come from that source. The program had to achieve a contract with parole, if it were to continue after its third year of seed money from the legislature.

While there is evidence that the director was overworked and his program coordinator underworked, their relationships had deteriorated to the point that increased delegation of work simply did not occur. The director spent far too much time in direct contact with the program residents, which was actually the responsibility of the program coordinator. The coordinator, who had considerable past experience in state agency work and who could have picked up many of the administrative tasks, was apparently not asked to do so. At the same time, however, the coordinator was developing a reputation with other service agencies and with several state agency officials as a crackerjack advocate, particularly with hard cases. On a number of occasions, she had assisted parole officers find residence for parolees who were AIDS victims. As a result of this work, as well as her work with parolees residing in Help House, a number of parole agents were developing favorable impressions of the program. However, this improved relationship seemed to be vested in direct ties between the coordinator and individual officers, and was not moving upward to the district supervisor, who was unaware that Help House had already served 24 parolees. At the same time, the officers, the coordinator, and several board members were firmly opposed to the physical conditions in the precinct station.

Phase V: Crisis and Stabilization

By the time that the previous president returned to Capital City in June, 1985, the internal dynamics of Help House were adversely affecting its positive public image. The director had not succeeded in filing the necessary planning documents to turn the renovation grant into an operational contract. The state was threatening to withdraw the money and give it to another shelter project. The parolee who had originated Help House resigned, as did the chairman, and the treasurer. The board was in disarray, rarely meeting.

The director announced his intentions to resign. The president and the professor, who had been re-elected to the board as first vice-president, asked him to stay on until a replacement could be found. Because of the tensions between the director and the program coordinator, the board had doubts that the coordinator was an appropriate replacement.

One morning in October, 1985, the professor was summoned by the assemblyman to an emergency conference. He rushed to the Capitol. The assemblyman reported that he had received a confidential phone call the previous day from a former board member. This person had reported to the assemblyman the squalid living conditions in the precinct, and went on to charge that the director was misappropriating program money. The assemblyman said that, on the basis of the phone call, he had spoken to the assistant supervisor of the district parole office and a parole officer. They confirmed the physical problems. The assemblyman told the professor that immediate action was necessary if Help House was to survive.

Shortly thereafter, the state planning agency announced a second program audit. The auditor said that he had heard the rumors of mishandling of funds and of the director's imminent resignation and therefore another audit had been ordered.

While this crisis was brewing, the state agencies were preparing their annual budget requests for the following fiscal year. For the third year in a row, parole requested money for a halfway house contract for the Capital City area. A legislative aid reviewing the request called the director of parole and said that she wanted to know why parole should get yet another year of funding for such a contract, when parole had yet to use the money and a halfway house existed in Capital City.

Immediately after that call, the director phoned the professor and said that parole was now prepared to contract with Help House. The parole director mentioned the phone call from the legislative aid, and also pointed out that the local district supervisor had recently been transferred to another district. Many of the local objections to Help House went with him. The professor said that he would put together a new contract proposal immediately. Although he was worried that the new audit and the other claims against Help House would affect relationships with parole, he was not aware of how bad the financial records actually were.

While the papers cementing a relationship between Help House and parole progressed, so did the investigation. Eventually, the parole director said he was suspending further negotiations until he had a report from the auditor. The report was issued in November and was scathing. The auditor listed a number of inappropriate accounting practices, and went further to charge that the board of directors was not giving proper oversight to the organization. However, the auditor also cleared the director of any missappropriation of funds and blamed the planning agency for not providing sufficient support and guidance.

While the crisis was breaking, the new president of Help House became very ill. The professor assumed duties as acting president. While he maintained his high personal trust in the director, he also could see that the director's effectiveness was irreparably compromised. He asked him to resign. An emergency meeting of the board was called in December, and the auditor's report distributed to each member. For the first time in months, all members of the board attended. The board appointed the program coordinator acting director. It also elected two new members, a financial expert who had been recommended by the director of parole, and a man who directed the oldest social service agency in the south side and had an excellent reputation among local and state officials. The board also retained a CPA whom the program coordinator had met when working with the local AIDS Council.

While the board was reshuffling and reorganizing, the state agencies closest to Help House also came together to exert both control and assistance. The state planning agency staff, and especially the auditor, worked closely with parole, the CPA, and the acting director to clarify and rectify the financial accounting. The acting president, the acting director, and an elderly volunteer who had been a high-ranking budget officer in state government before his retirement, worked nearly round the clock to finish the parole contract and the contract for the renovation project. The board ordered the acting director to shut down operations until a new building could be found.

The acting director, who lived in the south side, found a south-side real estate broker who was financially overextended with a number of renovation projects. He agreed to rent two floors of a newly refurbished townhouse to the program. The acting director got several district parole officials actively involved in inspecting the property and approving final renovations. Help House was closed in December, 1985, and reopened in mid-February, 1986 at its new location.

The state withdrew the shelter renovation money, but did invite Help House to reapply. The acting director, an architect on the board, and the acting president revised the proposal, and resubmitted it, requesting $190,000 rather than $90,000. The contract with parole was completed, with its budget integrated with the last appropriation from the state legislature. By March, 1986, Help House had cleared up its financial records, paid off all its back debts, and signed its first contract with parole. In May, 1986, the acting director was appointed director, the professor stepped down as an officer, and an entirely new cadre of officers took the helm—the first full replacement of board officers since the program began. The new president was a black man from the north side and president of the north-side Neighborhood Improvement

Corporation. The new vice-president was the executive director of the old south-side social service agency.

In the summer of 1986, Federal Bureau of Prison officials, who had been watching Help House from a distance since its inception, proposed that the Bureau would be interested in renting services from the program on a per diem basis. The district parole office immediately made the claim that it could use all the space that Help House could make available. The central office parole officials, however, approved of the entrance of the federal residents.

In October, 1986, at a second annual awards night, the assemblyman was presented with a large plaque commemorating his years of support. Many district parole people were in attendance. The professor announced his second resignation from the board. The new board officers were in firm control. The assemblyman, in his thank-you speech, recalled the years of struggle and crisis, and noted to the laughter of those who knew, that only a short time before it looked like Help House would die. Instead, it was now one of only three such programs in the state. He capped this off by announcing that the governor had just awarded the program $189,000 in homeless shelter funds. The program would have a larger, permanent home within months.

At this writing, the program has a capacity of 15 residents and is constantly full. A second contract with parole had been approved, and the per diem arrangement with the Federal Bureau continues. The shelter construction award has become an approved contract and renovation on the building, half a block from the parsonage, is about to begin. The program is a recognized member of Capital City social service agencies and appears, for the first time, to be on firm ground.

Lessons from the Struggle

There are a number of patterns in the above story that should be highlighted. It is these patterns, rather than the unique events, that provide for learning from this experience.

(1) *Key Individual Actors*. First, it is obvious that specific individuals are important to both the successes and failures of Help House. Often the successes and failures can be traced to the same individuals. However, it would be a mistake to see only individual

personalities as important. The key actors in this history provided force for organizational and community change, but they did so in the performance of organizational roles. The individual contributions were essential, but these contributions were possible because of the organizational resources made available as individuals took on organizational positions and as they provided links among organizations. Switches in organizational leadership highlight the connection of individuals to organizational positions. The parolee's detention just before the first officer elections, the professor's necessary absence from the city because of a job change, and the parole district supervisor's removal were all key organizational events.

(2) *Key Organizations.* There were also a number of key organizations in this story. The relative importance of various organizations shifted over time. All the organizations were located in one city, but their proximity alone does not explain their shifting influence. Their varying capacities to shape this process of change was related to their varying interests and constituencies, both in and outside of the city. Several types of organizational interests should be distinguished:

(a) Some organizations—including a few that were informal associations rather than formal organizations—had distinct neighborhood interests. These included neighborhood associations, and the black women's social club.

(b) Some organizations had a broader purview, perhaps city-wide or community-wide. These included the Council of Churches, the junior college, and the Emergency Shelter Association.

(c) Some organizations had even broader domains, defined as districts or regions that included, but were not limited to, Capital City. These included the Council of Community Services (serving a four-county area), the district parole office (covering a six-county area), the assemblyman's legislative district, the central parole office (concerned with the entire state), the state planning agency (the entire state) and the state university (which defined its mission in national terms).

As these organizations varied in the scope of their own jurisdictional interests, they necessarily had varying intensity and frequency of contact with other organizations within the local area. In
general, we could say that this level of interaction on the horizontal
level varied from very high interaction with other local organizations (e.g.: Council of Churches, Council of Community Services,
the junior college, the Emergency Shelter Association) to relatively
low interaction with other local organizations (e.g. the state university, the central office of parole, the district parole office, the state
planning agency).

Not only did the organizations vary in jurisdictional domain
and local interaction, they also varied on at least three other dimensions: size, responsiveness to non-local affairs, and their capacity to
provide local organizations with access to centralized resources.

(a) *Size* appeared important to differentiation of the internal interests within an organization. The parole district
office and the central office did not always display similar concerns. This is typical for large, decentralized
bureaucracies. The differences within that organization had a major effect on the ability of Help House to
achieve its goals. Similarly, the state planning office
was composed of a number of separate units with varying modes of operation providing for mixed signals.
The financial division had a very different approach to
the supervision of community contracts than did the
unit with the original contract monitoring responsibility. The first Help House director apparently
responded to the financial unit's first audit with the
same low priority that seemed appropriate to the very
relaxed approach taken by the contract unit. This
proved to be a major mistake, but it was based on two
years of implicit messages that any actions he needed
to take would be approved by the state agency.

(b) The organizations also varied in their *responsiveness to
non-local interests*. The local district parole office was
considerably more attuned to its central office than it
was integrated with other local service units. (Although
by the end of this history, that pattern had changed.
Either because of, or simultaneous to, interaction with

Help House, the local district office became much more interested in and committed to local affairs). The central parole office was far more concerned, in general, with its problems in the major downstate metropolis than with the problems in Capital City. Additionally, the central office was extremely concerned with legislative actions and the constraints placed on it by other state agencies (particularly the office of the budget).

(c) Lastly, these organizations varied in their capacity *to provide local organizations with access to centralized resources.* One should not make the mistake of assuming that all state agencies are equally broad (non-local) in their focus. The assemblyman, for example, was much quicker to support correctional innovation in Capital City than were the agencies of the executive branch. But then the assemblyman was elected by local constituents, not the governor. He also had access to discretionary legislative funds, while the state bureaucracies were limited to normal state program funds. The central parole office monies were not flexible enough that they could be applied to a specific neighborhood-focused program.

(3) *Coalitions of Organizations.* Help House was not an organizational effort. It was the product of a shifting coalition of organizations. The shape of that coalition changed over time. When the organization was just beginning (as a task force of another organization), the important coalition was very local in character—neighborhood churches, Council of Community Services, junior college. Later, Help House was far more connected with a state coalition (to such an extent, in fact, that several of the local organizations complained that it was no longer a community organization). Moreover, the second organizational crisis created a cooperative effort among the state organizations for the first time: the planning agency, the assemblyman, and both levels of the parole board worked in concert in 1985-1986, but had acted independently in previous years, relative to Help House.

As one reviews the mix of interagency linkages, it would appear that one crucial step for Help House was finding the right mix of local and non-local forces to create a viable organization force field. The force field that eventually emerged may have been created with less conflict and friction than in fact was the case, but it is unlikely that a harmonious, conflict-free effort would ever have worked. A number of commentators (Benson, 1975; Warren, Rose and Bergunder, 1974) have pointed out that cooperative action among organizations requires a relative balance of power: each organization must have something the other wants, and must be able to withhold cooperation if it does not receive some concessions. The ultimate balance of power that worked in this case did not come from within Help House, but did work through it. The legislative aid who threatened the parole budget request was important, and so was the fear of scandal by association for parole and the state planning agency. So was the removal of the parole district supervisor. But if Help House had not survived until those interactions occurred, nothing would have happened. Hence, Help House' ability to outflank initial parole resistance by getting an independent start through the assemblyman was crucial to achieving later cooperative relationships with parole. Although this separate funding of a neighborhood program ruffled a lot of feathers which later needed smoothing, this funding also gave Help House staff the opportunity to prove to parole agents that they were effective in providing services.

(4) *Images and Form.* It would also appear that for such an organization to survive, the image and form of organizing is just as crucial as the substance of its operations. Help House could not be accepted until it adopted the proper form and image. The form made the organization increasingly familiar to the state agencies that had the money and the clients. The state agencies were only satisfied when Help House had its own lawyers, accountants, and other professional-level staff. Operating as a neighborhood grass-roots organization was not effective, given the need for state approval and cooperation. The end result was a halfway house far different than the original conception by the Task Force in 1980. Yet the change was required if services were to be provided.

(5) *Limited Community Resources.* As a true community project Help House identifies some typical problems with community as opposed to organizational innovation. The community actors had to work by and large on their own time, not on organizational

time. It is possible that the Task Force would never have gotten its idea into motion without the massive infusion of time given by the professor. Part of that contribution was based on his previous experience with corrections, but part was simply that he worked for another organization (a university) which permitted him such flexibility in his organizational role that he could effectively incorporate Help House into his work duties.

(6) *Formalization as a crisis.* At the same time, the professor, the first director, and a number of the original board members were guilty of numerous errors, easily seen with hindsight, not so easily recognized when faced in the heat of the struggle. Quinn and Andersen (1984) refer to many of these mistakes as the crisis of formalization. The small cadre of community entrepreneurs responsible for getting Help House first moving were simply unable to find a smooth transition to organizational adolescence. On both the staff and the board level, the process of inclusion of new organizational members did not work smoothly. Delegation did not occur, workload kept building up in the original group rather than spreading out. The small group did not spend enough time trying to develop the skills and commitment of new organizational members to take over for them. The initial cadre got trapped in a vicious cycle. They saw that time put aside for such development would come directly from the time necessary to meet pressing day-to-day demands. As a result, the organization transition from birth to formalization required a crisis, a crisis of sufficient proportions that it almost killed the organization. But with the crisis, the organization did stop to reorganize. The reorganization took advantage of resources that were already available but that had not been mobilized.

(7) *Disadvantages of the private sector.* The professor's initial beliefs that voluntary sector halfway houses could be poorly managed and have trouble achieving effective relationships with the public correctional organizations would appear to be revalidated, up to a point, in his own Help House experience. Despite his previous knowledge, he could not avoid the same problems he had read about and which, in fact, contributed to many of the problems. However, his reading about these problems may have been incomplete. Could it be that the evaluations for other states that he had relied upon were also written of young voluntary organizations not yet through the formalization crisis?

(8) *Non-local dimensions of community.* While many observers would classify this effort as a community change, it would not have unfolded as it did if all the actors and interests could be circumscribed by the small geopolitical boundaries of the city itself. One important lesson would be that even relatively localized issues, such as one small halfway house in one small city, are affected by and, to some extent, are able to affect broad-based interests such as perceived solutions to prison overcrowding and concern for lack of minority group influence on correctional matters.

(9) *Advantages of Multiple Functional Ties.* Finally, not to be missed in this history is the strength that this organization gained by being associated with, and presenting itself as contributing to, non-correctional issues. Much of the original local-level support, and some of the later state-level funding, came from Help House as a contribution to the homeless problem rather than as a contribution to a correctional problem. Moreover, much of its eventual support from parole was tied to its ability to demonstrate a parole-related function that did not challenge parole itself—the residential rather than the service component. The concept paper which detatched it from treatment language made it less threatening, and the increasing parolee shelter problem made it more necessary.

Discussion Questions

1. To what extent was pure chance, or were random events, important to the development of Help House?

2. Could any program seeking to serve parolees actually be a community-run program?

3. What happened to Help House neighborhood goals as it drew closer to and became more dependent on state agencies?

4. How did conflicts and disagreements across the two levels of the state parole agency affect the development of Help House? When did the various state agencies actually agree to work together in this effort?

Chapter 3

The Development of Home Confinement and Electronic Monitoring in the United States

J. Robert Lilly and Richard A. Ball

Recent years have seen a dramatic explosion of interest in the development of what has been referred to traditionally as "house arrest." This term is often used loosely and it is probably preferable to refer to this correctional policy alternative as *home confinement*, a term that has the virtue of covering more specific practices such as *home detention* (in which the residence is used as a detention facility) and *home incarceration* (in which the residence replaces a jail or prison as a point of incarceration. The term "house arrest" tends to imply police action without much in the way of judicial process. Nevertheless, the term may be appropriate in a non-technical sense in that it offers a means of communicating the policy to the general public, a starting point in an effort to communicate more precisely the exact nature of this correctional alternative.

Home confinement has been both praised and damned. It has been praised as more humane and less "corrupting" than confinement in a correctional institution and promising as an economical alternative to building more jails and prisons. It has been condemned, or at least seriously questioned, because it seems to turn the home into a prison, setting a dangerous precedent and violating the sanctity of one's home as one's "castle," a last refuge from governmental intrusion.

In this article, we examine the historical context in which "house arrest" has suddenly become popular. We then consider the development of house arrest programs at two levels of analysis. First, we take a rather brief look at the emergence of these programs on a national basis. Then we move to a more focused analysis of the development of specific programs in Florida and

Kentucky. Finally, we return to a set of general questions about the effects of the house arrest movement on the nature of formal social control in society.

A History of Punishment

Until the mid-20th century, European and North American history had shown three fairly distinct periods in the punishment of offenders. However, the past two decades have seen a major historical shift, with both continents moving into a fourth phase of correctional policy, and the recent house arrest and electronic monitoring movement is part of this new phase.

Three Phases of Punishment

During the early Middle Ages, offenders were punished almost exclusively by undergoing voluntary penance through physical suffering or payment of fines. The acceptance of punishment often followed a confession to religious authorities such as a priest, with the offense defined as a *sin* and the penance as a symbolic repair of wrongdoing. Such policy was consistent with the social conditions of the time.

By the late Middle Ages, social conditions in Europe and the punishment of offenders had entered a second phase. The population had expanded significantly and available land had been settled. A quasi-capitalistic economic order had developed and so had a host of social problems familiar to us today, including unemployment, crowded living conditions, low wages, and crime. Traditional means of punishment gave way to new techniques as attention was directed toward the body of the offender (Foucault, 1977). Public whippings, branding, mutilation, and execution became the nearly universal means of punishment as the most gruesome tortures were applied to the body.

The early signs of what was to become a third phase in the punishment of criminals can be found in the "house of correction" and the acceptance of imprisonment that appeared in Calvinist Amsterdam in 1596, near the end of the Middle Ages. Here the city burghers sought to introduce labor and religious instruction as a means of correcting offenders. This development was associated with an expansion of trade and the growth of new markets outside Europe at a time when the plague had decimated the population, creating a shortage of labor. Although physical cruelty continued as the most popular means of punishing offenders, a new "humanitarianism" had begun to appear, a "humanitarianism" that happened to be perfectly consistent with the "work ethic" appropriate to the new economic order.

This shift has been described as a transition from a policy of "inclusion" dealing with offenders in the community to one of "exclusion" by which they were punished through incarceration outside the community.

Phase Four: Alternatives to Incarceration

By the 1960s, it had become clear that the policy of exclusion, which punished the offender by incarceration within a secure penal facility, was ill-conceived. Such facilities were troubled by idleness, overcrowding, and inadequate financial support. Inmates began to organize, and in some cases to riot, in an effort to call attention to their grievances. Some changes were made as a result of state and federal legislative reforms and decisions handed down by the U.S. Supreme Court. It is important to realize that all this took place during a major civil rights movement. To a considerable extent, what was happening in jails and prisons was a reflection of what was happening in the larger society. Many state legislatures created new programs, including educational programs, work release, home furloughs, and other innovations, all of which required additional funds. The period of the 1960s and early 1970s witnessed an extension of prisoners' rights. Incarceration became more and more expensive and more troublesome to administer.

Ironically, however, reported increases in crime rates throughout the United States in the late 1960s and early 1970s led to a proliferation of "get tough" laws with harsher and less flexible sentences. Parole boards became increasingly conservative, approving fewer and fewer paroles. The result of sending more offenders to jail or prison for longer periods of time while releasing fewer on the "other end" was predictable. Correctional institutions were subjected to severe overcrowding and tremendous social, legal, and economic pressures. From 1970 to 1979, the imprisonment rate increased an unprecedented 39 percent (Langan, 1985). This dramatic shift continued as the prison population in the United States jumped from 300,034 in 1977 to 463,866 in 1984 (Beck and Greenfield, 1985). It is now over 600,000. In fact, three of every 100 adult males in the United States were under correctional supervision at the end of 1985. Altogether, nearly three million men and women were under some form of correctional supervision, either imprisonment, probation, or parole (*New York Times*, Jan. 2, 1987:10).

Those faced with this problem perceived essentially two solutions. If imprisonment was to remain basic policy, then more institutions had to be built and maintained. If not, then it would be necessary to seek alternatives to incarceration and perhaps to move into a fourth phase in the European-North American tradition of punishing offenders. As was often the case in the past, a new direction was taken without abandoning the old. Many correctional facilities were constructed. There were, for example, 31 more state prisons and one more federal prison in 1984 than in 1983 (Allen and Simonsen, 1986) and President Reagan's proposed budget for 1988 allocates $65.4 million "to expand and repair the federal prison system, including $96.5 million to build two new medium-security prisons" (*New York Times*, Jan. 6, 1987:9). But there are limits to the former policy: one new prison cell may cost more than $80,000 and the yearly cost of holding each inmate may exceed $15,000. In some cases, the costs are even higher.[1] And other prison systems that have held down cost are faced with court orders to upgrade facilities and programs. Indeed, in some cases, the courts have assumed control of state prison systems to judicially implement the mandated improvements.

Despite the tendency to cling to and even to accelerate the old policy of *exclusion* of offenders in walled institutions, it seems clear that North America has entered a fourth phase of punitive policy, a phase that will lay heavy stress upon *inclusion* of the offender through what is usually termed "community-based corrections." Of course, probation has been an "alternative" for many years, but probation has come under fire as amounting to mere "leniency" that neither punished nor rehabilitated offenders but simply ignored them if they stayed out of further trouble for a certain time (see Petersilia, 1985). What was planned was nothing less than a "new justice" (Aaronson et al., 1977) that would provide alternatives in the form of halfway houses, weekend incarceration, diversion programs, restitution, community-service options, and a variety of other "community-based" strategies. Such alternatives have proved so popular in some circles that it can be claimed that "community corrections for the majority of offenders is the way of the future" (Allen and Simonsen, 1986:63).

One of the most recent of these new "alternatives" is home confinement or "house arrest." "House arrest" is a particularly dramatic example of the extent to which inclusion may develop in that it appears to take "community corrections" to the limit by converting the most private of realms, the home, into a place that actually *functions* as a correctional facility. Some have questioned the trend toward community corrections as another move toward repression under the guide of "humanitarianism," as a policy that is having the effect of turning the "community" itself into one vast prison (Cohen, 1985). If this is true, then the movement toward "alternatives" is a continuation of the imprisonment phase of punitive policy rather than a new phase. This is a subject beyond the scope of the present article.

Development of Home Confinement[2]

In the United States, "home detention" had been put in practice in St. Louis as early as 1971 (Rubin, 1985). By 1977, such programs for youth had been put in place in Washington, D.C.; Baltimore, Maryland; Newport News, Virginia; Panama City, Florida; St. Joseph-Benton Harber, Michigan; San Jose, California; Louisville, Kentucky; and Tuscaloosa County, Alabama. These programs, developed first as a means of dealing with youthful offenders within a context of home and family, were in part a response to widespread concern that increasing numbers of juveniles were being unnecessarily and unjustly detained in detention facilities prior to adjudication. In view of these concerns and the traditional use of such practices as curfews in dealing with troublesome youth, home detention seemed an attractive alternative and it had the additional merit of economic appeal. These first home detention programs were in essence much like current forms of *intensive supervision* (Gettinger, 1983). They proceeded on the assumption that youth can be kept out of further trouble by assigning paraprofessionals to them who would personally contact a juvenile at least once a day and maintain daily telephone contact with parents and teachers.

The later movement toward home confinement of adult offenders was somewhat less the result of a desire to protect the offender from the "corrupting" and "stigmatizing" effects of institutional incarceration (although this was one major consideration in proposals for use of the practice with drunken drivers, see Ball and Lilly, 1983b), than it was a consequence of jail and prison overcrowding and the perceived need for more careful supervision of offenders granted probation. The scramble to respond to the overcrowding crisis resulted in at least 30 states implementing some form of house arrest by 1986. Another dozen states were planning programs to be implemented within one year.

These developments were witnessed at the federal level as well. Beginning March 3, 1986, the federal government approved an experimental program for the U.S. Bureau of Prisons, the Probation Service of the U.S. Courts, and the Parole Commission that allows federal parolees' release dates to be advanced 60 days on the condition that "he remain in his place of residence during a specified period of time each night."

The surge of interest in home incarceration of adults as an alternative to jailing or imprisonment has been closely associated with the development of electronic monitoring technology. Electronic monitoring programs have received considerable attention in academic circles, the popular media, and in reports from the National Institute of Justice. The National Institute of Justice has not only provided publicity for this new technology but has also increased its funding of home incarceration and electronic monitoring projects.

While these developments provide an overview of the emergence and growth of home confinement programs in the United States, beyond their connection with the prison population crisis they tell us little about the dynamics behind program development in specific jurisdictions. In the following pages, we look more intensively at the development of these programs in two states.

Case Studies

Two programs at the forefront of the house arrest movement are those of Kenton County, Kentucky and the state of Florida. These programs are interesting because they contrast a locally administered, experimental project (Kenton County) with a comprehensive state program (Florida) considered the most ambitious in the United States. The comparisons are guided by four questions related to program creation, goals, support and opposition. The effort is to elucidate how a common impetus, prison and jail overcrowding, generated varied responses in two different jurisdictions. More specifically, we ask:

1. Who took the lead in the program's development and why did they support the program?

2. What was the response of probation/parole? Did they support the program? Why or why not?

3. Who funded the technology/equipment?

4. What types of communities have developed programs? Have any communities resisted house arrest and electronic monitoring?

1. Who took the lead in the program's development and why did they support the program?

Florida: In Florida, the Department of Correction's interest in house arrest initially grew out of a need to address their *statewide* prison overcrowding problems. By May 1983, the problem had become so severe that a group of criminal justice officials developed an alternative to traditional prison incarceration which they termed "community control." For these officials, community corrections was a concept that included, among other things, confining offenders to their residence as an alternative to incarceration. The concept was quickly formalized by the passage of the Florida Correctional Reform Act of 1983. It was intended and interpreted to provide a safe diversionary alternative to imprisonment and to help address "the problem of increasing prison population and associated high costs" (Flynn, 1986:64).

Unlike the 1986 Kentucky Revised Statute (KRS 200-250; see subsequent discussion) which defined home incarceration and electronic monitoring, the Florida Correctional Reform Act (1983) addressed Florida's approach to home confinement only. The Florida statute stated:

> Community control means a form of intensive super-
> vised custody, including surveillance on weekends and
> holidays, administered by officers with restricted case-
> loads. Community control is an individualized program
> in which the freedom of an offender is restricted within
> the community, home, or noninstitutionalized residen-
> tial placement and specific sanctions are imposed and
> enforced (FS 948:001).

Florida's efforts to design and implement community control and home confinement was, unlike Kentucky's effort, presented to the legislature, the public, and correctional employees, as being explicitly grounded in correctional philosophy. The argument was made, for instance, that community control was a form of punish-ment designed to develop a controlee's accountability and respon-sibility. To this end, the legitimating rhetoric claimed that punishment and reward were integral to "the backbone of democracy" and thus applicable to criminal offenders (Flynn, 1986). Punishment under conditions of home confinement would there-fore be consistent with values which stressed self-improvement, the work ethic, and the desire of offenders for better jobs and better pay.

Kentucky: While the supporters of Kentucky's proposed 1984 home incarceration law did not claim that it reflected or supported democracy, they did stress the argument that such an alternative had the potential to be cost effective and punitive. At a time when prison and jail overcrowding was a major concern, these argu-ments were persuasive, but whether they were convincing was another matter. The proposed 1984 bill (KY House Bill 8.305) was, in fact, deliberately killed in committee when it became embroiled in a tax reform controversy that threatened its passage.[3]

The decision to kill the 1984 bill did not, however, result in a moratorium on the subject. The interest in the topic was so intense in 1984 that the Kentucky Department of Corrections recom-mended and funded a pilot home incarceration and electronic monitoring program even though explicitly enabling legislation had not passed the state's General Assembly. Toward this end, a receptive audience for the pilot program was found in Kenton County (Covington), Kentucky, an area that had provided much of the initial support for the proposed bill. The county's popular and powerful Judge-Executive and the county jailer saw the pilot research project as a possible solution to jail overcrowding and as a possible avenue for avoiding court injunctions to reduce jail over-crowding. After a one-year research project which produced mod-est findings (see Lilly, Ball, and Wright, 1987: 189-203), the 1986 Kentucky General Assembly passed KRS 532:200-250 with mini-mal opposition. The statute, which defined and provided statutory guidelines for home incarceration and electronic monitoring, was signed into law in April of the same year.

2. What was the response of probation/parole?

Florida: Unlike Kentucky's proposal for home confinement, the Florida proposal had the benefit of a *statewide* implementation and evaluation plan. It included an implementation manual that was developed for the entire state, thus reflecting an effort to ensure programmatic uniformity. In addition, the statewide plan included special training for the "community control officers"; emphasizing the goals of the new program. The training of the officers also included self-defense, surveillance techniques (not high tech, elec-tronic surveillance), search and seizure, legality, identification of behavior disorders in the mentally ill, cross-cultural differences, and training in handling intensive relationships (Flynn, 1986:66). The new training, plus ample positive press coverage and a reduced caseload, enhanced the acceptance of the program by the community control officers. At no time was the program reported to have been interpreted as a threat to job security. In fact, addi-tional community control officers were reported to have been hired. Acceptance of the program by the community control officers may also have been enhanced by the fact that the program *did not* rely on electronic monitoring which could have been seen as job-threatening.

Kentucky: The situation in Kentucky was different. While the Kentucky legislation was constructed to provide statutory guidelines for home incarceration and electronic monitoring, there were no statewide implementation plans. In fact, the push for home confinement, as mentioned previously, came almost exclusively from *one* section of the state where a pilot project was conducted *before* passage of enabling legislation. Here, it is instructive to emphasize that the region of strongest state support for the home incarceration law came from northern Kentucky, an area with a long history of being different politically from the rest of the state. This distinction is often attributed to its location within the metropolitan area of Cincinnati, Ohio. With the majority of the state to the south, including the capitol, major cities, parks, universities and industries, northern Kentucky residents and politicians often express dismay over the General Assembly's history of "neglecting us." Major projects needing statewide political support that are initiated in northern Kentucky, often fail. This regional schism is exemplified by the fact that no governor has been elected from northern Kentucky in almost 100 years, despite the fact that it represents the state's third-largest concentration of population. For these reasons, it was not surprising that on more than one occasion lobbyists for the law reported encountering comments in and around the Kentucky General Assembly and the Department of Corrections (DOC) such as "you people up there are weird. We'd expect you to come up with something like this." In this instance, the only significant involvement by the state's DOC and probation officers was at the local level (Kenton County).

Several features of the Kentucky program contributed to the enthusiastic support at the local level. Key among these were the cooperation from one key probation officer who was designated to work with the program. Indeed, this officer's work was so integral that it appeared essential for the project's success. Her support was the most dependable feature of the project, a contribution made more significant because the support from county judges and the jailer vacillated during the time of the research. While it is difficult to be exact as to why, the strong support was no doubt influenced by the experimental and temporary nature of the research and the fact that it was conducted under the unusual conditions of cooperation among state officials, county judges and jailers. Further, local support was enhanced by the fact that it was the nation's first DOC-funded evaluation of home confinement *and* electronic monitoring and it generated a great deal of press attention for all involved.

There were, however, many moments of frustration for the probation officer in charge of the program, especially when the monitoring equipment failed to work. This did not prevent viewing home confinement and electronic monitoring as an additional means by which probation services could be enhanced. After the project was completed and it became clear that a statewide implementation program would not be developed, the probation officer sought and was granted a new assignment. At this point, a variety of reasons led to a decrease in the local probation office's support for the program. These developments included the election of new judges and changes in judicial interest in house arrest and electronic monitoring, the fact that the project did not generate anticipated funds from supervision fees, and an unexpected reduction in jail overcrowding.

3. Who funded the technology/equipment?

Florida: The first union of house arrest and electronic monitoring in Florida was accomplished in late 1983 when Judge J. Allison DeFoor (Monroe County) sentenced four people to house arrest and electronic monitoring (Ball, Huff, and Lilly, 1988:93). The equipment had been developed by Omni Communications, Inc. (Tavernier, Florida), and the offenders were supervised by Pride, Inc., a non-profit agency located in West Palm Beach, Florida. At this time the monitoring equipment was in the early stages of development and no purchase or lease was required.

Late in the same year, Pride, Inc. proposed a similar program for Palm Beach County where jail overcrowding was a serious problem. By late November, 1984, Pride Inc.'s proposal had been approved and Palm Beach County's first offenders were sentenced to home confinement and electronic monitoring. At this time, Pride Inc. was purchasing the monitoring equipment from Omni Communications. The purchasing funds were generated by supervisory fees charged by Pride Inc.

Kentucky: Between early November 1984 and late January 1985, the Judge-Executive of Kenton County, Kentucky decided to experiment with house arrest and electronic monitoring. With only one vendor demonstrating the operation monitoring equipment, the county decided to purchase monitoring devices from private vendors. There were no competitive bids.

4. What types of communities have developed monitoring programs?

The majority of communities (in both Florida and Kentucky) with monitoring programs are urban. There are, however, clients/offenders in each state who live in rural or semi-rural settings. The central offices of all programs are in urban settings.[4]

In each state, voices of opposition have been heard. The nature of the opposition, however, has generally been unorganized and concerned with easily answered technical questions such as the reliability of the monitoring equipment and cost effectiveness. The authors are unaware of any community which had sufficient opposition to this alternative to traditional incarceration to prevent implementation.

Contrasting the Florida and Kentucky Experiences

Contrasting the development of home confinement and electronic monitoring in Florida and Kentucky thus points to several similarities and differences in implementation patterns. In Florida, for example, the initial support for the community control program came from within the state's criminal justice system. It therefore had almost instant legitimacy in a state known for its conservative law and order legislation and law enforcement policies.

The extent to which the Florida proposal was readily accepted is witnessed by its rapid approval. It took less than six months between the time the law was proposed and its formal enactment, a process helped no doubt by the fact that it was sponsored by criminal justice officials and sold to the public and legislature as grounded in philosophies of democracy and punishment.

The passage of Kentucky's home confinement and electronic monitoring law, by comparison, took more than two full years of pluralistic lobbying. At no time did it have the benefit of a unified and concerted sponsorship from statewide criminal justice officials. Neither was the Kentucky proposal grounded in an explicit punishment or corrections philosophy being consistently presented to the legislature and public. Ironically, however, delayed passage of the bill did not seem to be merely reflective of this lack of official support or clear philosophical underpinning. Rather, the proposed bill was killed rather than defeated because other matters of more immediate concern were on the agenda of Kentucky's General Assembly.

Furthermore, the 1986 proposal was, in fact, passed not so much because of its broad political support but rather due to its lack of opposition. The Kentucky Department of Correction, which had sponsored the pilot evaluation that produced modest findings, chose neither to support or oppose the law. The result was that the law made legal what was already in operation in one section of the state, and provided guidelines for additional home confinement and electronic monitoring proposals in other sections of the state.

Although the Kentucky law did not have the same effect in terms of statewide implementation as the Florida law, it did address several concerns omitted in the Florida legislation. Included were issues such as prisoners rights, the types of information that could be transmitted electronically (no visual or audio information), and concerns with net widening and "big brotherism" (Lilly, Ball, and Wright, 1987:201). These latter provisions were intended to protect judges from public criticism. The Florida statute's silence on these issues seems to reflect the conservative law and order perspective and an insensitivity to prisoner rights, net widening, and big brotherism. The Kentucky law thus seems to represent more of a balance of interests.

It is impossible at this point to offer empirical support to the argument that the actual programs in each state reflect the tone and intent of each state's legislation. Anecdotal information and media accounts suggest, however, that the state sponsored programs are reflective of legislative intent. The home confinement programs in Florida have been reported in various media accounts as "tough" and "hard" on offenders. The lack of statewide programs in Kentucky render comparisons impossible. The Kenton County project, however, suggests that fairness and justice have been more important than "toughness."

Summary

Thus, the Florida and Kentucky experiences illustrate two different patterns of implementation. The commonality between the two was the effect of jail and prison overcrowding. In both jurisdictions, home confinement was considered a means of addressing the overcrowding crisis. In Florida, however, the effect was persuasive to state-level policymakers who developed a central plan for statewide implementation. In Kentucky, while the crisis ultimately pushed state-level policymakers to enact enabling legislation, there was no attempt to push local-level authorities to adopt. Consequently, the initiative of key officials at the local level was required for implementation.

The speed with which home confinement programs have developed in Florida, in Kentucky, and in other states, attests to the popularity of these programs. There are, however, a number of unresolved issues related to the home confinement movement that demand attention prior to the institutionalization of these programs on a national basis.

Unresolved Issues

One's evaluation of the home confinement movement is likely to be conditioned by one's reading of the history of corrections. To some, this has been, in general, a history of progress from brutal torture to imprisonment and, finally, to community-based alternatives to incarceration. To others, the history is one of good intentions that have tended to produce unanticipated, unfortunate consequences at every stage. To still others, the shifts in punitive policy described above really represent deep and very insidious trends toward *total social discipline* and the complete suppression of individuality under the guise of humanitarianism and progress (Cohen, 1985). Addressing these types of issues requires an examination of the context in which the house confinement movement has surfaced.

For those concerned that the house arrest movement represents the further intrusion of state control, the fact that the movement has coincided with the conservative political shift of the 1980s is telling. The house arrest movement is seen as part of two more general trends associated with this conservative era. These trends include the move to a crime control model (see Packer, 1968) of criminal justice policy and the increasing demand that behavior traditionally regarded as private be "accounted for" by some form of surveillance in the public realm.

The crime control model involves a reduced stress on due process rights of the accused, places heavier emphasis on the rights of society, and regards crime control as so important that greater state intervention is necessary. The dominance of the crime control model is witnessed in the Burger and Rehnquist (Supreme) Courts' move away from the due process emphasis of the Warren Court, in the trend towards determinate and mandatory sentencing policies, and the tremendous expansion of prison populations.

The trend toward expanded state involvement in private behavior is witnessed in the increasing governmental interest in drug use and sexual behavior. The federal government's well publicized "War on Drugs" involving proposals for urinalysis drug testing in the workplace and sanctions making users ineligible for federally insured student loans and mortgages is reflective of this trend. In the area of sexual behavior, the movement to recriminalize abortion and decisions such as the Supreme Court's ruling upholding Georgia's sodomy law criminalizing consensual sexual behavior between adults[5], also reflect the trend toward governmental intrusion in private behavior.

To a considerable extent, concerns expressed over possible invasions of privacy, either by the government or private agencies, have come about because of the enormously increased power of technology to penetrate the private realm. The federal Office of Technology Assessment has called for immediate federal legislation to control this technology, indicating that (1) the extent and use of electronic surveillance by the private sector is unknown, (2) the number of federal court-approved wiretaps and hidden microphone "bugs" was the highest ever in 1984 (the last year surveyed), (3) about 25 percent of the federal agencies responding to the 1984 survey indicated some use of electronic surveillance, and (4) a number of federal agencies were relying heavily upon such technology. The FBI, for example, was using nine different types of surveillance technology in 1984 with plans to implement eight additional types. In addition to new techniques in data transmission, "beepers," sensors, closed circuit television systems, satellite communication equipment, electronic mail, cellular telephone equipment, miniaturized cameras, optical devices, and a host of other surveillance devices, the Office of Technology Assessment (1985) identified at least 85 computerized record systems operated by federal agencies for purposes of law enforcement, investigative, and intelligence matters. These systems together include about 288 million records covering approximately 114 million citizens.

It is within this overall political context, involving the ascendance of crime control policy, extension of governmental involvement in private matters, and expanded surveillance technology, that the home confinement and electronic monitoring movement has emerged and spread. Recognition of these trends does not answer normative concerns about the desirability of these new correctional programs, but does suggest that the movement be viewed in light of very fundamental questions of liberty and the proper role of the state.

Conclusions: Questions and Reservations

Our interest in the possibilities of home confinement as an alternative correctional policy was triggered, in part, by a search for some option to be used in lieu of institutionalization. We were aware that "house arrest" was nothing new and that some such practice had often been used informally, especially with juveniles, and part of our concern had to do with protecting the due process interest of the offender and providing clearer, formalized policy to protect public employees such as probation officers from charges of arbitrary and capricious behavior. The National Advisory Commission on Criminal Justice Standards and Goals for Courts had made such concerns official, suggesting that a court-approved agreement be required whenever "diversion" involved actual deprivation of liberty as is the case with "curfew" or "house arrest." Our hope was for formal adoption through enabling legislation and careful evaluation of the policy through systematic research.

It is important to note that while home confinement has been adopted through the legislative process in certain instances (e.g., Florida), it has been more common to implement it through administrative or judicial fiat. This may pose a problem, if only because the policy may be altered with every new administrator or judge. Legislation allows for a full, public debate. This in turn serves to legitimize the practice and to provide for greater consistency in its implementation. As for the "systematic research," quantity is no substitute for quality. The evaluation research that has attempted to assess the effectiveness of home confinement has been troubled by many problems: a lack of random assignment of cases; the necessity of relying upon judges' opinions as to whether, for example, they would have sentenced a given offender to jail had home incarceration not been available as an "alternative;" and a host of other difficulties which call into question its validity. This is the product of circumstances rather than the fault of the researchers, but the need for more systematic work is clear.

Beyond these issues are others which are more difficult to address. As Marx (1981) has shown in his analysis of the "ironies" of social control, "It would appear that modern society increasingly generates ironic outcomes, whether iatrogenic effects... unintended consequences of new technologies...or the familiar sociological examples found in prisons and mental hospitals or in the careers of urban renewal and various other efforts at social reform." These "ironic outcomes" frequently mean that a "solution" to one problem creates one or more new problems that may be worse. To anticipate this sort of thing might be considered mere paranoia if it were not so clear that the tendency is built into the system, including the increasing complexity and interdependence of social life and the increased effort at intervention based upon expansion of professionalism and expertise. This may be the case with "house arrest" and there is an obligation to confront the possibility.

Although home confinement is still insufficiently developed as a formal correctional policy to allow for any early predictions, some trends seem to give reason to wonder about the future. In our earliest work with "home incarceration," for example, we advocated the use of volunteers to assist with monitoring of compliance (see Ball and Lilly, 1983ab; 1985; 1986ab; Lilly, Ball, and Lotz, 1986). The practical reason for this was to reduce pressures on probation offices. More generally, however, the suggestion was argued in terms of our theoretical perspective, which seeks to facilitate the reconciliation of offender and community. Given monitoring by volunteers, the offender would be involved with representatives of the local community rather than with government officials and it was hoped that the use of volunteers would contribute to the increased involvement of the public in the systems of criminal and juvenile justice. Given what seemed to be both practical and theoretical advantages of the use of community volunteers to monitor compliance, it is important to consider the extent to which the actual implementation of this alternative has been accomplished through the much more expensive and much less communal option of electronic monitoring.

The fact is that new correctional policies are rarely carried out as originally envisioned. They tend to be caught in a common pattern involving a "dialectics of reform" in which the established agents of social control who operate the criminal and juvenile justice systems on a day-to-day basis accept certain "reforms" but only on their own terms. Despite our theoretical position stressing the reconciliation of offender and community, we were troubled from the beginning by evidence that suggested the "community" might actually resist such reconciliation (Greenberg, 1975:1-10). The eagerness to embrace electronic monitoring now suggests that those operating the criminal and juvenile justice systems may be more interested in maintaining tight, bureaucratic control over offenders than in opening supervision programs to the public. Of course, it must be admitted that the electronic monitoring is likely to be a more reliable system, more free from problems of "human error." Whether this is good or bad depends upon one's point of view.

The socio-historical and social-psychological problems here are quite complex. We cannot go as far as the National Advisory Commission on Criminal Justice Standards and Goals for Corrections (1973:222) in assuming that, "The humanitarian aspect of community-based corrections is obvious." The use of the home as a jail, prison, or detention facility may contribute to the further blurring of the old distinction between what is public and what is private. As Hylton (1982) has pointed out, the President's Commission recognized years ago that any such blurring of lines between institutional treatment and community treatment might affect the rights of offenders. To what extent may it also affect the very concept of individuality?

As we indicated earlier, one's interpretation of the trend toward increased use of "house arrest" will be conditioned by one's reading of the history of correctional policy. Is it essentially a history of progress? Is it better interpreted as a history of unintended consequences and unfortunate "ironies?" Or is it really a history of the extension of total control over the individual? If the pattern is one of "progress," then it may be reasonable to accept "house arrest" as a continuation of correctional policy into more progressive and "civilized" practices. If the pattern is one of good ideas going wrong or leading to unforeseen and unfortunate consequences, it becomes especially important that those implementing "house arrest" do so with special caution and change course quickly if things begin to go wrong. If it is more accurately interpreted as a pattern of historical extension of control over the individual, the danger that "house arrest" is part of a larger trend that may lead toward the extinction of individuality is very real.

Notes

[1] A Minnesota correctional institution has reported direct and indirect *daily* maintenance costs at $103 per inmate or a total of more than $36,000 per year, which is twice the amount it would have cost to send the inmate to Harvard.

[2] "House arrest" has a long history dating at least to St. Paul the Apostle, who is reported to have been placed under house arrest (custodia libera) in Rome at about the age of 60. Galileo Galilei also experienced house arrest after a "second condemnation" trial in Rome in 1633. More recently, Czar Nicholas II of Russia and his family were kept under house arrest in 1917 until their deaths in 1918. This history is a cause for concern as it has traditionally been used as a means of silencing political dissent. South Africa, Poland, South Korea, India and the Soviet Union are all known to employ house arrest with political dissenters. On the other hand, France introduced the concept of *control judiciare* in 1970 as a fairly straightforward form of pre-trial detention involving a provision for home confinement as an alternative for common offenders (Gerety, 1980). In 1975, Italy initiated a policy of affidamento in *provo ai servizio sociale* (trial custody), which may be described as a form of parole following a shock period of three months incarceration. Other European countries have also experimented with some manner of home confinement as a means of dealing with a variety of offenders.

[3] The eventual passage of KRS 200-250 in 1986 required more than two years of extensive cooperation among several interested groups that were mobilized by self-interests and the tireless efforts of a fiscally conservative and civic-minded criminal defense attorney).

[4] In only one Kentucky location has it been necessary to establish an 800-number because of long distance phone costs associated with monitoring.

[5]In *Bowers v. Hardwick* (U.S. Sup. Ct. 1986) the Court upheld a Georgia statute that makes it a felony, punishable by 20 years in prison, for consenting adults to engage in oral or anal sexual relations.

Discussion Questions

1. Lilly and Ball discuss both broad, national trends and specific programs in two places. How do the broader changes in culture, policy, and politics affect specific program implementations?

2. Where would you place Florida and Kentucky home confinement programs on the horizontal and vertical community dimensions? To what extent does the entrance of private technology vendors complicate the community field?

Chapter 4
Accountability in a Decentralized System: An Organizational Dilemma of The United States Probation System

Thomas R. Maher

The U.S. Probation Service is responsible for a variety of functions relating to the sentencing and community supervision of federal offenders. Specific responsibilities include: (1) conducting pre-sentence investigations on individuals convicted in the U.S. District Courts; (2) community supervision of individuals placed on probation by the District Courts; and (3) community supervision of parolees released from the various federal correctional institutions.

Presently, there are 94 separate offices in the Federal Probation System (including Guam, Puerto Rico and the Virgin Islands) serving each of the Federal District Courts. Many of the district offices have one or more sub-offices in the outlying parts of the district. The area covered by each probation office and the staff size is determined by the geographic boundaries and workloads of the Court.

The Central office of the Federal Probation System is located in Washington, D.C., as a division within the Administrative Office of the U.S. Courts. The Probation Division is responsible for the administration and management of the entire Probation System.

During the 1970s, federal probation experienced increasing pressures and demands from Congress and the U.S. Judicial Conference for information on the impact and effectiveness of its service. While this new emphasis on accountability was felt by all branches and levels of government (Briar, 1973), it created a difficult problem for federal probation's management because of the

System's unique organizational structure; which is, quite simply, decentralized, dispersed and fragmented.

This chapter focuses on analyzing the response of this largely decentralized system to external demands for accountability. The intent is not to evaluate the system's response but rather to examine the response as a way of providing insight into two key issues of probation administration — centralization/decentralization and judicial versus executive control.

Probation developed largely as a local function administered by the courts. However, the long term trend has been toward centralizing probation services. Despite this trend, the debate over the relative merits of centralized versus decentralized administration and judicial versus executive control remains a live one. Further, although the centralization/decentralization and judicial/executive debates are usually geared at local and state probation agencies, several features of the federal probation system make it particularly appropriate as the focus of analysis. First, the administrative structure of the agency includes elements of both centralization (central office) and decentralization (94 district offices) within a judicially controlled system. Second, the federal system is often looked to as a model for the states. Third, the divergent responses of the central office and the district offices to the external demands for accountability illuminate key issues in the centralization/decentralization and judicial/executive debates.

The chapter begins by noting the pressures for accountability and then places the study in historical context by examining the origins and development of the federal probation system. Subsequent discussion focuses more explicitly on the organizational structure of the federal probation system as illustrated by the systems response to the accountability demands. The concluding section attempts to place these observations within the context of the centralization/decentralization and judicial/executive debates.

Accountability in Corrections

The pressure for accountability and evaluative research in corrections has been growing steadily during the past 20 years. Stuart Adams (1975:4) traced the beginning of the accountability movement to the California Department of Corrections by noting:

A notable early instance of this pressure occurred in California in 1957. The Legislative Auditor directed the State's Department of Corrections to request special funding for the purpose of systematizing and accelerating its ongoing research activities... The Auditor noted that corrections was becoming even more costly, yet there was apparently little impact on the behavior of ex-prisoners.

In the early 1960s, following the lead of California, several state correctional systems created Evaluation Units to begin the process of systematically assessing the impact of their correctional programs. In reviewing the results of 100 of these early evaluation efforts, Walter C. Bailey (1966:160) noted that "the more rigorous the research, the less likely it would be to show a positive result."

The publication of Bailey's work led to an even greater demand for correctional accountability. As Adams (1975:4) noted:

The late 1960s and early 1970s saw still more pressure for evaluation in corrections, particularly from the field of criminal justice itself.

Many works published in the 1970s added 'fuel to the fire. Perhaps most noteworthy was the review of some 231 studies conducted between 1945 and 1967 by Robert Martinson and his associates (Martinson, 1974). The Martinson review, which has since been labeled the "nothing works" study, concluded that "very few rehabilitative programs, whether institutional or community based and regardless of type of treatment have had any significant impact on recidivism" (Nelson, Ohmart and Harlow, 1978:3).

The end result of these and other[1] studies has been a tremendous pressure for corrections to demonstrate its value; and for correctional professionals to be accountable for results. As noted by Adams (1975:4) in his discussion of State Corrections and State Planning:

State Correction Agency administrators and State Planning Agency directors are being asked for continuing assessments of kinds and in volumes that are unprecedented.

Accountability in Federal Probation

Until the late 1970s the Federal Probation System had not experienced the kinds of accountability pressures that most state and local agencies had encountered. However, since 1978, this situation has changed dramatically as the Congress and the U.S. Judicial Conference have begun asking some pressing questions about the performance and utility of the system.

The reason for this sudden concern with Federal Probation's impact can be explained in part simply as a by-product or consequence of the system's phenomenal expansion during the previous ten years; and the substantial increase in Congressional funding which has been necessitated by this growth. While the system's expansion will be discussed in greater detail later in this chapter, it should be noted here that between 1970 and 1977, over 1,000 new probation officer positions were created, resulting in a 175 percent increase in the system's professional work force. But a more direct explanation for the new emphasis on accountability in Federal Probation is a report published by the General Accounting Office in October 1977, titled *Probation and Parole Activities Need to Be Better Managed.*

The GAO Report

The General Accounting Office, which is the investigative arm of Congress, examined the operations and performance of five federal district probation offices and concluded (Comptroller General, 1977):

(1) There are serious questions about the federal probation system's ability to help offenders adjust back into the community while protecting society.

(2) Probation officers are not making a sufficient number of contacts with the offenders they supervise.

(3) Identified case needs are usually not treated by probation officers.

(4) Rehabilitation planning receives inadequate attention.

(5) Probationers and parolees do not always receive needed services.

(6) When clients are referred for services, follow-up by probation officers is often inadequate.

(7) The Administrative Office of the U.S. Courts has not adequately managed or monitored probation activities.

(8) District-level monitoring is inadequate.

Attached to the document was a letter addressed to the President of the U.S. Senate and the Speaker of the House of Representatives from the Comptroller General of the United States. The letter stated, in part, that:

> The Federal Probation System is not adequately providing supervision and rehabilitation treatment to probationers and parolees. If supervision and rehabilitation are to become more effective, the Administrative Office of the U.S. Courts must begin to adequately manage and monitor probation activities.

It is clear from the report and the accompanying letter that the Administrative Office, and, more specifically, the Probation Division, is being held responsible for the management and performance of the U.S. Probation System. And since the publication of these documents, the Probation Division has taken several steps that are clearly in response to the GAO's criticisms. However, the impact of the steps taken to date has been very limited. The reasons for this assessment follow.

Efforts to Gain Control

There are numerous examples of efforts by the Probation Division to increase the performance, uniformity, and accountability of the Probation System. For instance, only six months after the GAO report was released, the Division distributed *Publication No. 105—The Presentence Investigation Report,* which mandates a uniform format for the presentence investigations conducted by federal probation officers. This monograph calls for the elimination of much of the excess verbiage that is found in many presentence reports and the inclusion of some new sections or headings relating to sentencing alternatives and sentencing patterns in the federal courts for the different types of offenses. A review of the district office's implementation of this monograph, however, shows that the efforts by the Division to attain national uniformity in the structure of presentence investigations has had only limited success. Some district offices have fully adopted and implemented the Publication No. 105 format. But many districts have adopted only part of the format suggested in the monograph; and at least one district has not changed to the new format at all. In still other districts, the format being utilized varies in accordance with the wishes of the different judges on the court.

Because the Division's work on the Presentence Monograph was initiated prior to the publication of the General Accounting Office Report, it would be inappropriate to suggest that it was produced in direct response to the GAO critique. However, the implementation of the monograph guidelines does exemplify the Division's problems in setting uniform probation policy.

A far more significant attempt to gain control on the part of the Division (and one that can be more clearly linked to the GAO Report inasmuch as it was started subsequent to the GAO Report and deals with the specific criticism by the GAO) is the Monograph on supervision procedure. *Publication No. 106—The Supervision Monograph* sets forth precise guidelines for the district offices pertaining to case classification, contacts with clients, the structure of supervision plans, the structure of case reviews, and the format and content of all case records (Keenan, 1980). The reaction of a few districts to an initial draft of Publication No. 106, provides insight into the difficulty of implementing uniform supervision procedures. One district office chief (from one of the largest district offices), for example, criticized the section of the monograph which mandates the use of chronological entries as the method of case recording. The Chief Probation Officer argued that this method is burdensome, time consuming, and, generally, not useful or necessary.[2] While most districts presently utilize the chronological entry-recording method, this district does not. And the chief has made it clear to the Probation Division that under no circumstances will he change to their system of record-keeping.[3]

In another major metropolitan district, several probation officers, working with their Chief, documented a litany of problems that they have with the standards and mandates set forth in the monograph (Reintegration Program Planning Committee, 1980). The group stated that, among other things, Publication No. 106 will:

(1) Limit the probation officer's professional judgment by requiring that all cases be classified and supervised in accordance with a standardized classification device.

(2) Limit the probation officer's ability to respond to unique situations in dealing with client problems by requiring specific actions on the part of the officer.

(3) Dramatically increase paperwork via a host of new forms and formats which are perceived as repetitive and time consuming; thereby impeding the agency's mission of working with and providing service to clients.

This kind of effort on the part of the Probation Division to increase standardization, uniformity and accountability (especially in terms of paperwork) is typical of what many agency/system managers have done in response to external pressure for evidence of performance (Tropp, 1974; Glisson, 1975). As noted by Thomas Cruthirds (1976:179):

The net effect of this cumulative effort (accountability) has been the inception and development of information systems in state social service agencies that place first line social service workers—those who render service directly to the clients— under increasingly intense pressure to provide feedback on their performance. The workers must record, case by case, both the process and the outcome of their intervention.

Also typical, and perhaps to be expected, are the kinds of arguments against standardization and record-keeping as set forth by these probation officers above (Federal Judicial Center, 1973).

What is unique, however, is that in the federal probation system, the position taken by the district offices may overrule the mandates established in Washington.

It should be noted, at this point, that the two Monographs referenced above are not the first attempts by the Probation Division to establish national guidelines for presentence investigations or supervision practices.[4] Rather, they are just the latest in a series of policies which have been issued in an attempt to unify the system and increase accountability. It should also be noted that the Division's efforts in this regard have not been limited to presentence investigations and supervision; but instead, have covered a wide range of areas, including hiring practices, staff utilization, promotions and even interagency relations (Guide to Judicial Policies and Procedures, Probation Manual, 1979). However, there is substantial evidence that the several district officers continue to have little in common in many of these areas; and, to some extent, are operating as independent and self-designed units.[5]

As noted in the introduction, the purpose of this chapter is not to defend or critique the positions taken by the district offices in relation to the two Monographs discussed above or, for that matter, the positions taken by district offices on any of the policies issued by the Probation Division. Nor will this chapter attempt to justify or disclaim the merit of specific guidelines established in Washington. Instead, an effort will be made to explain the unique organization/system structure that enables this kind of diversity and independence on the part of the district offices and to examine its consequences; especially as it relates to the future of the Federal Probation Service. Of special interest in this regard will be the dilemma faced by the Administrative Office and the Probation Division, in terms of their being held accountable by Congress for a system over which they exercise limited control.

In order to place the dilemma described above in perspective, it will be necessary to first examine the historical development and phenomenal growth of the Probation System.

Historical Origins and Growth

The Federal Probation Service was created through the Federal Probation Act, which became law on March 4, 1925. The

Act enables the Federal District Courts to appoint probation officers "to obtain essential personal data and social background information about individual offenders before the court and to provide a system of effective supervision over offenders" (Chappell, 1950:30). The initial growth of the system was very slow; in fact, the first three probation officers were not appointed until 1927.[6] By 1930, there were only eight officers in the United States (Moore, 1950:22).

Between 1927 and 1930, the probation service was administered by the superintendent of prisons. However, an amendment to the original Probation Act signed into law by President Hoover on June 6, 1930, transferred responsibility for the system to the Attorney General. In discussing this Act, Victor Evjen (1975:8) noted the responsibilities and duties of the Attorney General relevant to probation:

> Provision also was made for the Attorney General to investigate the work of probation officer; to make recommendations to the court concerning their work; to have access to all probation records; to collect for publications, statistical and other information concerning the work of probation officers; to prescribe record forms and statistics; to formulate general rules for the conduct of probation work; to promote the efficient administration of the Probation System...and to incorporate the operation of the Probation System.

The Attorney General delegated these responsibilities to the Bureau of Prisons. During the Bureau's administration of the system, which lasted ten years, the system grew dramatically from the eight officers appointed in 1930, to 233 officers in 1950 (Gooch, 1977).

On August 7, 1939, President Roosevelt signed a Bill that established the Administrative Office of the U.S. Courts (Gooch, 1977). Initially, the Probation System was excluded from this Act and remained under the Executive Branch. After a heated argument between the Department of Justice and the U.S. Judicial Conference, however, the position of the Congress changed; and on July 1, 1940, the responsibility for supervision of the Probation System was transferred to the Administrative Office. This transfer resulted in the creation of two new positions within the Administrative Office—Chief U.S. Probation Officer and Assistant Chief U.S. Probation Officer—and these two constituted the initial central office staff of the Probation System under the Judicial Branch of Government (Gooch, 1977).

The growth of the Probation System was slow but steady from 1940 to 1970. The growth was not caused by a dramatic increase in the use of probation by sentencing judges, but was more an effort to get caseloads down to manageable levels. Persons under supervision during this period increased by only about 12 percent (34,562 to 38,409); but the number of probation officers increased by about 163 percent (from 233 to 614).

A tremendous increase in the number of persons under the supervision of the Probation System did begin to occur in the early 1970s with the increased use of probation as a sentencing alternative by judges throughout the country (U.S. Department of Justice, 1978). From 1970 to 1979, the number of persons under supervision increased from 38,409 to 65,795. Congress responded to this growth in workload by authorizing over 1,000 new probation officer positions between 1970 and 1977; and as of 1984 there were 1,902 U.S. Probation Officers. Hence, the real growth of Federal Probation has been most recent.

This expansion of the Probation System has, of course, resulted in a host of new costs and funding needs. As the system grew, new office space, new equipment, and additional clerical positions were required.

The financial impact of the System's expansion is demonstrated, in part, through the Congressional appropriations for Probation. The total appropriation for 1928, 1929 and 1930 was only $25,000 (Bates, 1950). In 1931, it was increased to $200,000 (Evjen, 1975:7). In 1979, almost $7,000,000 was spent on just the salaries of probation officers and support staff (Administrative Office of the U.S. Courts, 1979:54).

In view of Federal Probation's growth and consequential costs, it is not surprising that Congress instructed the General Accounting Office to examine the impact of the System. It is perhaps more surprising that the Congress continued to support the expansion, especially during the early to mid 1970s without any hard evidence of the System's performance and impact.

The Consequences of Decentralization

The scathing General Accounting Office report seemed to set off alarms in the halls of Congress. Following the publication of the document, the Probation Division continued to claim a need for additional probation officers and formally requested funding for this purpose. However, from 1977 to 1983 neither the Judicial Conference nor the Congress agreed to any of these requests and no new positions were authorized.

The pressures on the Probation Division were clearly reflected in a September 15, 1980, announcement that:

> The Probation System faces a reduction of 70 probation officer positions and 45 probation clerk positions over the next two fiscal years. The House Appropriations Committee in its report on the Judiciary Budget for Fiscal Year 1981 directed a reprograming of resources and transfer of positions from Probation Offices to Clerks Offices to meet the demonstrated need for 175 additional deputy clerks.

In discussing these staff cuts at an Executive Board Meeting of the Federal Probation Officers Association[7] in Philadelphia, Pennsylvania, in September 1980, the Chief U.S. Probation Officer, William Cohan, noted that the system is still highly vulnerable for an even greater personnel reduction. In an effort to counter this, the Chief requested that a work measurement study be initiated immediately in an effort to demonstrate that an additional staff cutback is not feasible.[8]

In the short run, the work measurement study proved successful as the findings were used to persuade Congress to authorize 205 additional probation officer positions between 1983 and 1984. Whether this somewhat "crisis-oriented" effort to save probation officer positions will be successful in the long run remains to be seen. It is clear that the pressure to demonstrate performance and impact is squarely on the shoulders of the Probation Division. The problem, however, and the point of this chapter, is that the *organizational structure* of this system will make the attainment of evidence to demonstrate the system's utility extremely difficult, if not impossible.

In order to clarify this argument, it will be necessary to examine in greater detail the organizational structure and intra-organizational relationships of the Probation Division and the district offices.

Organizational Structure and Roles

The Probation Division

The two-man central office staff of 1940 has also grown during the last 40 years. Today, there are 23 central office (Probation Division) positions—15 professional and 8 support staff (Administrative Office of the U.S. Courts, 1975). The professional staff consists of the Chief U.S. Probation Officer, two Assistant Chiefs, five Regional Probation Administrators (RPA) and seven Probation Program Specialists. Organizationally, both of the Assistant Chiefs report to the Chief Probation Officer.[9] One of the Assistants supervises all of the Program Specialists who perform a variety of support functions, including the development of new data systems; monitoring Congressional activities relative to corrections, training, publication of the System's Newsletter; and assisting in several ongoing projects and programs coordinated by the Assistant Chief.

The second Assistant Chief supervises the five RPAs who are directly responsible for field operations in five geographically distinct parts of the country (Northeast, Southeast, Western, North Central, and South Central). It is the RPAs who are the primary links between the Administrative Office and each of the 94 district probation offices.

A clear statement of the authority of the RPAs (and, in turn, the Division and the Administrative Office) over the district offices is difficult to produce. The statutory authority given to the Attorney General relevant to probation in 1927 (as listed earlier in this paper) was transferred to the Administrative Office in 1940. However, that language is vague, at best, and subject to several interpretations. The Probation Division (1975:2-3), for example, states that among other things, it has direct responsibility for the field offices in terms of:

(1) Establishing standards of professional performance (including presentence investigations, case supervision, report writing, and case records).

(2) Formulating rules for field office operations, record management, professional services, and statistical data processing.

(3) Development and maintenance of procedure manuals.

(4) Investigating and evaluating the work of probation officers through direct observation, review of reports, and analysis of statistical data.

(5) Administering the Personnel Program of the Probation System, including recommending standards to the Judicial Conference, assessing personnel needs, developing budget estimates, and allocating positions.

While this appears to be a fairly clear statement of both responsibilities and authority for enforcement, the authority becomes somewhat watered down upon closer examination. The method of enforcement is through "requiring compliance where authority exists and consulting with court and probation staff, *and making use of persuasion.*"

But precisely where the "authority exists" and where "persuasion begins" is not statutorily defined. Nor is it defined in the mandates issued by the United States Judicial Conference.[10] This lack of clarity has resulted in the situation described earlier in this chapter in terms of the Probation Division lacking control over the Federal Probation System. To understand this situation more fully, we must analyze the organizational structure and various relationships that exist at the district level.

The District Offices

The five regions managed by the Regional Probation Administrators differ greatly in terms of their geographic size, the number of district offices they include, and the number of probation officers working in the region. The Northeast Region, for example, is geographically the smallest regional area; but it encompasses the largest share of the 94 district offices (23), and the largest number of probation officers (466) (Federal Probation Workload Statistics, 1980). By comparison, the South Central Region includes a much larger area, but has the fewest number of district offices (13) and it is also last in terms of probation officer staff (219).

The several district offices within each region also differ greatly, especially with respect to the number of authorized positions. The State of New Hampshire, for example, has only one district office with only two probation officers; while the State of New York has four separate district offices with a total of 127 probation officers. The largest of the New York State Offices is the Southern District which covers only Manhattan Island. The office has 55 probation officers. The largest single district office in terms of staff size is California/Central (Los Angeles), with 112 probation officer positions.

It should be noted, too, that the assignment of personnel to the various districts is not based solely on workloads; hence, there are also great differences in the average caseload and presentence investigation workload of officers in different districts. According to statistics released by the Statistical Analysis and Reports Division of the Administrative Office for Fiscal Year 1979, the range in workloads is: from the Virgin Islands District Office, where the average number of investigations conducted by each officer was 77 and the average caseload was 96; to the Nevada District Office, where the average number of investigations was only five and the average caseload was only 34.

The organization structure in each district office varies in accordance with the size of the office. A district office classification system used by the Probation Division is perhaps the best means of describing the structural differences. This classification system identifies the districts as either: (1) major metropolitan, (2) medium, or (3) small.

Major metropolitan districts typically include a chief probation officer and a deputy chief (California/Central has two deputy chief positions). Depending on the number of staff positions authorized, the deputy chief will have between three and 12 supervising probation officers reporting to him/her. Each of the supervisors will monitor the work of six to nine line probation officers. In most major metropolitan districts, the chief, deputy chief and supervisors do not do any casework or investigative work.

Middle-sized districts typically cover small, metropolitan areas and their surrounding counties (i.e., Pittsburgh). Organizationally, the middle-sized districts are much like the major metropolitan districts, with the differences being that there are fewer supervisors (i.e., one to two) and no deputy chief position. Supervisors report directly to the chief, and, as is the case in the major metropolitan districts, chiefs and supervisors generally do not carry caseloads or conduct investigations.

The district offices classified as "small" by the Division differ greatly from the two types described above. In these districts, there are six or less staff positions, and while one of the officers will be appointed chief, he/she will usually carry a caseload and conduct investigations.

Major metropolitan, middle, and small districts are found in each of the five regions of the Probation System. In the Northeast Region, for example, the Eastern District of Pennsylvania is classified as a major metropolitan district. The agency serves Philadelphia and surrounding counties. It consists of a chief, deputy chief, six supervisors, and 43 line probation officers. None of the management personnel carry caseloads. Also in the Northeast Region is Pennsylvania/Western (a middle district), which includes Pittsburgh, Erie, and their surrounding counties. The office staff consists of a chief, two supervisors, and 18 line officers. Here too, none of the management staff do casework. And, finally, an example of a small district office in the Northeast is Vermont, in which a chief and two line probation officers all carry caseloads and do investigative work for the entire state.

The common element in all of the district offices throughout the country is the position of chief probation officer. As demonstrated above, the range and scope of responsibilities of the 94 chiefs vary greatly (it should be mentioned that the pay for the chiefs differs in accordance with the district size). But in every instance, chiefs are responsible for the operation of the federal probation service in the districts. The authority of the district chiefs and their mandate is established by statute as follows (U.S.

Code Title 18, Section 3654, as Amended August 2, 1949, C383, 2, 63, Statute 491):

> Whenever such court shall have appointed more than one probation officer, one may be designated chief probation officer and shall direct the work of all probation officers serving in such court.

As noted earlier, the primary function of the probation system is service to the court through presentence investigations and the supervision of convicted federal offenders. It is important, therefore, to examine the role of the court and its relationship to the probation office in discussing the organizational problems of Federal Probation.

The Court

By definition and as used in this chapter, the term *court* refers to one or more federal district judges responsible for deciding the civil and criminal litigation within a district. As of mid-1983, there were 515 authorized judgeships in the 94 districts; and like the distribution of probation officers, the number of judges on a court varies in accordance with the district's workload. At present, this variation ranges from the few courts authorized only one judgeship (including Washington/Eastern and Guam) to the Southern New York Court which is assigned 36 judges (Administrative Office of the U.S. Courts, 1984:4).

Judges are appointed to Federal District Courts by the President of the United States with the advice and consent of the Senate. The appointments are for life, as the judges can only be involuntarily removed from the bench through impeachment by the Senate—an extremely rare action in the history of the American Judicial System. Specifically, upon appointment, a judge continues to hold office as long as he/she maintains "good behavior" (Guide to Judiciary Policies and Procedures, 1980).

In those courts consisting of more than one judge, the "one who is senior in commission and under 70 years of age is the chief judge of the district court" (Federal Judicial Center, 1976:15). In multi-judge districts the workload is distributed among all the judges "as provided by the rules and orders of the court," with the chief judge having the authority and responsibility for the observance of such rules and orders. The chief judge also assigns cases when rules have not been established or in instances where they do not apply.

The authority of the district courts over their probation offices is defined by statute. As amended in 1940, the Probation Act vests in the district courts the power to appoint all probation officers; and specifically states that these officers shall "serve within the jurisdiction and *under the direction* of the court making such appointment" (U.S. Code Title 18, Section 3654, as amended August 2, 1949, C383, 2, 63, Statute 471). Lest this authority be misunderstood, the following interpretation is offered from the publication, "An Introduction to the Federal Probation System" (1976:15):

> In all matters relating to probation, unless otherwise specifically provided by law, the district court is the final authority.

The courts differ greatly in terms of the extent to which they set policy for probation offices. Some courts, for example, take an active role in establishing policy and procedures pertaining to both the direction of the probation office and its internal operations. Most courts, however, delegate this responsibility to the chief probation officer—rarely intervening or overriding their chief probation officer's decisions.

The courts also differ in terms of the method of interaction with the probation department and their adherence to policies established. In some instances, the court will act as a body and follow standard procedures; however, it is not uncommon for one or more of the judges to instruct the probation office to ignore policy and handle their cases in a fashion directly contrary to established procedures. An example of this is found in one major metropolitan district, where, by policy, the probation officer in court at the time of sentencing is usually not the officer who conducted the investigation; but is, instead, any one of several duty officers assigned to sentencing on that particular day. Recently, however, one of this district's judges instructed the probation office that, for his cases, the investigating officer must be in court on the day of sentencing. While this directive is clearly contrary to established procedures and creates a great deal of inconvenience (particularly for the officer who must come in from the field for the sole purpose of attending the sentencing), the probation office has adhered to the judge's wishes.

Examples such as this are numerous and most probation offices can cite a wide range of unique and different procedures that are followed for individual judges on the court. The point, however, is that the probation offices in the federal system do not always serve just a single entity, i.e., the court; but instead, must be responsible to each of the independent judges assigned to the district.

A district probation office then is subject to at least two external authorities. On the one hand, there is statutory accountability through the Administrative Office policies and guidelines; but, at the same time, the office is in existence through statute to operate "under the direction of the court." And, as noted above, in most instances, the court (which may include up to 36 independent managers) is the final authority.

It should be reemphasized that, operationally, there is little question as to which of these authorities (judges vs. Administrative Office) is superior. Clearly, the judges, both individually and collectively, carry far more influence and power. This point would be obvious to anyone who observes the daily operations of the federal probation office. When the Probation Division makes a request for information or assistance, and/or issues directives, chief probation officers may react promptly and comply with the Division's wishes; but, frequently, the chief will react when and if he has the time. A request or directive from a judge, on the other hand, is much more likely to receive the immediate and full attention of the chief probation officer and his/her staff.

In closing this section, it should be re-stated that the focal actors in this unique organizational configuration are the district chief probation officers. Through the support and influence of their judges, the chief probation officers are usually in a position of near total authority over the operation of the district probation service. In a sense, they have become "power brokers" who, through the influence and support of their court, are able to affect local policies and procedures which are often inconsistent with Administrative Office directives.[11] The result of this, as noted in a

1975 federal probation publication, is that each probation office continues to function as an independent operation responsible only to its own court.

Hence, the federal probation service is, in reality, a largely decentralized system. As noted by Merrill A. Smith (1975:26), a now-retired chief of the Federal Probation System:

> Unlike the majority of government agencies, the federal probation system, from its inception, has been a decentralized organization.

Where consistency does exist between the policies of the probation division and actual operations in the district field offices, it is usually the result of mutual cooperation or common interest, rather than enforced mandates (Smith, 1975). As one Probation Division staff member recently noted, "we manage district offices *through persuasion and subtle manipulation.*" And, as explained by Smith, in discussing the early efforts by the Administrative Office to obtain probation system uniformity:

> *With persuasion as their only weapon,* the Director (of the Administrative Office) and his aids pressed vigorously for observance of the standards.

If the reality is that persuasion and manipulation are the primary management techniques available to the Administrative Office, why has the General Accounting Office and, in turn, Congress placed responsibility for the performance of the system on the shoulders of the Probation Division? One explanation may be that the organizational structure has been misinterpreted. By simply examining the organizational chart of federal probation, one could easily surmise that there is a direct authority relationship extending downward from the Administrative Office to the field offices. A less than thorough review of the statutory mandates pertinent to federal probation could reinforce this assessment since the language is vague, if not contradictory, and requires careful analysis. As evidence of this, consider the fact that federal probation was characterized as a "centralized system" in at least one LEAA publication (Allen, Carlson, and Parks, 1979:56).

But what, in fact, does a careful review of the statutes show? In discussing this question, Chester McLaughlin (1975:32) noted:

> The responsibility of administering the system (federal probation) *is shared, by statutory direction,* by the local court and the Probation Division of the Administrative Office of the U.S. Courts.

While this "shared responsibility" is perhaps an accurate interpretation of the law and of Congress' intent, it ignores two basic realities. First, that the Probation Division has little, if any, real power to carry out its responsibilities; and, secondly, local courts, which have the power, are, to a great extent, not accountable for their actions.

What then is the answer to this "organizational dilemma" of obtaining accountability in a highly decentralized federal probation system? Should the Administration of the system be truly centralized with real authority placed in the hands of the Probation Division; and/or should the probation function be placed within the Executive Branch of Government, thereby limiting the influence of the judges? Certainly, there would be some advantages to this structure in terms of the problems identified in this paper, but there may be dysfunctional consequences as well.

Centralization vs. Decentralization

The literature on probation management offers several arguments on both sides of the probation centralization/decentralization question. For example, the National Advisory Commission (1973) noted that centralized probation systems are less likely to be subject to local political influences, and are more likely to result in an efficient utilization of system resources. The President's Commission of Law Enforcement and the Administration of Justice (1967) noted that in centralized systems it is more likely that uniform policies and procedures will be developed resulting in a "greater likelihood that the same level of services will be provided to all clients in all cases." The President's Commission also noted that centralized state probation systems are more likely to be "in the forefront of developing innovative programs, demonstration projects and correctional research."

The counter arguments to centralized probation administration are equally persuasive. Allen, Carlson and Parks (1979:54), for example, noted that decentralized probation systems are "generally characterized by participation, access, and responsiveness." Along these same lines, Killinger, Kerper and Cromwell (1976) observed that decentralized systems are bound less by "bureaucratic rigidity and are thus able to experiment with new methods and procedures." Other arguments on this side of the issue—relating, however, more directly to state systems, include the potential for greater community support and a more thorough familiarity of the community on the part of line workers (President's Commission on Law Enforcement and the Administration of Justice, 1967).

In reviewing the administrative structures of probation services in the 50 state governments, Carlson and Parks (1979:47) noted that "the current trend in corrections appears to be in the direction of centralization." The Council of State Governments (1977) made a similar observation, noting that while these systems (those moving toward centralization):

> may benefit from the overall increase in funding for corrections, from more sophisticated information systems, and from greater visibility to the state legislature...the price for these benefits...may be the loss of their independent status, a consequent limitation in policy making discretion, escalating political pressure on controversial programs, and a possible loss of financial resources to institutional programs.

Judicial Branch vs. Executive Branch Control

The question of centralization in probation administration is usually discussed hand in hand with the issue of judicial vs. executive control. While this is actually a separate issue, a review of the literature does show that most centralized systems are under executive branch management, and most decentralized systems are under judicial branch control (Allen, Carlson and Parks, 1979:56).

Common arguments in favor of judicial control are (1) since most probation work comes from the courts, the system should be under court management (Wahl, 1966:371); (2) probation can be more responsive if it is under court direction (Allen, Carlson and more responsive if it is under court direction (Allen, Carlson and Parks, 1979:56); (3) the court as a manager can obtain more rapid feedback on the effect of probation as a sentencing alternative (Allen, Carlson and Parks, 1979:56). On the other hand, however, the National Advisory Commission (1973) noted that:

> Since all other subsystems which carry out court dispositions of offenders are in the executive branch, inclusion of probation could insure closer coordination of programs, more rational allocation of staff, and increased access to the budget process and the establishment of priorities.

Summary

Unfortunately, there are no clear or definitive answers to these questions, as several strong arguments can be made for maintaining the decentralized and judicially controlled structure that presently exists in federal probation. But given the current pressures on the system, it is likely that these kinds of questions and various other alternatives will soon be under consideration. In discussing the issue of probation administration, Allen, Carlson, and Parks (1979:56) reported that:

> If we ask what is the proper location for probation administration, we find that there are strong arguments for centralized administration, for decentralized administration, for placement in the Executive Branch of Government, and for placement in the Judicial Branch of Government. It appears that this question is not amenable to definitive answers; what is important though is a thorough consideration of the tradeoffs which characterize each alternative.

The decentralized and judicially controlled structure presently in existence in Federal Probation is characterized by many of the strengths and weaknesses listed above for this organizational/system type. For example, many of the district offices are (as the National Advisory Commission warns) supposedly affected by local politics, especially in terms of hiring practices. "Who you know" as opposed to "what you know" is, unfortunately, still said to be the key variable for job applicants in a few districts. Centralizing the hiring function would probably go a long way toward eliminating this kind of activity; and perhaps on a system-wide basis, the Service would benefit through the elimination of political appointments. However, it must be recognized that centralizing the hiring function would almost certainly be an expensive undertaking; and more importantly, it could place great restrictions and limitations on those districts that are already free of political pressures and which are already hiring the most qualified local applicants.

On a different level, a move toward centralization would, as the President's Commission noted, enable increased uniformity and standardization; and consequently would result in a greater likelihood of similar levels of service being provided across districts. At present, the level of service does vary greatly from district to district and, as has been noted in this essay, the Probation Division has difficulty in even setting in place the devices for recording and monitoring district office activity. But here again, the question of "trade-offs" must be considered. Would the administrative paperwork necessitated by a centralized monitoring system prove to be a major hindrance to those districts already active in the service delivery area? And, can a single mechanism for monitoring service delivery be utilized in the highly diverse districts of this system? The answers to these kinds of questions can not be derived from the limited analysis provided in this chapter, but these are the types of issues that should be thoroughly reviewed prior to any structural change.

Before closing this narrative, it should be mentioned that there have been some efforts in the past to place the federal probation system under a centralized, executive-controlled structure. However, in each instance, the attempts have been thwarted by the judiciary. Not surprisingly, the probation district offices have consistently supported the current structure and are clearly not interested in resurrecting the question of reorganizing federal probation.

What is perhaps different now, however, is that the federal probation system is under tremendous pressure to demonstrate its utility. It is not likely that this pressure will diminish. Although it may be overstating the case to suggest that federal probation's survival is at stake, it is not an exaggeration to note that the survival of the system in terms of its present size is clearly in jeopardy. Federal probation has fought a long and hard battle to obtain the resources and personnel it now holds. However, it is quite likely that these gains will be greatly reversed in the absence of substantive information demonstrating the system's performance.

It is not the conclusion of this chapter that the Federal Probation System should be placed under the executive branch of government. But, it is hoped that this alternative, along with others, will be considered in the very near future. The trade-offs involved in adopting the various structures available must be examined and analyzed with survival as a fundamental concern. It is hoped that this chapter will provide a first step in sorting out those trade-offs and in pointing out what is at stake.

On a broader level, it is hoped that this essay will contribute to the resolution of the kinds of questions that have been raised by Allen, Carlson, and Parks (1979:56), who proclaimed:

> It is clear that comprehensive, descriptive studies of the experiences of agencies placed in different administrative locations could assist in accurately and completely delineating the advantages of each location.

Notes

[1]See especially von Hirsch, Andrew and Hanrahan, Kathleen, *Abolish Parole,* National Institute of Law Enforcement Assistance Administration (September 1978), and U.S. Comptroller General, *State and County Probation Systems in Crisis,* Washington, D.C., General Accounting Office (May 1976).

[2]California Central, the largest district in the Federal Probation System, uses quarterly summaries of supervision activity and case progress as the sole method of case recording. The summaries are based on handwritten notes that are kept in the file by the probation officer. No "running log" of case activity is maintained.

[3]Interestingly, with the endorsement of their Chief Judge, this district has also refused to adopt the Publication No. 105 mandates pertaining to sentencing data being included in the presentence reports.

[4]See Administrative Office of the U.S. Courts, *Publication No. 102* and *Publication No. 103,* Washington, D.C., Administrative Office of the U.S. Courts.

[5]An example of the variance in terms of both hiring practices and staff utilization is found in a review of the Probation Officer Assistant positions. These slots were created and authorized several years ago in an effort to "bridge the

gap" between probation officers and "hard to reach" clients. According to the Administrative Office regulations, POA's should not have a college degree, nor should they assume caseload responsibilities. Some district offices however, have ignored these guidelines, hiring applicants with a bachelor's or master's degree who are now carrying regular caseloads.

[6]The first U.S. Probation Officers were assigned to the Southern District of New York, the District of Massachusetts, and the Southern District of West Virginia.

[7]The Federal Probation Officers Association is an organization consisting of and representing the interests of federal probation officers. The Executive Board meets twice each year to address a variety of issues of concern to the membership.

[8]As noted in the Probation Division's biweekly newsletter — *News and Views* (September, 1980):

The Probation Division has requested that the Management Services Branch in the Administrative Office conduct a work measurement study of the Probation System. The purpose of this study will be to develop a staffing formula which can be used to accurately determine the number of positions, both professional and clerical, that are needed. The Management Services Branch has scheduled such a study to begin not later than November 1980.

[9]It should be noted that the Pretrial Services Branch of the Probation Division is not included in these figures inasmuch as the program is still in "pilot project" status.

[10]The U.S. Judicial Conference is the policy-making arm of the Federal Judiciary. It is comprised of the Chief Justice of the United States, the Chief Judges of the 12 Appeals Courts, the Chief Judge of the Claims Court, the Chief Judge of the Court of Appeals for the Federal Circuit, and one District Judge from each circuit.

[11]It should also be noted that this process occasionally works in reverse. Although less common, Chief Probation Officers sometimes solicit support for a position from the Administrative Office and then use this support to persuade Judges to adhere to a policy they initially opposed.

Discussion Questions

1. According to Maher's observations, how does pressure for accountability affect diversity among local units of a community-placed system? How could this change in diversity affect the district office capacity to respond to other organizations within the district?

2. How does the long-standing probation debate over centralized or decentralized administration relate to the community vertical and horizontal dimensions? For example, how might decentralization strengthen the horizontal interactions among district officers and other organizations in a community? Would that necessarily happen? Or could some very decentralized systems fail to interact frequently with other organizations in a community?

3. Consider the advantages and disadvantages to offenders to be clients in centralized rather than decentralized organizations?

PART TWO
THE OPERATION OF COMMUNITY CORRECTIONS ORGANIZATIONS

The chapters in the first part of this book focused on the interaction of correctional organizations and other community units (including other correctional organizations) during periods when correctional programs were being developed and changed. That is, those chapters examined correctional programs when the community fields (as defined in Chapter 1) were shifting. In contrast, the chapters in this section focus on correctional programs themselves rather than on changing relationships between the correctional organization and other actors in community fields. The focus here is on the operations of correctional programs in which the locus of policymaking and the sources of legitimacy and financial support have (for the time being) been determined.

Organizations have been studied in various ways. It is common to focus on (1) organizational goals and the means of attaining them, (2) the structure of roles and interaction patterns and the strategies for controlling them, (3) the culture, or values and social climate in the organization, and/or (4) the interaction of the organization with its environment. The first part of this book studied the last of these four dimensions. The three chapters in this section deal with the first three dimensions: goals and means (or technology), culture, and structure.

In a book of this size, these dimensions cannot be completely or evenly represented. In the chapters which follow, organizational culture receives the least attention, although Jester's description of parole and probation departments includes some important comparisons in the value differences between the two kinds of field supervision.

The concern for organizational goals and means receives the greatest attention. In Chapter 5, Jean Jester provides a thorough and perhaps unique account of the activity of probation and parole officers in eight departments. Her theoretical framework is that of organizational technology: The process by which organizations translate goals into daily production activity through the arrangement of resources around particular tasks. She is successful in identifying and measuring three distinct technologies, both in the work of individual officers and in the overall operations of eight different agencies. This analysis provides one of the most complete pictures of the actual work of probation and parole. Moreover, by examining how beliefs are translated into actual resource distributions, she is able to resolve some important and long-standing questions about whether the ideological conflict between service and control accounts for significant differences in the actual behavior of correctional officials.

In Chapter 6, Nora Harlow and E. Kim Nelson continue to examine correctional technology. However, rather than focus on the activities of individual probation or parole officers, these authors explore several technological strategies used by probation managers as a response to budgetary pressures. Based on their observations of probation agencies located in widely varying communities across the United States, Harlow and Nelson are able to identify a number of strategies that may, or may not, be useful to probation managers facing a common environmental threat—budget cuts.

In Chapter 7, David Duffee and Kevin Wright focus on variation in organizational structure and technology among correctional transitional release programs in four states. They show that despite very similar general policy goals (i.e., reintegration), the state programs vary on characteristics such as organizational auspice, assumptions and objectives, staffing, client selection, technology, and linkages to community service providers.

These chapters focus more attention on the internal operations and structure of correctional programs than they do on the position of the organization in its community field. Consequently, the dynamics of community forces are more submerged in this section of the book. However, there are important questions to be asked about the relationship between the local/extra-local dimensions and the internal operations described in this section. For example, Harlow and Nelson's review of strategies to cope with budgetary pressures clearly demonstrates how these technological choices are influenced by a host of organizational and political forces.

What may be an appropriate strategy for the chief probation manager in rural New Hampshire may be entirely inappropriate in Contra Costa County, California. Duffee and Wright note how the transition programs in Michigan, Minnesota, New York and Pennsylvania varied considerably in terms of community linkages. Further, they begin to develop a picture of how various program dimensions may be related to the nature and extent of community interaction.

The relationships between the community-level variables and the technological factors covered by Jester are not so clear at this point. The ambiguity of the connection may, in fact, be the nature of the beast. The Duffee and Wright chapter, like a number of reports on correctional as well as other public agencies such as schools, welfare agencies, and mental hospitals, indicates a loose-coupling of the technical and policymaking levels in such organizations. It may well be that the nature of correctional supervision makes this activity less dependent than some other organizational functions upon the source of policymaking and financial resources. In other words, issues such as due process, standardization, and uniformity may be more dependent on the mix of local and non-local forces surrounding the agency than are the issues of which offenders' needs are met or which supervision technology is practiced by an officer.

The possibility that technology is less determined by community setting than some other factors, if true at all, is true only in matter of degree. Jester convincingly documents, for example, some significant differences in resource distribution between the statewide parole departments and the more local probation departments. Moreover, what Jester calls the "environmental control technology" cannot be effectively promoted in an agency which has poor quality interactions with referral agencies or in communities which have few human services to offer. If, as Duffee and Clark (1985) have predicted, this technology becomes more frequently practiced in the future, it will mean that correctional agencies will have successfully changed their position in the community field. They will succeed by formalizing their attachments to other organizations in the community.

It is important to remember, however, as the Duffee and Wright findings indicate, that this type of formalization will not occur simply through the adoption of reintegration goals. Rather, community linkage will be determined by a number of dimensions of organizational structure and technology. These dimensions, in turn, are not so much the product of goal statements as they are the result of the mix of political, legal, and social forces surrounding the program. These concerns, of course, lead us back to issues of environmental relationships and the array of community values and interests. We return to these concerns in the following section.

Chapter 5
Technologies of Probation and Parole

Jean Jester

Technologies are means to an end. The ends of the criminal justice system are generally classified as retribution, deterrence, incapacitation, and rehabilitation. Corrections, including community corrections, as part of the larger system of justice, would be expected to share these goals. Thus, among the observable activities of community corrections organizations, we would expect to find examples of technologies which are oriented towards these various goals.

Three Technologies of Probation and Parole

The first three of these goals, deterrence, retribution, and incapacitation, appear to share a common or related technology. That is, the pursuit of these goals generally ends in some degree of pain, suffering or discomfort for the offender. The nature of the pain and discomfort in our present system is, for the most part, according to Packer (1968:58), some deprivation of liberty, although some public humiliation may also be involved. In any case, if we focus on the predominant feature of this pain as the deprivation or limitation of liberty, the means for achieving this end constitutes a technology of corrections which may be called behavior controlling technology. The existence of such a technology in community supervision has been agreed upon by several scholars and practitioners who have focused on what has variously been called authoritarianism and community protectionism.

In addition, there would seem to be little doubt that, as an ideal at least, rehabilitation or treatment is also considered a legitimate goal of community corrections organizations (Dressler, 1969). One key element of rehabilitation is the attempt to help individuals function well, or better, in society. This approach often focuses on changing certain personal qualities of the offender by building inner strengths, developing a better self-image, increasing personal awareness or altering commitment. Vinter (1965) describes such efforts to achieve inner change as the technology of mental health. That such efforts are elements of probation and parole work seems undeniable (see Dressler, 1969; Grupp, 1971; Diana, 1960; President's Commission on Law Enforcement and Administration of Justice, 1967).

In addition to this mental health technology, there is another element of rehabilitation which is important in community supervision work. Dressler (1969:218), in his discussion of the helping process in community supervision, notes that:

> Manipulating the environment in favor of the client is extremely important with the offender group, for this facilitates the solution of immediate environmental tensions which so often lead to recidivism.

This aspect of rehabilitation does not seem to center on verbal exchanges as much as on a re-ordering of certain environmental conditions which impinge on the offender. For example, an agent may be involved in an effort to secure a job for an offender or to improve his or her living arrangements. This rehabilitation-oriented technology may be termed the environmental manipulation technology.

It seems, therefore, that there are three identifiable technologies of probation and parole. The first, associated with the goals of retribution, deterrence, and incapacitation, is a behavior controlling technology and involves deprivation of liberty. The second, associated with the goal of rehabilitation, is a mental health technology and relies on personal communication and stresses attitudinal or personal change. The third, also associated with rehabilitation, is an environmental manipulation technology and focuses on changing certain negative environmental conditions to the benefit of the offender.

These goals of corrections have been discussed frequently, as have the means for achieving them. Some have even suggested creating new technologies (Clear and O'Leary, 1983). Rarely, however, have the specific practices of probation and parole been studied quantitatively. Consequently we do not know whether the goals most often espoused in corrections are actually transformed into work elements which can conceivably achieve these goals. Nor do we know which, if any, of these technologies actually predominates in real work settings. This study sought to determine (1) whether probation and parole work could be described in technological terms and, (2) if so, which kind of technology was most often implemented in different field supervision settings.

Observing and Classifying Work Processes in Probation and Parole[1]

For the purposes of this study, a method was needed which could be utilized to provide a relatively specific description of the operations of community treatment agencies such as probation and parole departments. Past efforts in this area have, for the most part, taken two routes. Either the researcher has attempted to assume the role of observer and to catalogue the activities of workers (e.g., Studt, 1972), or a self-report system has been employed (e.g., Glaser and Wohl, 1970). The observation method, while yielding rich detail, is limited to a small number of workers and activities. The self-report method, while covering more workers and activities and yielding quantifiable data, provides less detailed information.

An alternative method of observing employee activity, work sampling (e.g., Heiland and Richardson, 1957), was employed in this study. Work sampling allows for accurate and precise descriptions of activities and also provides quantifiable data. Its two main features are the use of random observations of the work situation and the use of pre-established categories of activity descriptions.

The first step in the work sampling study involved a preliminary analysis of the parole and probation officer's job, with the intent of developing a listing of activities performed. This was accomplished through a series of meetings between the researcher and a group of officers. A list of approximately 60 activities was developed in these meetings. The second step was to obtain reports on activities using these categories. Eight groups of parole and probation officers (N = 62) from seven departments were included in the sample. Information was collected through use of coded time sheets in which officers would record their activities for each 15-minute time segment of the day. In a 22-day period (assuring that a beginning and end of month were included for each group studied), three days were randomly selected for each officer.

The final step of the work sampling phase involved classifying activities according to technology (mental health, control, or environmental manipulation). Based on the literature on punishment and treatment (Menninger, 1971: Newman, 1978; Packer, 1968; Street, Vinter, and Perrow, 1966) tasks which involved involuntary participation, held the potential for depriving an offender freedom, encouraged conforming behavior and which seemed to focus on the needs of the community were called control-oriented tasks. Tasks which appeared to deal with personal or emotional problems of the offender or the establishment of a therapeutic relationship between worker and client were treated as elements of mental health technology. Tasks which seemed to involve brokerage, advocacy, mediation or the provision of tangible services such as employment or housing were treated as elements of environmental manipulation. Some activities, such as conferences with supervisors, traveling, etc. involved support activities and were classified as maintenance activities. Interrater agreement on classification of activities according to technology ranged from 64 to 100 percent.

In an attempt to assess the validity and reliability of the work sampling data, open-ended interviews were conducted with 64 of the officers. Officers were then classified on the basis of these interviews as primarily control, mental health, or environmental manipulation-oriented. Cross tabulating these results with the work sampling data indicated a high correlation ($Q = .70$) between reported descriptions of activities and the outcome of the work sampling analysis. This seemed to indicate that the work sampling method provided a reliable and valid measure of task activity.

Analysis of Work Processes in Probation and Parole

The work sampling method was designed to yield detailed and specific information on the nature of the work performed in community supervision agencies. First, and most importantly, it was intended that this information be used to make comparisons between the groups with respect to the technologies which appeared to dominate in the different organizations. A second concomitant goal was to describe the nature of the job of the community supervision agent.

In this section, the data obtained from work sampling in each location will be discussed and analyzed. It will be discussed both in terms of what it says about the nature of the work and how it was used to draw a technology profile for each office and each officer.

The Nature of the Parole Officer's Job

Four groups of parole officers were examined in this study. Groups I, II and III were all part of a state department of corrections. Group VII was also a unit in a department of corrections from an adjoining state. Each of the groups will be discussed separately. A brief narrative introduction describing the features of the office garnered from observations and interviews with the officers will also be presented. This will be followed by an analysis of the work sampling data for the groups.

Group I

This was a parole office covering a largely rural area and two small urban areas. Although not situated in a wealthy community, the facilities used by the agency were impressive when compared to the other agencies. They were located in a downtown, business district of a small metropolitan area in an office building which was used by other non-state organizations. The fact that this parole office was located where it was and shared facilities with the type of organizations that it did seemed to indicate that the group was well integrated in the community.

This was further underlined by comments made by the officers that one of the intangible rewards of their job was the measure of respect which the community awarded them. They were often asked to speak to community groups and participate in local functions such as parades and local celebrations. One officer, when asked what he found appealing about the job, responded that "people, not just parolees, but people in the community respect what I am doing." Several officers mentioned that their position in the community made them more effective in their job by allowing them to use personal contacts to place parolees in jobs and by helping them receive information about the activities of their parolees. This ability to capitalize on personal relationships was also recognized as a particular feature of this office by officers in other offices who were asked to comment on how the officers differed statewide.

Officers expressed a general satisfaction with all aspects of the job. Each officer stressed that he was in the location by choice, often having waited years for transfer to this location. The recent appointment of a director who was unanimously well received added to other factors in producing a group which appeared highly content. The one disharmonious note in this setting was a general disenchantment with their "central office." This headquarters, field-office schism which is, perhaps, the inevitable consequence of such an arrangement was heightened by the belief of the officers that their own headquarters leadership was committed to the dissolution of the entire parole program in the state.

The office consisted of 22 persons, 13 of whom were parole officers. Professional staff, including supervisors and director, amounted to 16 people—all male, all white. The relatively small size of this office precluded specialization and all parole officers in this office were expected to perform the same job functions. The lack of specialization was considered a positive feature by most of the officers. There were three hierarchical levels consisting of a director, two senior parole officers operating as first-line supervisors, and the parole officers. There were no para-professionals below the parole officers. The same officers were responsible for both supervision and investigations. All thirteen officers responsible for these activities participated in the study.

Table 5.1 presents a comparison of the distribution of time spent by each parole group on the different categories of activities. As can be seen, administrative duties and travel accounted for the largest bulk of time in this organization. Travel alone accounted for over one-fifth of the total work time. Offender contact and extra-agency contact were quite similar—30 percent of the work time was devoted to offender contacts and 26 percent to extra-agency contacts.

A more detailed picture of the specific interactions is presented in Table 5.2. From this we see that 12 percent of the officers time is spent on interactions offering support, counseling or encouragement—in short, classical casework activities. Approximately 10

Table 5.1

Distribution of Time Spent on Different Classes of Activity for Parole Groups (Percent of Total Time)

Classes of Activity	I %	II %	III %	VII %	All Parole Groups %
Officer-Offender interactions	30	31	27	27	29
Extra-Agency contacts	26	17	22	21	22
Administrative tasks	22	36	25	29	28
Travel	21	15	24	23	21
Other	1	1	1	—	.8

Table 5.2

Distribution of Time Spent on Officer-Offender Interactions for Parole Groups (Percent of Total Time)

Classes of Activity	I %	II %	III %	VII %	All Parole Groups %
Supportive, counseling, casework	12.1	12.3	11.5	9.8	11.
Risk evaluating, rule enforcement	9.8	9.4	4.5	6.3	7.5
Voluntary service referral	.5	.5	.1	.4	.4
Mandatory service referral	.6	.6	.3	.4	.5
Investigatory, aggressive enforcement	3.8	7.2	8.9	4.9	6.2
Material assistance	3.1	.9	1.5	6.3	3

percent of the officers' time is spent on discussions about rules or attempting to enforce rules through verbal persuasion and four percent is spent on interactions that are of a more investigative or control-oriented nature. Interactions in which services of a material nature are offered account for three percent of the officers' time. Referral activities, whether mandatory or voluntary, are inconsequential, taking only about one percent of overall work time. The interactions, then, appear to center on either counseling and supportive efforts or rule enforcement with very little difference in time spent on these two types of interactions (12 percent for the former, 14 percent for the latter.)

Table 5.3 shows the tabulation for activities associated with the community. As can be seen, participation in hearings does not account for a large portion of the officers' overall work time (approximately two percent). Searching for absconders is of little importance, as is contacting witnesses for hearings or for other reasons.

Table 5.3

Distribution of Time Spent on Extra-Agency Contacts for Parole Groups (Percent of Total Time)

Classes of Activity	Parole Officer Groups				
	I %	II %	III %	VII %	All Parole Groups %
Exchange of information with law enforcement	4.4	5.6	4.7	4.8	4.9
Hearings	1.8	1.1	1.9	—	1.2
Searches	.7	.9	2.6	2	1.6
Witness contact	.8	.1	.3	—	.3
Community assistance and supportive	9.5	4.6	7.2	4.6	6.5
Community contacts investigatory	5.2	2.3	3.8	1.8	3.3
Non-offender related community contacts	3.7	2.5	1.3	6.5	3.5

Although exchange of information with the police accounted for four percent of the officers' time, contacts with other agencies and individuals in the community were far more important and took more than three times as much time. These contacts, in reference to particular parolees, were also more often an effort to be of assistance or service to the parolee than for the purpose of investigating his/her activities and compliance with rules. Apparently the main thrust of the control efforts in this office was towards rule enforcement and follow-ups in face-to-face interactions rather than investigations in the community.

Aside from travel, the maintenance activities which were the most time-consuming were recording and report writing and participation in conferences and meetings (see Table 5.4). Intra-office contacts alone were more time-consuming than such activities as exchanging information with the police or providing material service to offenders. Travel time (21 percent) came very close to taking as much time as actual offender contacts (30 percent).

Table 5.4

Distribution of Time Spent on Maintenance Activities for Parole Groups (Percent of Total Time)

Classes of Activity	Parole Officer Groups				All Parole Groups
	I %	II %	III %	VII %	%
Conferences, training, meetings	6.8	11	9.9	7.9	8.9
Checking procedure and resources	2.4	2.9	2.3	4.5	3
Recording and report writing	8.7	14.7	9.6	12.5	11.3
Reviewing cases	4.1	7.9	3.2	3	4.6
Travel	21.4	14.6	24.4	23.4	21
Other	.8	.5	1.3	—	.7

In comparison to the other parole groups, this office spent more time in interactions with the community than any of the other parole offices. It also seemed to spend the least time on administrative duties.

Group II

This group was the largest of the offices studied. The area covered was a large metropolitan center. The office was centrally located within the area of service, a ghetto area which was among the most economically deprived of the city. Physical conditions in this office were much worse than in any of the other offices examined. Although the building which housed parole was in overall poor repair, the facilities relegated to parole were among the worst in the building. Rather than giving the impression of being an integral part of the community, as was the case in the preceding office, this building resembled a fortress built to separate the inhabitants from a hostile environment. Indeed some of the officers in this office were given to wearing combat attire—fatigue jackets, combat boots, etc. The surrounding neighborhood was perceived as dangerous and several officers noted that they often made visits in pairs although this was technically a violation of organizational rules.

Although there was less need to travel in this office since the geographic area covered was not extensive, officers at this agency were less accessible than in the other offices and more difficult to contact. Often, even supervisors were unaware of the whereabouts of their subordinates.

Contacts with other agencies, even law enforcement agencies, were considered difficult. One officer explained that after dealing with the same police precinct for seven years, he was still unrecognized when contacting someone at the precinct. Community networks were non-existent because agency personnel were constantly transferred within their departments and it was not possible to count on getting to know key people in these agencies. Even within this organization there was a degree of instability especially with respect to offenders since officers were constantly jockeying for "better caseloads" when they became available. Officers here rarely held onto a caseload for more than one year unless it was considered a highly desirable one, which meant one of the few socially stable neighborhoods covered by this office.

One of the distinctive features of this group was the alienation the officers appeared to feel from the community. The surrounding community was not viewed as an asset on which to draw, as was the case in the previously described office, but something which had to be contended with. In questioning one of the administrators about which community groups had an influence on the officers' work, the surprising response was, "Oh, we get some people from legal aid giving us trouble occasionally but we've learned to deal with it." Another officer, who was one of the few who lived in the community serviced by the office, noted that it was nearly impossible for his fellow officers to maintain good working relationships in the community because none of them were part of it.

In addition to feelings of alienation from the community, there was also a general disenchantment with supervisors in this office. The feeling appeared to be that supervisors were not malicious but simply unaware of the conditions that front-line officers faced in their daily routines. The supervisors, on the other hand, felt obligated to make excuses for some of their officers by noting the fact that the men often operated in a manner which they did not approve of but over which they had little control.

The one feature that appeared to be a source of pride for all the members of the organization was the fact that it was generally believed that this office was called upon to deal with more serious offenders and more serious social problems. Invariably, when asked to specify how this office differed from others, the response was that the offender populations were different—more hardened, more disturbed and living in more disorganized environments.

This office had a total staff of 70 and a professional staff of 50. Forty-two of these were parole officers and 37 of the parole officers performed supervision duties. There were two female officers and four were minorities. There were no women middle managers. The director was male. Ethnic integration existed at both the management and officer level. Specialization of functions was evident in the fact that there were four distinctive job titles assigned to parole officers. However, two of these titles were actually held by a single person—indicating that specialization was not an important feature. In fact, 88 percent of the parole officers were doing the same work. There were two levels above the officers and none below giving a total of three hierarchical levels with parole officers occupying the lowest professional rank. The bulk of the officers were assigned supervision duties with investigations being handled by the remaining officers. The director of this office answered to an area director making this office less autonomous than the other three parole offices. Twelve officers representing two supervision units participated in the study.

As Table 5.1 indicates, here as in the preceding group, travel and administrative tasks take up the bulk of time (52 percent). However, travel only accounts for 15 percent of the time. Maintenance activities such as meetings and report writing and record-keeping account for a larger percentage (36 percent) with this group. There is more officer-offender contact than time spent with the community. Since this was the largest office studied, this may account for the larger proportion of time spent on maintenance activities.

In this group, the officer-offender contacts appear to be more oriented towards controlling behavior and enforcing rules than any of the other parole organizations (Table 5.2). Altogether, approximately 17 percent of work time is devoted to officer-offender interactions of this type.

In Table 5.3, we find that attending hearings, searching for absconders or contacting witnesses accounts for only two percent of the officers' time when considered together. The single activity in this group which demanded the most time was exchanging information with police which took up almost six percent of the officers' time. As was the case with Group I, control and rule enforcement in this office appeared to be primarily a matter of officers interacting personally with offenders rather than being heavily dependent on developing or tracking down information in the community.

Group III

This office was located in a rather affluent suburban area. Moderate in size, its facilities were adequate, although not centrally located. The officers here tended to be older than in Group II and came to the office generally as a result of exercising seniority rights. Although employing 52 people, it tended to appear more tightly organized than Group II. Officers' whereabouts were always known and each officer was easily traced and contacted.

Stability and even a degree of rigidity appeared to characterize this office. Leadership's authority appeared to be based on official position rather than the charismatic appeal that was found in Group I. When asked to identify the single most important influence in his work, one officer observed, "We all have different feelings about what the job should be like, but we all end up doing the job that is expected of us." When asked how he knew what was expected of him, he replied that it amounted to following standards set by the office director. When another officer was asked whether his own interpretation or an official order would take precedence, he answered without hesitation that the official order would prevail. Some officers admitted feeling conflict about following procedure when it seemed at variance with their own judgments, but admitted that resolution of the conflict was inevitably in line with "company policy."

It was not difficult for the officers to identify with the community which they served since many of them lived either in the communities they covered or close to them. Since many of the areas serviced were affluent suburbs of a large metropolitan area, there were many community resources available to the officers. In addition, the office maintained a professional presence in the community and good relations with the service agencies. On at least two occasions while the study was being conducted, the office was visited by representatives from volunteer community agencies. Several institutions of higher education sent students to the office as observers and a number of the professional staff held positions as adjunct faculty at these institutions. It appeared then, that public relations was an important consideration in this office.

This office was the second largest group observed. Of the professional staff of 28, 23 were parole officers. Of these 23, 17 were responsible for supervising offenders. Thus, even though there were four different job titles associated with parole officers, 74 percent of all officers were similarly engaged. All officers, except one, were male. One officer was a member of a minority group. There were three hierarchical levels for the professional staff with parole officers occupying the lowest rank. The bulk of the officers were engaged in providing supervision, and investigative duties were assigned to the remaining officers. Sixteen of the 17 officers responsible for supervision participated in the study.

As Table 5.1 indicates, 27 percent of work time in this office is spent with the offender. Somewhat less time (21 percent) is spent interacting with the members of the community. Maintenance, including travel, accounts for half of all work time. The ratio of offender community interactions is not much different here than in the other two groups. As in the case of the other groups covering similar geographic areas, travel accounts for a very large portion of the work day.

When the nature of the officer-offender interactions is examined (Table 5.2), one finds that as in the other two parole offices in this state, approximately 12 percent of work time is spent on casework and counseling interactions. However, a much smaller percentage of time is spent discussing rules or evaluating the potential for rule infractions with offenders. This group of officers does, nevertheless, appear to emphasize discipline by spending more time on such activities as arrests, searches, covert operations, physical examinations, etc. As in the other offices, time spent rendering material assistance in face to face interactions is minimal, and time spent on referrals for services amounted to less than one-half of one percent. If one considers counseling and casework interactions and material assistance as activities on behalf of the offender and risk evaluation and investigations as activities on behalf of the community, it appears that this offices' interactions are almost evenly divided between the two commitments (13 percent for offenders and 14 percent for the community). Of all the work activities not associated with actual offender or community contacts (Table 5.4), travel accounts for the most time.

Group VII

This was a parole office in a state adjoining the other three groups already discussed. Although two groups in this state were solicited, only one would cooperate. Even in this group, two officers refused to participate. This office was also a part of a larger super-structure known as the Department of Corrections. The duties of these parole officers were more limited since there existed other correctional agencies to provide counseling for drug and alcohol abusers and for maintaining community contacts with various social agencies. This meant that many of the counseling and supportive duties assigned to the parole officers in the other groups were not required of this group. At the time of the study, the

Department of Corrections was supporting a move in the state legislature to phase out the parole system. While the plan called for an eventual phase-out rather than total dissolution of the parole program, the officers were, nevertheless, aware of the fact that their efforts were not highly valued by their central office.

The area serviced ranged from highly affluent suburbs to depressed inner city areas and some rural areas where underemployment was a problem. The office itself was located on the outskirts of one of the urban areas it serviced.

To this observer, the office represented the classic example of an organization in decline. Leadership on the local level was weak. A satellite office existed and had been in operation for two years, but the supervisor in charge of the office had never visited the premises. Job definitions appeared unclear. When asked to define what he considered his primary duties, one officer replied, "I was hoping you could tell us since you talk to the people at central office and I don't." Although unable to clearly define their job, the officers seemed to agree that their central office did not wish them to engage in a great deal of rule enforcement. While sitting in on a parolee-officer meeting, the writer heard an officer inquire of the parolee if he was working or still being supported by his girlfriend. The parolee, who had been on parole for eight months at the time, responded that his girlfriend was still "taking care of me." The officer's response to this was, "You're lucky." When asked about this after the interview, the officer shrugged and indicated that at one time he would have insisted that the man take a job, but that to do so today would mean he would be open to criticism by his superiors.

Another officer indicated that it was not his job to enforce rules. "My position is to offer assistance, not to impose my standards on people," he explained. When asked what kind of assistance he supplied, the response was, "Whatever comes up."

The office appeared to have little contact with the surrounding community. For example, when a policeman was asked directions, he could not say where the office was located.

This office was the smallest of the parole offices studied. It had a total staff of eleven and a professional staff of eight, seven of whom were parole officers. There were no special job titles for parole officers and only one hierarchical level above parole officer.

There was, however, a level below parole officer, that of parole aid. Minority members and one woman made up part of the professional staff. Duties for all parole officers involved both supervision and investigation. Five of the seven parole officers working in the office participated in the study.

Although this group was part of a different correctional system, its overall use of time was not very different from that of the other three parole groups. As Table 5.1 indicates, 27 percent of its time was spent on officer-offender interactions. As in the case of the other parole groups, over half of all work time was needed for administrative tasks and although the geographic area covered was not as extensive as that of Group I, 23 percent of work time was devoted to travel.

In looking at the officer-offender interactions (Table 5.2), one finds that the officers spent approximately 10 percent of their time on counseling and supportive interactions—this was less than any of the three other parole offices, although not very much less. They spent approximately six percent of work time on discussions about rules and evaluating possible rule infractions and approximately five percent on investigative activities or aggressive rule enforcement. As in the other parole offices, referrals to service agencies did not account for much time. However, this group did appear to spend more time providing material assistance (six percent) than any of the other three parole offices.

In Table 5.3, the analysis of the extra-agency contacts indicates that this group spent approximately five percent of its time on exchanges of information with the police. This makes all the parole offices very similar in this respect. Contacts for the purpose of investigating compliance required only 1.8 percent of the officer's time—the least time spent by any parole group. Apparently here, as well as in the other groups, the search for information about conduct or behavior is primarily carried out through face to face contacts with offenders rather than through third party reporting. This office appeared to spend considerably more time on general outside contacts than the other offices. A closer look at these figures not included here reveals that these contacts were almost exclusively in two areas—evaluating service resources and extra-agency conferences with other agency personnel. This was an office in which many of the counseling and supportive duties had been assigned to other correctional agencies. It is not surprising, therefore, that more contacts with these agencies would be required.

If one were to include extra-agency contacts such as participating in meetings and conferences as administrative duties along with those specifically designated as administrative duties, this parole office, although the smallest of the four, would appear to spend the greatest amount of time on maintenance tasks since 56 percent of their time is spent on such activities.

Composite Description of Parole Officer's Job

Despite the apparent differences in group climate and morale, it appeared obvious that there was a great similarity between the operations in the four offices. Even though there were considerable environmental differences and even differences in organizational affiliation, there was a consistent pattern of operations which was observed. For example, it was clear that each of the groups devoted approximately one-third of their work time to interactions with offenders. Interestingly, this did not change even in the one agency, Group II, which seemed most at variance with the others. The two classes of activities which revealed the most variability were "extra-agency contacts" and "administrative and maintenance." Even here, it appeared that the variations were not very great. It would seem that barring the unusual inhospitable surroundings of Group II, approximately one-fifth of the parole officers' time is spent interacting with the community. Hence approximately 50 percent of work time involves inter-personal contacts of one type or another. Clearly the interpersonal skills of the officer are a major factor in determining effectiveness in the job as presently structured.

Administrative tasks, excluding travel, appear to place only limited demands on the officer's time. However, travel (taking almost one-fifth of all work time) accounts for a large portion of work time. Since this time cannot be considered productive, this is a rather disturbing finding.

Interactions between parole officers and offenders are consistently carried out in such a way that approximately half of the interactions provide some kind of assistance to the offender either in the form of counseling or material assistance to the offender, and half are directed towards community protection, either in the sense of rule enforcement or risk evaluation.

In terms of the interactions with other agency representatives or community members, we found considerable consistency in the amount of time spent interacting with the police—approximately five percent of work time for all the parole groups. Looking at the total picture of extra-agency contacts, it appears that in parole offices more time is spent on activities associated with protecting the community than on activities or tasks in which the officer is operating as an agent or advocate for the offender.

While the administrative tasks were only described in broad terms in most cases and were therefore not very useful in terms of describing this particular aspect of the work, one fact was obvious. Recording and report writing, which is often described by officers as inordinately time consuming, accounts for a mere 11 percent of work time. It would seem that this aspect of the job is neither unduly time-consuming nor heavily deterministic in terms of effectiveness.

The Nature of the Probation Officer's Job

Four groups of probation officers participated in the study. Generally speaking, gathering information from the probation groups was a considerably easier task than dealing with the parole groups. There was less apprehension and more enthusiasm for the study among the probation officers. One reason for this was, undoubtedly, the fact that they were more secure since, unlike the parole officers, they were not facing the possible dissolution of their departments.

Group IV

This group was composed of four probation officers operating as the adult supervision section of a county probation department. Although the group was small, it was part of a relatively large and highly specialized department. The adult supervision unit initially consisted of five officers; midway through the study, one was dropped as a result of civil service requirements which left four officers to participate. The community serviced was predominantly rural. It was set in an economically depressed area where the main source of employment was provided by a single industry.

This agency's position was somewhat unique compared with the others studied in that its director, although a career probation worker, was well connected politically. This placed the agency in a pivotal position with respect to community resources. Although the salaries were not high, the facilities were impressive and relationships with police and other local agencies were cordial. All the officers who discussed their jobs indicated a fondness for the director and a belief that they benefited from the director's favorable reputation.

Business in this office appeared to be conducted on an informal level. The relationship between the supervisor and the officers, all of whom were in their twenties, appeared to be almost paternal in nature with the supervisor essentially directing the supervision of the cases through his officers. While carrying what they considered to be large caseloads, the officers admitted that because they were responsible for supervision and not investigation, they did not feel pressured in their work. These officers appeared to be less conscious than the other probation officers of the demands of the County Board of Supervisors. They tended to describe their jobs in introspective terms, referring to fulfillments and satisfactions. There was an obvious lack of urgency in their approach to the job which appeared to be a general reflection of management style. When asked to describe management's philosophy, two officers suggested that there didn't seem to be one other than "to keep things running smoothly."

This department consisted of 32 people, 21 of whom were professionals. Thirteen of these were probation officers. There were four job descriptions for probation officers and just 31 percent of the officers were responsible for adult supervision indicating that specialization was emphasized. There were several women professionals at different levels. No ethnic minorities were represented on the staff. In all, five hierarchical levels existed—three above the probation officer and one below. This was an autonomous organization with a director who answered to the County Board of Supervisors.

Table 5.5 provides a breakdown of the time distribution of the four probation groups. As can be seen, a large portion of this group's time is spent in interactions with offenders. Forty-one percent of all work time is spent in this way. Only a minor portion of the work day appears devoted to contacts with other agencies or individuals. Administrative tasks also account for 41 percent of work time, but travel, unlike parole, accounts for only five percent of the work day. Clearly, then, the nature of the job, while certainly office bound, is very offender-oriented in that almost half of all work time is spent in interactions with offenders.

Table 5.5

Distribution of Time Spent on Different Classes of Activity for Probation Groups (Percent of Total Time)

Classes of Activity	Probation Officer Groups				
	IV %	V %	VIa %	VIj %	TOTAL %
Officer-Offender interactions	41	36	26	26	32
Extra-agency contacts	11	16	19	22	17
Administrative tasks	41	42	49	46	45
Travel	5	5	5	4	5
Other	2	—	2	—	1

In Table 5.6, we find a categorization of these offender interactions. The activities which predominate in this group are very definitely those associated with offering support or providing counseling. Almost a quarter of the entire workday is spent on such activities. Referrals to service agencies demand very little time. Providing material assistance also seems unimportant. Investigatory contacts with offenders, as well as contacts related to obtaining restitution payments, are not important either. Some rule enforcement via clarification and discussion of rules and behavior does go on, accounting for 11 percent of the workday. By and large, one would have to say that officer-offender interactions are primarily supportive and offender-oriented. Of the three probation offices studied, this was the one in which officers were not responsible for pre-sentence investigations while they were doing supervision. This appears to result in many more offender-officer interactions of a supportive nature.

Table 5.6

Distribution of Time Spent on Officer-Offender Interactions for Probation Groups (Percent of Total Time)

Classes of Activity	Probation Officer Groups				
	IV %	V %	VIa %	VIj %	TOTAL %
Supportive, counseling, casework	23.9	11.4	10.6	12.1	14.5
Risk evaluation, rule enforcement	11.2	13.2	5.4	3.5	8.3
Voluntary service referrals and followup	.7	5	.5	1.4	1.9
Mandatory service referrals and followup	1.7	1	2.8	1.1	1.7
Investigatory, aggressive enforcement	2.3	3.8	4.1	2	3.1
Material assistance	1.3	1.5	1.8	4.1	2.2

In Table 5.7, which presents a breakdown of the extra-agency contacts for the probation group, we see that exchanging information with police accounts for approximately two percent of the work time. Activities such as participation in hearings, contacting witnesses, and processing restitution payments amount to less than one percent of work time. Contacts with agencies or individuals in the community account for only about six percent of work time. These contacts tend to emphasize assistance slightly more than investigation in this office.

Table 5.7

Distribution of Time Spent on Extra-Agency Contacts in Probation Groups (Percent of Total Time)

Classes of Activity	Probation Officer Groups				
	IV %	V %	VIa %	VIj %	TOTAL %
Exchange of information with law enforcement personnel	2.4	6.8	2.9	.3	3.1
Hearings	.1	2.2	2.7	.8	1.5
Witness contact	.1	—	.2	.3	.2
Restitution processing	.5	.6	—	—	.2
Community contacts: assistive and supportive	3.6	5	4.1	10.9	5.9
Community contacts: investigatory	2.6	1.4	3.4	2.6	2.5
Non-Offender-centered community contacts	.9	.4	5.9	6.6	3.5

The amount of time spent on administrative duties (Table 5.8) is far greater in probation offices than in parole offices. Conferences and meetings occupy approximately 11 percent of the work time, and recording information in the case record and writing reports take one-fifth of the work time. Even checking procedures and resources occupies a sizable chunk of time (three percent) as does reviewing of cases (five percent). Travel, as has been noted, accounts for very little time, especially when one considers the amount of time spent with offenders.

Table 5.8

Distribution of Time Spent on Maintenance Tasks in Probation Groups (Percent of Total Time)

Classes of Activity	Probation Officer Groups				
	IV %	V %	VIa %	VIj %	TOTAL %
Conferences, training meetings	11.5	9.7	13.4	22.3	14.2
Checking procedures and resources	3.4	3.9	4.1	3.5	3.7
Recording and report writing	20.9	21.4	24.5	9.8	19.2
Review of cases	5.2	6.7	6.7	4.8	4.8
Travel	5.3	4.7	4.9	4.4	4.8
Other	2.5	.6	.3	3.2	1.7

Group V

This was the smallest of the three probation departments studied. It operated in a rather affluent bedroom community of a large urban center. The offices of the department were located in a county office building in a small town. Despite the small size of this agency, the atmosphere could not be classified as informal. This appeared to be a highly organized group who took the question of accountability to the community (as represented by the County Board of Supervisors) seriously. When asked to sketch an organizational chart, the director indicated the Board of Supervisors as the head of the organization rather than herself, and the officers invariably referred to the Board in comments about agency operations.

The small size of the group made the assignment of specialized duties impossible. Therefore, all members of the group were responsible, to some degree, for preparing pre-sentence reports and for supervising offenders on probation. This lack of specialization appeared to be a source of satisfaction to the officers, all of whom mentioned it as an advantage of working in this department.

Morale appeared good here. Officers believed that they had good working relationships with law enforcement agencies and the judiciary, who they believed were highly responsive to their recommendations. The officers responded well to their director, who in turn, appeared to consult with them regularly rather than issue instructions. The line of authority was clearly drawn, however, with officers deferring to her on important issues. All recommendations for probation, for example, were carefully reviewed by her, and officers admitted their judgments were not regularly upheld. Three officers were young, having less than two years field experience and readily accepted this arrangement. A third officer accepted it with resignation but noted that efficient operation required the director to exercise this type of control. Satellite offices were used but were tightly controlled, with officers who worked at these locations calling in several times a day.

This office consisted of ten people, five of whom were professionals. Four of the professionals were probation officers. Only two hierarchical levels existed—director and probation officer. There were no specialized assignments, and officers were responsible for both supervision and investigations. This was an autonomous unit answering only to the County Board of Supervisors. All four of the officers participated in the study.

This group spent about 36 percent of its work time with offenders and 16 percent in extra-agency contacts. The largest portion of time was devoted to administrative tasks. Travel in this office, as in the other probation offices was not very time-consuming (five percent of work time).

The officer-offender interactions (Table 5.6) appeared to be more evenly distributed between supportive and counseling activities and rule enforcing activities. Also of some importance in this office was time devoted to making referrals to services most of which appear to be done on a voluntary basis. Providing material assistance in these interactions appeared to require only a minor amount of time (1.5 percent) and investigatory and aggressive disciplinary activities do not appear to require much time (3.2 percent).

However, those extra-agency contacts which resulted in exchange of information with police were relatively important in this office, requiring about seven percent of the officer's time

(Table 5.7). Participating in hearings did not account for much work time (2.2 percent). The community contacts here, outside of police contacts, seemed to be more often for the purpose of assisting offenders (5 percent) rather than for ferreting out information about behavior (1.4 percent). The control efforts in this office appeared to be largely in terms of interacting with police or discussing and evaluating rules and infractions in face-to-face contacts with offenders.

The time devoted to maintenance tasks (Table 5.8) in this office, as in the other probation offices, was considerable. Conferences and meetings took up approximately 10 percent of work time. Checking procedures and resources accounted for four percent of work time. Recording and report writing were among the most time-consuming of all activities, requiring 20 percent of work time. Reviewing cases called for almost seven percent of work time and travel approximately five percent. The fact that as much as 47 percent of work time was spent on administrative and maintenance tasks was particularly impressive for this office, since it was the smallest office examined. If we take factors such as time devoted to record keeping as an indication of bureaucracy, then it seems clear that the size of an organization has little to do with the degree of bureaucratization.

Groups VIa and VIj

These groups were part of a moderate-sized county probation department. The service area covered was extensive, and covered both rural and urban areas. Because the office was sufficiently large to permit it, and because the administration appeared to be supportive of innovation, there was a considerable degree of specialization in this office. For example, not only were officers divided among juvenile and adult groups, but individual officers were assigned responsibilities for various special projects. There were special positions for community liaison work and for police and court liaison. Investigations and supervision were handled by the same officers, however.

The atmosphere in the office was cordial. Officers appeared to work closely with one another and with their supervisors. Supervisors and officers interacted socially outside the job and efforts requiring full staff cooperation were common. For example, co-ordination of the use of staff cars was easily achieved through informal arrangements. Further, conferences and staff meetings included considerable give and take, with the director and super-visors consulting staff rather than passing on information.

There appeared to be a commitment on the part of manage-ment to involve the agency in the community. Contacts with volun-tary agencies were consciously sought and efforts to maintain relationships with these agencies were encouraged by supervisors. Voluntary personnel were invited to participate in supervision efforts and considerable agency time was devoted to supporting and assisting this personnel.

Despite the cordiality of the staff, it was obvious that officers felt under considerable pressure to adhere to time schedules. Sev-eral officers indicated that there were organizational priorities with respect to investigations that were detrimental to their super-vision efforts. Nevertheless, the overall impression was one of satis-faction and fulfillment. As one officer observed, "At (another probation department) they're always overworked but nothing seems to get done. They're never on time with their investigations and they don't even talk to their supervisors. Here we get a lot of work, but at least you know something is getting done."

This was the largest probation office to participate in the study. It had a staff of 35, including 20 professionals. Fourteen probation officers worked here. Seven were responsible for adult supervision and six for juvenile probation supervision. Only 50 percent of the officers were engaged in the same job. In all, there were four job descriptions for probation officers. Specialization was an important feature of this office. There were four hier-archical levels, with two above probation officer and one below (probation aides). This was an autonomous organization answer-ing to the County Board of Supervisors. Of the 14 probation officers in this department, 13 took part in the study.

The juvenile unit was administratively separated from the rest of the organization, with its own chain of command and work assignments. The officers in the juvenile unit tended to be the most experienced officers in the organization. They had been hand-picked for the job because management believed that they pos-sessed qualities which would make them effective juvenile probation officers. These qualities were described as empathy, imagination and commitment. In effect, this group of officers was considered the cream of the organization. They answered to a supervisor who had been with the department longer than the director and who was given considerable autonomy by the director. Consequently, the juvenile unit operated independently from the rest of the organization. Their caseloads were smaller, and specialized assignments were arranged for the officers.

Group VIa was responsible for adult supervision and investigation. As Table 5.5 indicates, this group spent less time with probationers than did the other two probation groups discussed earlier. Twenty-six percent of their work time was spent with offenders and 19 percent of work time was spent interacting with other agencies or individuals. The administrative burden appeared the heaviest here requiring 49 percent of work time. Travel required only five percent of work time in this group as in the other probation groups already described.

In looking at the officer-offender interactions delineated in Table 5.6, we see that 11 percent of work time was spent on counseling and supportive interactions. Discussing and enforcing rules required 5.4 percent of the officers' time and investigative and aggressive disciplinary actions took approximately four percent of work time. Referrals which were more than twice as likely to be mandatory than voluntary accounted for 2.8 percent of work time. Providing material assistance in face-to-face interactions appeared to be no more important here than in the preceding groups. This group engaged in slightly more extra-agency contacts than the other two. Non-offender-related community contacts appeared more important here. No doubt the administration's support of outreach programs contributed to this increased time spent on such activities.

The exchange of information with law enforcement took very little of the officers' time—less than three percent. Hearings, searches and restitution payment processing amounted to only three percent of work time. Approximately three percent of work time was spent on community contacts of an investigative nature. Here, as in the other probation groups, control seemed to rely more on face-to-face contacts than information obtained from the community.

Maintenance tasks required the largest portion of time in this group (Table 5.8). Conferences and meetings and training sessions required more time here than in the two preceding groups, but less time than in the juvenile unit. Record-keeping and report writing demanded the most time in this group calling for almost a quarter of all work time. If one considers the maintenance activities listed in Table 5.8 and such activities as maintaining extra-agency relationships as further examples of organizational maintenance, one finds that as much as 60 percent of work time was taken up by administrative tasks.

Group VIj worked exclusively with juveniles. They spent less time with offenders and the most time in interactions with community members. As Table 5.5 indicates, only 26 percent of work time was spent with the offender while a very nearly equal portion (22 percent) was spent on extra-agency contacts.

Their client-office contacts involved considerably less rule enforcement and risk evaluation than was the case in the other groups (Table 5.6). They did not appear to engage in a great deal of casework activity, but they were the group which spent the most time providing material assistance to offenders in face-to-face contacts. However, even as the most active group in this area, they spent only four percent of their time on such activities.

Their community contacts were mainly devoted to contacts with agencies and individuals in which they were providing assistance and support for offenders. They also spent more time on non-offender-related contacts than did any of the other groups. Exchange of information with law enforcement personnel played virtually no part in their activities, nor were they much involved in hearings or obtaining restitution payments or dealing with crime victims or witnesses.

Their major activity appeared to involve participation in conferences and informal and formal meetings with their co-workers on which as much as 22 percent of their work time was spent (Table 5.8). They were involved in considerably less record-keeping and report writing than any other probation group. This was probably the result of their smaller caseloads. They also engaged in less travel time than any other group.

Composite Description of Probation Officer's Job

There appeared to be less consistency among the probation groups than among the parole groups. Nevertheless, one aspect of the job appeared consistent in all four groups, and that was the fact that a very large portion of work time was spent on administrative tasks in these agencies. An average of 45 percent of all the work time of probation officers' was devoted to administrative tasks. This was more time than was devoted to either officer-offender interactions or extra-agency contacts. It was apparent that the probation officers' job, despite considerable variations in environments, called for administrative skills as much as it did for interpersonal skills.

In terms of the interpersonal skills called for, it appeared that contacts were more heavily weighted towards the offender. This is to say that considerably more time, almost twice as much, was spent dealing with the offender face to face than with members of the community or other agency personnel. The officer-offender interactions were also likely to be directed more towards assisting the offender than protecting the community. Of all the tasks in this class of activities, those related to counseling and casework were most prevalent.

In their extra-agency contacts, the officers operated as community protection agents about one-half of the time and as advocates or spokespersons for the offender about one-half of the time.

Record and report writing required approximately one-fifth of work time in all but one of the groups. Clearly skills which facilitate this task are important components of the job. Interactions among organizational members were also important. About 15 percent of work time was spent on such interactions and in one group 22 percent of work time was spent in this manner. Apparently, organizational maintenance is of considerable importance in probation agencies.

Parole and Probation Compared

In terms of general impressions, it appeared that the most outstanding difference between probation and parole officers was the fact that probation officers, to put it simply, appeared happier in their jobs. They were less dissatisfied with the organizations they worked for than were parole officers. To be sure, parole officers' dissatisfaction was primarily with their central offices, and the fact that the probation departments were autonomous units may explain these differences to some extent. However, much of the satisfaction with the jobs described by probation officers appeared to be derived from interactions on the job with co-workers—this was often described as being part of a united effort in pursuit of organization goals. These sentiments were never expressed by parole officers. Indeed, when parole officers discussed the satisfactions of their jobs, it was primarily related to satisfaction with the officer-client relationship, and secondarily with the respect of the community for the position of the parole officer but never with satisfactions growing out of the interactions with other officers.

In a critique of the concept of probation, Blumberg (1970:154) notes that probation officers derive vicarious satisfaction from dealing with lawbreakers. Very little of this came through with respect to the probation officers interviewed. Indeed they spoke surprisingly little about the offenders unless specifically questioned on the subject. Parole officers, on the other hand, spoke at length about their charges without prodding and did, in some cases, appear to derive pleasure from working with offenders. One officer even showed the writer a scrapbook of newspaper clippings of his most "fascinating" cases in which he clearly took great pride.

Probation officers seemed less in conflict about their dual roles as guardians of the community and assistors to offenders. They readily admitted that individual officers tended to emphasize one or the other of these roles, but did not seem troubled by this. Parole officers more often took the position that all parole officers operated, for the most part, in a similar manner with respect to these goals, and that only slight variations existed in style. Alternatively, variations in operating styles were acknowledged, but were referred to in pejorative terms. Thus, one found parole officers who disagreed so vehemently with the approach of other officers that they literally would not speak to one another. Interestingly, displays of intolerance could not be associated with a single methodology. One officer who could be classified as an advocate of leniency in dealing with offenders observed that he could easily be tolerant of a client's weaknesses, but found the "hardnose" approach of fellow officers totally unacceptable and could not relate to them on any level. Another parole officer indicated he would resign his position before accepting as a partner an officer who "believed that the social work approach can work on this job."

On the whole parole officers seemed to give more thought to their jobs and less to their organizations, while probation officers were more concerned with the types of organizations in which they were operating and would be operating in the future.

Although there were some differences in the work patterns observed in parole and probation groups, there was also a degree of similarity which suggested that a pattern of operation peculiar to community supervision agencies existed. In order to measure the similarity in the patterns between the groups, the various tasks which would logically be thought of as similar were grouped to provide a manageable list of job elements. This allowed statistical measure of the similarities between the four parole groups and the four probation groups, as well as the similarities between probation and parole.

There were 62 separate activities or tasks associated with the job of the parole and probation officer. By combining tasks with similar characteristics, 36 task groups or elements were identified as relating to both the work of the probation and parole officer. A mean for each of the 36 elements was obtained for the four parole groups, and a similar mean was obtained for the probation groups.

The 36 means representing the parole work pattern were correlated with their counterparts representing the probation work patterns, and a Pearson Product Moment Coefficient of .63 was obtained. This suggested that there was considerable similarity in the two work patterns but that they were not identical by any means (see Table 5.9).

A second correlation was obtained by comparing the means for the parole groups with those of the probation groups in that class of activities identified as officer-offender interactions. For this class of activities, a correlation of .91 was obtained between probation and parole. This suggested that, in terms of how officers interact with offenders, probation and parole are very similar. It

Table 5.9

Correlations Between Probation and Parole Groups with Respect to Time Distribution on Different Job Elements

Total Distribution of Time for Probation and Parole on 36 Job Elements	.63
Distribution of Time on 11 Elements Relating to Officer-Offender Interactions	.91
Distribution of Time on 10 Elements Relating to Client-Related Extra-Agency Contacts	.94
Distribution on Time of 6 Elements Relating to Extra-Agency Contacts of a General Nature	.94
Distribution of Time on 9 Elements to Administrative and Maintenance Tasks	.36

was apparent that what transpired between officer and client was very nearly identical in both groups. There was clearly something about the nature of community supervision which transcended organization affiliation, differences in structure and geographical environments, and resulted in similar types of interpersonal interactions with offenders.

Perhaps even more surprising was the equally strong correlation between that class of activities identified as client-centered, extra-agency contacts. A correlation of .94 was found between time spent on the different elements of this aspect of the job in both types of agencies. There was also a strong correlation in the area of general community contacts. Apparently here as well, what was done in the community was very similar in both probation and parole. Interestingly, the similarities emerged even in the face of differences in the caseloads between the two groups. Probation groups were responsible for managing much larger caseloads than parole groups, yet their pattern of activities with respect to their clients did not differ radically.

There were great differences, however, in the way in which administrative or maintenance responsibilities were carried out. A correlation of .36 was obtained, which suggested very little similarity between probation and parole in this area. Table 5.9 summarizes the correlations discussed above.

Although there were considerable differences between parole and probation in the administrative area, there were great similarities within probation and parole groups for this group of tasks as well as for the other classes of activities. These correlations are summarized in Tables 5.10 and 5.11.

Table 5.10

Correlation of Time Spent in Activity Classes Between Individual and Aggregate Parole Groups

	Group I	Group II	Group III	Group VII
Officer offender interactions	.95	.92	.86	.89
Extra-agency contacts: client-related	.94	.95	.98	.91
Extra-agency contacts: general	1.00	.9	.4	1.00
Administrative and maintenance tasks	.99	.92	.97	.97
Total activities	.97	.92	.97	.97

Table 5.11

Correlation of Time Spent in Activity Classes Between Individual and Aggregate Probation Groups

	Group IV	Group V	Group VIa	Group VIj
Officer-offender interactions	.98	.84	.95	.89
Extra-agency contacts: client-related	.95	.8	.89	.81
Extra-agency contacts: general	.22	.46	.95	.96
Administrative and maintenance tasks	.89	.81	.96	.8
Total activities	.94	.91	.95	.85

As can be seen, the probation groups tended to be less consistent in their distribution of time than did the parole groups, but, except for that category of activities identified as General Extra-Agency Contacts, they were also highly related to each other. This similarity is even more striking when one takes into account the fact that three of the probation groups were operating in autonomous agencies totally independent of each other. Yet despite this isolation, they appeared to follow very similar patterns in at least four of the major classes of activities. It would seem that definitive patterns for both probation and parole are detectable in these data.

Drawing the Technology Profile

In addition to providing a description of the nature of the work, work sampling, in this study, was designed to provide information which could be used to determine the technological orientation of the groups. This is to say that the data generated by work sampling could be used to determine whether a particular group made relatively greater use of either of the three technologies of community supervision described earlier—control, mental health, or environmental manipulation.

Since it was decided earlier that tasks which composed the role of the community supervision agency could, in most cases, be identified with one of the three technologies, drawing a profile involved determining which types of tasks predominated in the operations of the different groups. We have already seen that some variations existed in the groups with respect to how they apportioned their time with respect to the various classes of activities. By using the criteria developed earlier in this study to identify the tasks according to the technological orientation, it was possible to determine how the different groups apportioned their work time with respect to the three technologies.

Of the 36 elements extrapolated from the original 62 tasks, 24 dealt with processing the offender. The 12 remaining were either related to administrative tasks or of such a general nature that they could not be directly related to the actual processing of offenders. Of the 24 elements associated with processing, 15 appeared associated with control technology, 3 with mental health technology and 6 with environmental manipulation technology. This rather awkward distribution resulted from the fact that many of the control tasks were of such a nature that they could not be easily combined to form elements of multiple tasks. There were also more tasks which could be associated with control described by the officers when they were asked to draw up lists of tasks for which they were responsible.

Table 5.12 indicates the amount of work time devoted to each group of tasks associated with the three technologies. As can be seen, while there is considerable similarity among some of the groups, there are also some marked differences in the amount of time each group devoted to the three categories of tasks. Group VIj clearly spent much less time on control tasks than any of the other groups. Group IV clearly spent much more time on mental health tasks than any other group.

It was also apparent that control tasks appeared to take up the most work time in all the groups except one. Apparently, control of offender behavior was the major goal of the majority of the probation and parole groups examined. To be sure, some emphasis on control technology was to be expected in view of the fact that the officers tended to identify more control-oriented tasks than any other type when asked to describe their jobs. However, since

Table 5.12

Ratios Obtained when Comparing Time Spent on Control, Mental Health, and Environmental Manipulation Activities

	Parole and Probation Groups							
	I	II	III	VII	IV	V	VIa	VIj
Total Percent Time Spent on Control Activities	28	28	28	30	29	29	22	11
Relative to Other Technologies[1]	1.1	1.5	1.3	.86	.61	1.3	1.2	.35
Total Percent Time Spent on Mental Health Activities	13	13	12	11	25	16	11	14
Relative to Other Technologies[2]	.31	.38	.32	.34	1	.44	.38	.5
Total Percent Time Spent on Environmental Manipulation Activities	13	6	9	12	6	7	7	17
Relative to Other Technologies[3]	.31	.15	.22	.39	.94	.15	.21	.68

[1] $\dfrac{a}{b+c}$, where a = percent time spent on control activities;
b = percent time spent on mental health activities;
c = percent time spent on environmental manipulation activities.

[2] $\dfrac{b}{a+c}$, where a = percent time spent on control activities;
b = percent time spent on mental health activities;
c = percent time spent on environmental manipulation activities.

[3] $\dfrac{c}{a+b}$, where a = percent time spent on control activities;
b = percent time spent on mental health activities;
c = percent time spent on environmental manipulation activities.

officers were asked to name the tasks associated with their work and not to rate them in terms of importance, there was no indication that control would play such a prominent role in the overall picture of their work.

In six of the eight groups examined, control tasks accounted for the greatest portion of the processing time. In five of the groups, officers appeared to spend more time on control tasks than on mental health and environmental manipulation combined. However, since we are primarily interested in how the groups differed in terms of their relative dependency on the three technologies, a formula for determining the relative importance of the technologies in the organizations was devised.

Time spent by each organizational group on control activities was divided by combined time spent on mental health activities and environmental manipulation activities. Time spent on mental health activities was divided by the combined time spent on control activities and environmental manipulation activities, and time spent on environmental activities was divided by time spent on mental health and control activities (see Table 5.12). This produced three ratios for each organization. In order for a group to be considered dependent on or dominated by a particular technology it was determined that they should be seen to devote as much or more time to that technology as they did to the other two technologies combined, which is to say that the ratio for the dominant technology should equal or exceed one. This definition for technological dominance was a stringent one, but in view of the somewhat subjective designation of activities as control-oriented, mental health-oriented, or environmental manipulation-oriented, it was felt that the inference of dominance should be as unequivocal as possible. Hence the requirement that, for an organization to be considered dominated by a particular technology, it should demonstrate an unquestionable preference for a specific type of activity. As Table 5.12 indicates, five of the eight groups appeared to devote far greater resources, at least with respect to time, to control oriented activities than to either of the other two technologies. Thus, Group I, II, III, V, and VIa could be considered as dominated by control technology.

Of the remaining three groups, one group, IV, appeared to be dominated by mental health technology. Groups VII and VIj did not show a clear dominance by our earlier definition. However, VIj, when considered in relation to the other seven groups, made the greatest use of environmental manipulation technology. While this technology accounted for very little time in the other groups, it did consume 17 percent of the work time for Group VIj. This group was also the one which made the least use of control technology— half as much as any of the other groups. It was reasonable, therefore, to assume that this group probably practiced environmental manipulation as much as any community supervision agency is likely to, given their propensity to emphasize control.

This left Group VII, which could not be considered dominated by control technology even though the greatest proportion of their time was spent on such tasks. In view of the clear pattern of dominance by control in five of the eight groups examined, it appeared that any group which did not follow this pattern must be significantly different in some respect. Clearly, Group VII was operating to diminish the importance of control technology since, in combination, it spent more time on mental health and environmental manipulation than on control. Group VII appeared to have a slightly greater tendency to emphasize environmental manipulation than to emphasize mental health. Hence, for comparison purposes, Group VII was chosen as a group which could be considered as leaning towards environmental manipulation as an organizational orientation. This interpretation left us with five groups dominated by control, one which appeared dominated by mental health (IV), and two which appeared oriented towards environmental manipulation (VIj and VII).

On the individual level, a similar procedure was followed using the mean time over three days spent by each officer on each group of activities. The daily percent of time spent by each officer on each of the categories of activities was calculated and the means computed. The ratio for each technology was then calculated for each officer. The method of computation was identical to that described above for the organizational ratios. As with the organizational ratios, those officers whose ratio was one or above were considered as displaying technological dominance. Of the 62 participating, 33 appeared to display control dominance in their work patterns. Only nine displayed either mental health or environmental manipulation dominance. However, since control dominance was clearly the normal operating pattern, officers whose work patterns were not dominated by control were considered as leaning towards one of the other two technologies, whichever accounted for the greater amount of time. Thus, for comparison purposes we had 33 officers dominated by control technology, 13 leaning towards mental health, and 16 leaning towards environmental manipulation.

When the officers in each organizational group were distributed according to their technological preference, it was found that five of the eight groups had 50 percent or more of their officers displaying control dominance. This information is presented in tabular form in Table 5.13. As can be seen, Group IV had most of its officers oriented towards mental health, Group VIj had the largest percentage of its officers oriented towards environmental manipulation, and Group VII had as many officers oriented towards environmental manipulation as it had dominated by control. This seemed to further support the earlier decision to designate Groups IV, VIj and VII as groups representing technologies other than control.

Table 5.13

Number of Officers in Each Organizational Group Distributed According to Technology Preference

Group	% Officers Control Dependent	% Officers Mental Health-Oriented	% Officers Environ. Manip.-Oriented	N
I	50%	8%	42%	12
II	87%	13%	0	8
III	50%	19%	31%	16
VII	40%	20%	40%	5
IV	25%	75%	0	4
V	75%	25%	0	4
VIa	71%	14%	14%	7
VIj	17%	33%	50%	6

Ideology, Goals, and Technology in Probation and Parole

This study of work processes in eight probation and parole units sought to determine (1) whether the specific work activities of field supervision agents could be described in terms which linked those tasks to the goals espoused for correctional systems, and (2) whether those technologically grouped tasks could serve to distinguish the various units from each other. The answers to both questions are affirmative. Specific tasks can be designated and measured and both the officers themselves and independent raters reach at least rough agreement on the relationship of those tasks to traditional correctional goals. Further, not only do individual officers differ in the degree of time they devote to the implementation of the three technologies, but also those individual differences are not randomly distributed across offices. It would appear that technology preference is not simply a matter of individual discretion, despite the relative operational independence of probation and parole workers from each other, compared to other kinds of front-line work.

These discoveries have a number of implications for the study and management of probation and parole. The first of these concerns the varying ideologies of corrections and the extent to which these are transformed into policy, or organizational goals that shape operations. In a study of welfare organizations, Street and his colleagues (1979) discovered that ideological positions adopted by individual welfare caseworkers did not have the expected influence on their actual behavior with clients. Through a variety of processes, the welfare organizations produced homogenous worker behavior, despite the fact that worker attitudes toward the purpose of welfare work differed. Hypothesizing a similar possibility in corrections, Duffee (1984) suggested that the often-discussed variations in agent styles of supervision (Glaser, 1964; Studt, 1972) might, in fact, have more significance for how agents understood their work than for how they actually did it. The data in this study would suggest that expressed concerns for control and rehabilitation are descriptive of work processes themselves. They would also verify Studt's suggestion, however, that technology for control is more elaborate and time-consuming in probation and parole than are technologies for rehabilitation, despite complaints that community corrections is "soft" on convicted criminals and despite the general insistence in corrections literature that the community setting provides opportunity for treatment.

A second implication is that there may be more opportunity for managerial control of probation and parole work than is often assumed. Probation and parole supervision is often described as highly discretionary work affording considerable independence and self-determination by individual agents. While this may be accurate, if one is interested in comparing this work to other occupations, the patterning of technological preference within units and the differences across them indicate organizational and environmental sources of technological concentrations.

Where there are such concentrations, a logical next question is whether management may choose the technology it desires to implement or whether the technological concentration is determined by organizational or environmental factors which are essentially out of managerial control. Organizational structure and technology variables have been shown to vary with variables such as size and community context. But comparative studies have indicated that there is ample room for managerial choice both in the enunciation of goals and the selection of technology (Pugh, 1984; Langworthy, 1986). How managers in community corrections can most effectively choose to maximize a technological concentration, and whether those technologies have significant impact on the lives of those organizations, are also important topics for investigation.

Notes

[1]For further information on the methodology employed in this study, see Jester 1980.

Discussion Questions

1. Why might there be greater differences among probation offices than among parole offices?

2. Would you agree with Jester's basic premise that control activities can be distinguished from mental health and environmental manipulation activities? Why should a controlling behavior, for instance, be considered more closely associated with punishment than rehabilitation?

3. Does Jester describe any organizational or environmental characteristics of offices IV, VIj, and VII that might explain why these offices were not control-oriented?

Chapter 6
Probation's Responses to Fiscal Constraints*

Nora Harlow
E. Kim Nelson

There is a new mood evident throughout the land, and it manifests itself increasingly in restrictions placed on public spending and growing expectations for accountability in government. Vocal portions of the public no longer support unregulated growth in the public sector. Even those who call for maintenance of existing service levels seem less willing to pay the escalating price. We now must learn to make do with less, or find new and more resource-conscious ways of providing the services we have come to expect from government.

At the same time, we must avoid a preoccupation with efficiency at the expense of other social and institutional values on which our public programs, and government itself, are based. It serves no one well to perform more proficiently a function that has lost its connection to the social fabric. Government is weakened when its agencies lose sight of the reasons for their existence, even more so than when they are simply inefficient, bureaucratic, or "fat."

Public agencies today are struggling to find just the right combination of efficiency in operations and centrality in the public mind. As the economic pie becomes effectively smaller, there is some sifting out of functions and services, with less valued (or less politically secure) activities feeling the pinch sooner or with more

---

*This chapter is a revised version of material excerpted from Nora Harlow and E. Kim Nelson *Management Strategies For Probation in an Era of Limits*, prepared under a grant from the National Institute of Corrections, U.S. Department of Justice (1982). Reprinted with permission.

devastating results. Being able to demonstrate operational efficiency or cost-effectiveness helps; but those agencies that some-
how project an image of *essentialness* are in an enviable position
when budget cuts become the order of the day.

The Case of Probation

For several reasons, probation departments are maximally
affected by the squeeze on public revenues. They often are loosely
linked to the political and executive powers-that-be in state or local
government. Traditionally, they have had no informed and active
public constituency. Their goals are vague, and their accomplishments difficult to measure. In some cases they are overextended,
having expanded into areas of unfilled need when resources were
plentiful. As public revenues begin to shrink (or at least stop growing at the same rate), these weaknesses are magnified by the shift
in public opinion toward harsher penalties for convicted offenders.
In this setting probation agencies have difficulty both in establishing a clear need for the functions they perform and in proving that
they perform them well.

There is great diversity in responses of contemporary probation managers to assaults on their funding base. Some are cutting
back to basics, with "basic" defined by statutory mandate or by
management's understanding of what probation does best. Others
are seeking opportunities to expand into new areas, taking on functions for which there happens to be funding or that match local
preferences for particular programs. Because of their inclinations
and expertise, some managers concentrate on building public
constituencies and political support, while others streamline and
document internal operations to upgrade performance and
accountability.

First-hand observation of successful administrators makes it
clear that there is no one best way of organizing and managing a
probation agency, even in affluent times. It is also clear that not all
strategies touted as resource-conserving are cost-effective for all
agencies under all circumstances. If managers are to choose wisely
among realistic options for an era of limits, they need to be able to
estimate the likely effects of a given approach in their particular
situation. This becomes more important as budgets tighten. Under

conditions of growth and ready availability of funds, an error in implementation often can be corrected, or its effects obscured, by an increase in spending or a new program. Under fiscal limits, it becomes more important to do it right the first time, as implementation errors may result in opportunities lost.

This chapter looks at selected examples of strategies that probation managers have turned to in recent years to deal with fiscal constraints: formalizing the classification process; substituting workload measures for caseload measures; using alternatives to regular supervision; and streamlining the presentence investigation process. Thoughtfully implemented under appropriate circumstances, each of these can aid in resource conservation, but cost savings are in no way guaranteed. Success depends on organizational and environmental factors—the context of implementation—as much as on the design of the technology itself.

Formalizing the Classification Process

Classification and differential handling of cases have long been the norm for probation agencies dealing with varied caseloads. Distinguishing among different types of offenders, and then treating them in appropriately different ways, is a logical way to meet offender needs and minimize risk to the community. Where caseloads are large, differential treatment becomes essential if resources are to be focused on those who need it most.

In recent years there has been a trend toward systematizing and formalizing the classification process. Many probation departments have developed their own classification instruments or adapted instruments developed elsewhere. Many also are refining and standardizing their case management modes to match available resources to client groups (e.g., specialized units) or to promote more consistent and measurable handling of cases (specifying the components of different levels of supervision).

The rationale for systematizing procedures used informally for many years generally involves some combination of the growing concern for equity in the handling of offenders—given impetus by the concept of "just deserts" (Fogel, 1975)—and the need for more objective, explicit, and replicable bases for making resource allocation decisions. The need for detailed information for purposes of accountability and budget defense is a recent, but increasingly prominent, reason for moving to more formal classification and case management schemes.

Classification and Resource Conservation

But can formal classification serve as a major resource conservation device? Should probation managers look to these systems to help them cut costs? It depends. An important fact about classification instruments and case management schemes is that they are, at heart, neutral management tools. They can be tailored to the needs and policy concerns of almost any jurisdiction. They can expand the use of resources as easily as conserve them. Classification and differential case management will not reduce resource use unless probation managers and judges are intent on using them for this purpose.

Classification instruments themselves may contain biases toward increased resource use. For example, the well-known Wisconsin system (at least as originally designed) involves the collection of kinds and amounts of information that may place higher than normal demands on data collection resources. Still, it is more often the policy element of the classification process—the decision rules—rather than the instrument, that makes a system cost-conserving or not. In the Wisconsin system it is the decision to include the needs assessment score in classification for supervision level (which may place a low-risk client with high service needs on intensive supervision) that holds the potential for increased resource use.

In both cases, the tendency toward increased costs can be reversed. In some places where modified versions of the Wisconsin system have been introduced, for example, information considered less important is simply not collected, while needs assessment is used only for case management, not for assignment to supervision level.

The flexibility this implies is what makes formal classification and differential case management potentially so useful in resource conservation. Where a well designed and maintained system is in place, management has access to the information needed to move scarce resources around as policies, client characteristics, or resource levels change. By modifying decision rules and raising or lowering cutoff points to move more offenders to higher or lower levels of supervision, management can use the classification system to respond quickly to a changing situation, maintaining ongoing balance between available resources and needs for them.

Some Examples

Some managers report that, without their classification system, they could not handle the growing workload with the resources provided by their budget. The sentiment expressed by Connecticut's director of adult probation is not uncommon:

> There is no way that we could continue to be described as a service-providing agency or agency concerned with protecting the community if we did not have this [differential caseload management] system. We have had no new positions assigned to this agency by the legislature since 1977, and the caseload since that time has increased by 6,500 cases.

Connecticut's classification system, called Differential Caseload Management by Objectives (DCMBO) guides officers in assigning clients to one of three management modes. Clients in Model I are unsupervised for the most part, contacted by telephone and written correspondence as needed. Model II clients are those who demonstrate no willingness to change their behavior; they are placed in a "surveillance" mode and are returned to court immediately when they violate probation conditions. Model III clients are relatively high risk, but ready to change and capable of being helped. Supervising officers generally carry caseloads of Model II or Model III probationers, seldom taking on both types. This enables officers to more clearly define their roles, and gives clients a better understanding of what is expected of them.

In Connecticut, formal classification and differential case management have made it possible to take on constantly growing workloads by sorting out those cases that can be "banked" into unsupervised categories. Data on 48,000 cases provided information on client characteristics for use in designing supervision modes, making supportable recommendations to the court, and assigning officers to different locations. As such, formal classification is a vital resource allocation tool for this jurisdiction's probation managers.

It is instructive to contrast the situation of a small probation agency serving a geographically dispersed rural clientele. A district probation office in New Hampshire used formal classification to equalize officer caseloads until budget cuts reduced professional staff to two. Since that time, the classification system has been overshadowed by the logistics of travel, but even when the office had more staff an offender's classification was seen as no more than a general guide for decision-making. The chief of one of California's more rural probation agencies agrees with this approach: "No classification system that ignores geographic location would be cost-effective for us."

Informal classification will always be useful, when resources are scarce, to determine which cases can be banked, terminated early, or assigned to unsupervised activities such as restitution or community work. The move to formal classification, however, may be more useful to some probation agencies than others.

The utility of the DCMBO to the Connecticut system seems to derive in part from the size and structure of the agency (including the need to allocate resources among a number of offices) and the large numbers involved (up 6,500 cases in less than five years). To a small, single-office agency, formal classification may provide a rationale for differential handling of offenders (and protection against charges that offenders are inappropriately "unsupervised"), and it may aid the functional specialization of caseloads and officers—a boon to some managers looking for ways to reward and motivate staff. It may be less important to the small, rural agency as a resource allocation or conservation tool.

A Low-Cost Option

One type of classification instrument that may be useful to the smaller agency (or to any agency that does not make use of specialized caseloads) is the intake screening tool. The probation division of the Hamilton County (Ohio) Municipal Court uses an instrument based on information commonly gathered at intake to divert 40 percent of the caseload to non-reporting probation status.

This instrument, developed in-house by the intake supervisor, identifies probationers who have no significant life problems and little likelihood of being rearrested. Typically, these clients have some education, a stable marriage, few convictions, and no indication of serious substance abuse.

Hamilton County probation managers tested other screening instruments (including Base Expectancy), but felt they were not sufficiently accurate to warrant labeling cases as potential "failures." They found it easier and more productive to identify those most likely to succeed (this does not include all potential successes, which are simply the inverse of predictions of failure, but only those very low-risk cases that can be easily spotted). In this way they avoid what they feel may be the self-fulfilling prophecy of high-risk classification, and their predictions of success are wrong only 2 percent of the time (compared to 50 percent of the time when they tried to predict success or failure for the entire population).

Definite cost savings are claimed for the Ohio approach, which has enabled caseloads to be reduced to the point where they are manageable, rather than intolerable. Implementing the screening program costs the agency little beyond the printing of forms, since volunteers handle the intake interview and then set up the conditions and complete the paperwork for non-reporting status.

Formalizing Classification: Summary

Field experience suggests that cost savings can be achieved if classification is used to screen out a significant proportion of probationers from active supervision. Without such screening, there may be no immediate cost savings associated with implementing a case classification system. In fact, there probably will be an initial increase in costs to develop or adapt such a system to local needs and to train staff in its use. There may be other resource-related benefits, including long-run cost avoidance (if not actual reductions) through improved resource allocation, but this requires judicial and probation management willingness to use the system for this purpose. The tool and the policy go hand-in-hand.

The increased equity, accountability, and control over resource use associated with systematic classification are themselves important values for public service agencies in an era of fiscal limits. When combined with workload measures, classification aids in resource allocation and equalization of workload among officers and offices. When integrated into a management information system, classification provides detailed information on offenders for evaluation purposes, as well as for projection and defense of resource needs.

Substituting Workload for Caseload

The debate over ideal or appropriate caseload size has gone on for decades without coming any closer to consensus than a general feeling, at least within the field, that "caseloads are too high."

One reason for the failure to come to closure on this central resource-allocation issue undoubtedly is that caseloads differ. Not all cases require or tend to receive the same amount of time and effort. Without a systematic means of equalizing the distribution of different kinds of cases among officers and offices, a caseload of any given numerical size may be light or heavy, large or small, depending on the work involved.

Workload measures have been developed to improve upon caseload as a means of assigning cases (and other responsibilities) to officers, as well as for allocating officers (and other resources) to offices, functions, or divisions of the agency. Because of the demonstrably greater equity that such a system permits, states that subsidize locally administered community corrections operations also are moving to replace caseload with workload in their formulas for allocating funds.

Workload measures are an adjunct to formal classification, since consistent means of assigning clients to different supervision intensities (reflecting staff time and effort) are necessary to a determination of workload "size." Classification provides a basis for deciding where to invest resources; workload measures enable resources to be optimally and equitably applied.

The steps involved in developing or instituting a workload system are fairly straightforward. Time studies (see Jester, this volume) are used to obtain a measure of the amount of staff time that goes into the activities associated with various supervision levels, as well as that devoted to such tasks as investigative work and hearings. Other activities (program development, community work, administrative tasks, etc.) also must be assigned some unit values expressed in terms of time. Total agent time available (minus personal time, sick leave, and vacation) then is used to compute both the combinations of cases and activities that a single officer can reasonably carry and the number of agents an office with a given workload should be assigned.

Advantages of Workload Measures

In addition to increased equity and precision in resource allocation, the most commonly cited advantage of these workload measures seems to be the increased specificity they permit in supporting budget requests. Those responsible for budget appropriations reportedly are tired of hearing the yearly plea for more officers to handle what is claimed to be a constantly growing caseload. Use of workload figures provides a consistent measure of departmental workload relative to available staff, and this allows budget decisions to be based on some knowledge of their likely effects on operations. Connecticut reportedly has built in "a tremendous amount of accountability" in recent years:

> We utilize a work unit system and attach a numerical work unit to every aspect of the probation job. We are now able to show the percentage of time spent in the field, in the office, in investigative work, court work, serving of warrants, etc. The day is gone when one can simply try to justify the budget request based on caseload sizes and the number of investigations completed during a given year.

The chief in Contra Costa County, California, uses a workload system to keep tabs on his various divisions' actual and "earned" (meaning what they "ought" to have if resources were sufficient) staffing levels. When resources do become available, these figures help to settle the question of where they will be applied. They also are useful in depicting areas and extent of understaffing and the likely effects of any proposed cuts in the salary line.

Perhaps the most important contribution of the workload measure, at least from the taxpayer's point of view, is that it halts the practice of rewarding the accumulation of ever-larger case-loads. Managers throughout the public sector have long decried the lack of incentives for efficient management of government services. In probation, awarding funds on the basis of caseload counts has discouraged efforts to conserve resources by moving people off probation as rapidly as possible. Without this fundamental change in the reward system, other measures to conserve may have unacceptable costs. The director of a locally administered department in a Community Corrections Act state made this point:

> As long as the State hands out dollars for every case retained on probation, it hardly makes sense to look for ways of improving productivity. We may do so anyway, because we believe it's right; but if we do, the money we save will go to those counties that are least efficient. First we've got to replace caseload with workload in the State's allocation formula.

There are ways of avoiding increased productivity even where workload measures are used. The policies that drive the classification system (e.g., how many and which offenders are placed on maximum) and case management scheme (how much goes into each supervision category, how quickly cases are moved to lower levels) will determine, to a large extent, how many officers are "needed." By assigning high time values to a function such as maximum supervision, and then routing a large proportion of offenders through it, any department can use workload measures to "prove" its need for more resources.

Workload Measures: Summary

Like classification, then, workload measures can aid resource conservation or they can serve the opposite purpose. They do, however, provide a basis for equitable allocation of scarce resources among jurisdictions, offices, and functions. Workload measures make explicit the assumptions that underlie resource allocation decisions and budget requests, thus encouraging a more responsible and responsive budget allocation process. Finally, they provide managers with information needed to use resources in a more thoughtful manner, including the ability either to make optimal use of shrinking resources or to demonstrate the department's need for more.

Using Alternatives to Regular Supervision

Increased use of less costly alternatives is the policy element that makes classification a resource-conservation tool. Unless low-cost alternatives are available, classification may have no cost-reducing or cost-avoidance effects. The information generated by systematic classification likely will be useful in other ways (e.g., increased accountability and control over resource use, better data for budget defense). But for managers looking for ways to cut costs, alternatives to the normal probation routine are an indispensable concomitant of formal or informal classification.

Alternatives to regular or intensive supervision come in many different forms, their variety reflecting the conditional nature of the probationary sentence. In most jurisdictions, the judge can use considerable discretion when it comes to designing a sentence appropriate to the case. Within limits set by the court, and with the judge's tacit or express approval, the probation department then can apply any of a range of resources over a defined but alterable period of time in managing the case.

That alternatives to regular supervision can be found becomes most evident when departmental funds are sharply reduced. Although we might rather learn this fact in other, less unpleasant ways, even already-high caseloads can be handled with fewer resources through greater reliance on court diversion, "banked" (no service) probation caseloads, conditional discharge, and early termination. These, in fact, may be among the few immediately available options for a resource-poor department faced with sudden and significant budget cuts.

Some Simple Low-Cost Alternatives

A small district probation office in New Hampshire, pared to a professional staff of two, makes heavy use of formal and informal alternatives. Early termination is a major resource-conservation strategy. Cases are reviewed as often as once a month to determine who can be taken off probation and, wherever appropriate, petitions to do so are filed with the court. "It is rare," the district manager reports, "that anyone stays on probation for their entire term."

Another mechanism for minimizing resource use is a contract developed with offenders that sets out what will be accomplished by specified points in time. The probationer is asked where he would like to be in six months or a year; then the officer helps him to "backplan," to set monthly goals in a matrix of "key result areas" that will lead to the stated objective. As long as an individual is progressing toward his goal and staying out of trouble, little supervision or service is provided.

In this same district, a court-funded diversion program siphons off some cases before they reach the probation department (others are diverted informally at later points). Many of those who remain are given some form of conditional discharge or placed in no-service caseloads contingent upon paying a fine or victim restitution or doing some type of volunteer community work. All of these measures combined allow officers to concentrate on those offenders for whom no alternative to close supervision is appropriate.

Restitution and Community Work

Victim restitution and community work programs are enjoying an upsurge in popularity throughout the country, in large part because such dispositions are seen as fitting the current public mood. Requiring offenders to "pay for" their crimes, or "make good" the losses they have caused, certainly seems to have wide appeal. Because both dispositions involve the collection of money or the contribution of volunteer work, it is sometimes loosely implied (especially for restitution) that these programs also are unusually cost-effective for the probation department, or in other ways inherently good strategies for an era of limits.

The important fact to remember about all such "alternative" programs is that they cut costs only when used in lieu of regular supervision. If used as an enhancement, they may add qualitatively to service offered, but they also will increase its costs. The ability to take on a larger workload could lead as well to a widening of the probation "net."

The district court of Quincy, Massachusetts, is well known for its *Earn-It* program, which combines community work and restitution in an attractively packaged program. Referral to Earn-It often serves as an alternative, not an enhancement, and it is credited with diverting from one-quarter to one-third of the caseload from traditional forms of supervision. The existence of these special sanctions permits a judge to order restitution and/or community work as a condition of court diversion, a condition of suspended adjudication, a condition of probation (sole sanction or supplemental), or a condition of a split sentence (permitting early release from jail).

One of the most striking aspects of the Quincy program is the extent to which the business community has been mobilized in its support. An offender referred to Earn-It for a job (as many must be in order to pay restitution) is put in touch with one of 50 or 60 participating employers. Those sentenced to volunteer work go to one of about 70 cooperating community service sites. Through careful screening and matching of clients to jobs, assurances to employers that they can reject anyone they have questions about, frequent contacts with work sites, and responsiveness to employer concerns, *Earn-It* staff maintain the involvement of business sponsors and volunteer work sites. Free publicity is one of the ways they reward them for participation.

The success of this kind of program may depend on factors outside the control of the probation agency—the availability of low-skill jobs, for example, or the acceptability to the business community of the kinds of clients the department generally handles (this does vary from place to place, even among those that deal with the same kinds of crimes). Much, however, can be accomplished by a skilled job developer, especially with aggressive marketing of the program by top management and support or leadership from the court.

The Quincy program shows impressive completion rates: about 80 percent of restitution orders are paid, and about 90 percent of those sentenced to community work comply. And such success is not unique to that setting—a restitution program operating in ten cities in Ohio, Indiana, and Illinois (called *Prisoner and Community Together*) reports that 98 percent of its restitution orders are paid.

Minimizing Costs of Alternative Case Management

Some alternatives (e.g., banking of cases, early termination) may produce immediate and direct cost savings by cutting resource investments, not replacing them with others. Community service and restitution may or may not cut costs, depending on how they are used.

Even if used as alternatives rather than enhancements, restitution and community work may increase costs of service. (Some programs, for example, have ended up costing more than the jail incarceration they were designed to replace). Even at a low level of staffing and programming, there will be development costs and ongoing expenses associated with program management and job placement (or contracts with others to perform these functions). Directors of many programs spend a good deal of time looking for ways to fund them.

It is possible, of course, to use restitution and community work as alternatives or as enhancements without setting up a formal program if an agency wants to go this route. In the New Hampshire district office, these dispositions are handled without fanfare. Restitution is the responsibility of the defendant rather than the probation department. Direct payment to victims means that probation generally does not have to go through setting up a case, monitoring collections, and so on. If verification of payment is presented within the time frame ordered by the court, the resources of the probation department may not be called upon at all.

Alternatives: Summary

"Probation too often plays games with figures in order to protect our 'overworked' image," one probation manager observed. "We have to realize that it is not how many cases we have that is important; it is how we handle them. A great many probationers do well without our help."

Certainly if cutting costs is the goal (rather than proving a need for increased revenues), the use of lower-cost alternatives to regular supervision is an obvious way to go. Combined with careful screening or classification, dispositions such as diversion, banking, conditional discharge, fines, and restitution/community work can serve as cost-effective alternatives. In addition, any means of ensuring that offenders "pay for" their crimes can enhance the public image of probation as an instrument of justice and a mediator between lawbreaker and society.

Streamlining the PSI

Most efforts to alter and improve the presentence investigation process have been aimed at increasing the accuracy, utility, and consistency of information and recommendations contained in the PSI report. The goal of reform in this area generally has been more equitable and more appropriate decision-making about offenders.

Experience gained in a two-year demonstration program adds new motivation for change in the PSI process (Beckley et al., 1981). In this nationwide action-research program, probation agencies in nine state and local jurisdictions experimented with PSI format, content, and processes. Increased efficiency in the PSI process was only one of the goals of these experiments, but the short-report format (which all projects developed) and some of the other innovations adopted in different sites did reduce report preparation time and associated costs.

In Pima County, Arizona, for example, the probation department cut preparation time by 33 percent and costs (even with a 10 percent salary increase) by more than 21 percent through the use of short reports in appropriate cases, interfacing of forms to eliminate duplication, and use of lower-cost personnel and volunteers in data collection tasks.

The Washington, D.C., department experimented with a team approach to investigation. Officers in a specialized PSI unit handled interviews and report-writing individually, but worked as a team in data collection and verification. One officer, for example, might be responsible for verifying employment status on all cases referred to the unit, while another performed all residence checks. A paraprofessional hired with grant funds assisted officers in data collection tasks, especially those requiring time-consuming trips out of the office. In this manner, six probation officers and one paraprofessional assumed the workload of seven officers.

The range of activities undertaken by study sites suggests that streamlining the PSI process is a strategy available to any probation agency, regardless of size, resources, or authority to innovate. As a group, these jurisdictions showed that cost savings can be achieved through the use of short reports, as well as through changes in data collection and report preparation processes. Using these savings to "rationalize" resource allocation, however, may prove more problematic.

In theory, at least, savings in the PSI area can improve resource allocation in two ways. Agency resources no longer devoted to presentence investigations can be targeted on other functions (e.g., supervision), and, if more efficient report preparation results in speedier sentencing, the resources saved by reduced pretrial detention become available for use in other ways. The first adds resource flexibility to the probation agency; the second, to the justice system as a whole.

Impact on Other Functions

For various reasons, the impressive cost reductions achieved in some PSI experiments did not have the effects on resource allocation that might be expected. In some jurisdictions, the experiment, although a success, was discontinued. In others, the savings generated simply failed to spread to other areas, within or outside the agency.

Implementation problems of the first type occurred in at least two locations. The team experiment in Washington, D.C., was abandoned after six months, largely because of officer dissatisfaction with the approach. Probation officers disliked having to rely on the scheduling of others, and they preferred to control the work that goes into their final products. In Multnomah County, Oregon, a cost-effective change in report format did not get beyond the experimental phase because state approval of the new forms was not obtained. The project had received state go-ahead to experiment with report formats, but neglected to pursue the necessary authorization to make the change more permanent.

Even where change is institutionalized, savings may not be transferred to other functions. Where court workloads are growing, more efficient production of PSIs is just as likely to result in more referrals. In Pima County, for example, the substantial efficiencies achieved helped this department to accommodate a 36 percent increase in referrals with no increase in staff.

The Connecticut probation department created a specialized PSI unit with the expectation that relieving supervision officers of presentence tasks would give them more time for client contacts. With the help of short reports and some procedural changes to make the process more efficient, this department did succeed in reducing report preparation time. However, for reasons that are still under investigation, supervision contacts did not increase.

Cutting preparation time also may not speed delivery to court, nor will faster delivery necessarily produce earlier sentences. The Pima County reductions in preparation time did not result in faster delivery, and thus did not impact sentencing. But even where delivery time was dramatically advanced, the referral-to-sentencing interval was not necessarily affected. Judges, attorneys, and supervising probation officers all must cooperate if sentencing is to occur earlier. Changes in the presentence process are not, by themselves, enough.

Keys to Success

Most jurisdictions involved in the PSI project are still working out implementation problems of one kind or another. The process of change in this "swampy" area is inherently political, and anything other than straightforward cost-cutting takes time, determination, and ongoing effort. Some lessons learned from this nationwide experiment may be useful to those considering productivity increases through changes in the PSI, as well as changes in other areas of the criminal justice system.

Most of the LEAA sites found the system-wide advisory committee (required of all sites by the national program design) to be extremely useful in an area where any change can impact other justice agencies. Some jurisdictions felt that the committee itself was a major product of the experimental effort. Working together to deal with a system-wide issue such as the PSI opened up channels of communication that had never before existed. "Now when you have a problem," said one enthusiastic participant, "you have a person you know to talk about it with. Some problems can be resolved in a phone call and not even take committee action."

Certainly if planned changes will require the cooperation of other agencies, key agency representatives (not just the judge, but the "right" judge) must be coopted by the project and feel some ownership of problems that may arise, as well as of any products that come out of the group effort.

Changes should be designed and sold as an experiment, with ongoing assessment and modification as indicated. Nonetheless, everyone should understand that some change will occur, and that management is committed to improvement in this area. "Staff should not be allowed to interpret projects such as this as temporary," advised one manager, "or feel that they will probably go away after a short time. They must not be allowed to revert to the old way when anyone's back is turned."

All participants should be encouraged to communicate their reactions to new formats or procedures, and this feedback should be considered in making modifications. Formal evaluation, at whatever level is feasible, will be necessary in determining whether change has been successful. But "data" will not be a sufficient guide for action; people and their roles in the interorganizational setting will heavily influence success.

Streamlining the PSI: Summary

Field experience with efforts to streamline the presentence process suggests that costs associated with report preparation time can be reduced with little or no adverse effect on the quality of service to the courts. Reductions in preparation time and costs may or may not produce added resources for supervision, earlier sentencing, or reductions in jail populations. All of these will take special efforts and skilled management of implementation problems. Finally, where probation takes a leadership role in a joint effort to increase system-wide productivity, there are many opportunities for building public constituencies and political support. Streamlining the PSI is a good focal issue for initiating this process, while at the same time generating some real cost savings.

Conclusion

It makes no sense to talk of "management strategies for probation" as if different approaches were equally appropriate for all of the varied situations in which probation managers find themselves. There are numerous organizational and environmental factors that determine the options available to a manager and affect the success or failure of any strategy he may adopt. Also, as even the few examples offered here suggest, policy decisions determine the utility of many probation technologies for agencies hoping to reduce costs.

In the literature on criminal justice and corrections one often reads that "increased coordination" will reduce duplication and cut costs, that "alternatives to incarceration" are cheaper and just as effective, or that functional specialization of staff enhances the productivity of the unit and the agency as a whole. Yet it is clear to any experienced manager that such general statements are not always true.

Because there has been no pressing need to worry about implementation errors in the past, there is not a great deal of information to aid probation managers as they tailor strategies to deal with resource constraints. This likely will change. If the field is sincere about its new interest in organizational and administrative issues, it will produce, in time, a body of knowledge about context and its effects on the implementation of strategies designed for an era of limits.

Discussion Questions

1. Jester's chapter demonstrates the existence of different probation technologies and varying patterns of resource allocation.
The Harlow and Nelson chapter, in contrast, argues that technology and resource allocation decisions can be, and, in some
agencies, are being, more systematically made. Could the
resource-conserving strategies described by Harlow and Nelson
be successfully implemented in the type of system described by
Maher in Chapter 4? Why or why not? How could resistance to
resource conservation be overcome?

2. Are some types of correctional organizations more likely to be
pressured for accountability than other types? For example,
Harlow and Nelson argue that probation is particularly suscepti-
ble to resource cuts? Why might prisons be less vulnerable?
Would all kinds of probation agencies be equally vulnerable? In
what kinds of community fields might probation be viewed as
more essential?

Chapter 7
Reintegration Policy in Practice: Transition Programs in the 1970s

David E. Duffee and Kevin N. Wright

Organizational ideology and practice are always related but rarely identical. Mission statements may define the outer boundaries of operation and provide guidelines for implementation. They may also serve to justify or rationalize organizational actions by highlighting some plausible connections between certain program elements and long established value premises while downplaying or ignoring other forces equally important to the shape of the actions taken. The program elements which are rationalized are often those having greatest currency within a social service sector: they are the program elements which are likely to be widely recognized as efficacious within the current beliefs about social practice. The program elements that are downplayed or ignored are often those more specific to the organization in question: they are the program elements which are responses to local constraints rather than cosmopolitan beliefs about good practice. The result of this differential attention to enunciated program qualities is selective public and expert attention to the nature of programs. We tend to focus attention on the commonalities in goals and missions and to focus away from those aspects of programs which make them unique.

The correctional programs of reintegration are no exception to this general process. Reintegration policy focuses on the issue of graduated release and related programmatic efforts to change, over time, the relationship of the correctional client both to the system of punishment and to the free community. Policy statements tend to ignore, or treat as idiosyncratic, the variations in client/organization relationships that are attributed to exigencies of specific locales. The result is that very different programs are justified with resort to the same policy language. The effect of exigency in program history often receives less attention.

Reintegration programs are not new. The 19th century prison programs of Maconochie and Crofton included graduated reduction in custody and increased inmate exchange with communities prior to expiration of sentence. The mark system and the ticket-of-leave were the forerunners of modern parole practice. But they were also the origins of prison policies which would not become popular until the 1960s. By that time, parole had become the normal means of release from prison, and complaints arose that the transition from prison to parole was not an easy one for many offenders to negotiate.

The Momentum for Reintegration

The ascendancy of reintegration as preferred, official policy can probably be tied to the publication of *The Challenge of Crime in a Free Society* (1967) by the President's Commission on Law Enforcement and Administration of Justice. This document marked a move away from the client-centered changes of rehabilitation and toward a concern for changes in the relationship between the client and the environment.

Three passages from the report outline the transformation of preference. In the first passage, the Commission concludes that traditional means of corrections had failed and that the usual conditions of confinement probably worked against change of behavior by the prisoner:

> For a great many offenders, then, corrections does not correct. Indeed, experts are increasingly coming to feel that the conditions under which many offenders are handled, particularly in institutions, are often positive detriments to rehabilitation (1967:159).

The Commission then outlined the problems encountered in institutionally based efforts:

> Life in many institutions is at best barren and futile, at worst unspeakably brutal and degrading. To be sure, the offenders in such institutions are incapacitated from

committing further crimes while serving their sentence, but the conditions in which they live are the poorest possible preparation for their successful reentry into society, and often merely reinforce in them a pattern of manipulation or destructiveness (1967:159).

The Commission justified the need for reintegration by noting the failure of institutions to prepare inmates for reentry into the community. It condemned the conditions of confinement. But in the next passage, the Commission also criticized the rehabilitative mission. It proceeded to shift the explanation for criminal behavior away from the inadequate individual and toward an inadequate linkage between certain individuals and social resources.

Correction of offenders has also labored under what is coming to be seen as a fundamental deficiency in approach. All of the past phases in the evolution of corrections accounted for criminal and delinquent behavior primarily on the basis of some form of defect within the individual offender. The idea of being possessed by devils was replaced with the idea of psychological disability. Until recently, reformers have tended to ignore the evidence that crime and delinquency are symptoms of the disorganization of the community as well as of individual personalities and that community institutions—through extending or denying their resources—have critical influence in determining the success or failure of an individual offender (1967:164).

Based on this general perspective, the Commission identified a major strategic fault in correctional design. It proposed that many specific difficulties faced by offenders during the transition to parole had a source in correctional practices occurring well before release. The Commission argued that prisoners should be engaging in activities that (1) focused on the development of skills which improved chances of legitimate employment and (2) increased their legitimate opportunities once released. Simultaneously, correctional staff should be: (3) helping inmates to select and test new skills and (4) developing the opportunities in the prison and in the community through advocacy and referral.

This program strategy became known as reintegration (O'Leary and Duffee, 1971; Studt, 1973; Conrad, 1973). Proponents of reintegration recognized that previous correctional programs had similar goals of reducing recidivism, and even provided some of the recommended program elements, such as graduated release. However, the reintegrationists insisted that a system of graduated release was not sufficient for reintegration to take place. What happened during the reduction in custody was equally important. Incremental reduction in custody, by itself, could be a means of rewarding inmates for good behavior, and therefore a security strategy rather than a means of influencing post-release behavior. Other prison programs, said the reintegrationists, focused on change within the inmate rather than on changes between the inmate and his social environment. Programs stressing attitude and motivation rather than skill and opportunity were misdirected because they ignored the practical realities of most prisoners' post-release situations (Miller and Ohlin, 1985).

Implementation of Reintegration

Like many other correctional policies before it, reintegration was more often invoked than followed. It became a popular buzz word more readily than a set of implemented programs. Probably the most frequently adopted aspect of reintegration policy has been more widespread use of graduated release. Probably the most ignored aspects have been the recommendations for limiting the use of prison and the recommendation for coupling skill development with increased opportunity for testing those skills under controlled conditions. Regarding the latter, many correctional departments seem to have taken the position that increasing the offender's contact with the community is itself the required change in opportunity. Such a position ignores the growing body of research findings in both corrections and mental health documenting the empty, unstructured, and resourceless lives of many persons deinstitutionalized without support (Scull, 1977; Miller and Ohlin, 1985; and see Minnesota Governor's Commission on Crime Prevention and Control, 1975 and 1976, as discussed later in this chapter).

Very often, implementation of reintegration has been restricted to either the tail end of an inmate's prison sentence or the initial portion of parole. Many systems have introduced means of increasing an inmate's contact with community as he nears parole or expiration of sentence. Work release, educational release, and home furlough are three examples of such program efforts. Other programs often included in this group are pre-release programs occurring in institutions, pre-release community residences, and halfway houses for parolees (see LeClair, 1979, for an example of program coordination in one state system).

One possible reason for the popularity of this particular form of reintegration programming was that it could be tacked onto existing programs and did not require extensive changes in sentencing patterns or large capital budgets. Graduated release could be coupled with retributive and deterrent sentences.

Federal legislation provided funding which made the development of many transitional programs possible. After the publication of *The Challenge of Crime in a Free Society* in 1967, the U.S. Congress passed the Omnibus Crime Control and Safe Streets Act of 1968. This legislation provided block grants to the states to develop crime control programs. Block grants gave the states considerable flexibility in their approach to criminal justice funding. Initially much of the federal money was used for police programs. But an amendment to the Act in 1970 assured attention to correctional programming by establishing a special category of funds for that purpose.

During the period from 1970 to 1975, state correctional systems received an infusion of federal dollars to fund innovative programs. It was a time of change and experimentation. President Nixon's National Advisory Commission on Criminal Justice Standards and Goals (1973) continued to press for reintegration:

> It is clear that a dramatic realignment of correctional methods is called for. It is essential to abate the use of institutions... The institution should be the last resort for correctional problems.

It was early in this period that new transitional programs were initiated in New York, Michigan, Pennsylvania, and Minnesota. The programs in New York, Michigan, and Pennsylvania are pre-release programs, while the program in Minnesota was a post-parole transition program. The programs in Michigan, Pennsylvania, and Minnesota take place in community residences or halfway houses, while the New York program takes place in prison, just prior to parole release.

The two programs that have the most in common are those in Michigan and Pennsylvania. In both of these cases, inmates are transferred from prisons to residential centers located often in the city of parole release. In both programs, the residents are not yet eligible for parole. Because inmates in these programs are still serving their minimum sentences and are still under the authority of the prison administration, they are in pre-release status. If the residents do not follow the rules of the program, or if they commit another crime, they can be returned to a regular prison with less rigorous due process than if they were on parole. If such pre-release centers are defined by statute or administrative directive as prisons, then their residents can be moved in and out at the discretion of administrators under *Meachum v. Fano* (but see Duffee, Maher and Lagoy, 1977, for an example of procedures when such centers are statutorily distinguished from prisons).

While the propriety and legality of the pre-release center selection and revocation process will not get full coverage in this chapter, certain aspects are important. The fact that the residents in these centers are not on parole, and not even eligible for it, is one important distinction between centers in Pennsylvania and Michigan and those in Minnesota. In that latter state, halfway house residents were parolees. They could, on occasion, abscond from a center or be terminated from a center for unsatisfactory performance without losing their parole status. And, if officials in Minnesota wanted to return a halfway house resident to prison, they first needed to go through the double revocation hearing required by *Morrissey v. Brewer*. Consequently, a very important aspect of the Michigan and Pennsylvania programs is that the halfway house staff has a considerably greater hold over its residents than is the case in Minnesota. One would assume that the greater ease of revocation (or transfer) of pre-release status as compared to parole status, would give pre-release staffs greater implicit control over the behavior of residents.

On the other side of the same coin, one could argue that the residents in Michigan and Pennsylvania would perceive their center residence as considerably more advantageous to themselves than would the residents in Minnesota. In the former states, the legal alternative to the halfway house is a prison cell. In the latter state, halfway house residents are more likely to compare themselves to other parolees than to prisoners. Hence residents in Minnesota are likely to see themselves as under much greater control than their peers.

Finally, in New York, the transition program takes place in the prisons rather than in the community. Inmates attending pre-release programs are neither eligible for parole nor residing in communities. They are still in prisons. Pre-release in New York, in most instances, takes place behind walls. Prisoners who choose to use the services of the pre-release program report to the pre-release center when not engaged in other duties. In the center, they can participate in a number of activities that may help them prepare for parole. These broad comparisons among the four programs are summarized in Figure 7.1.

Figure 7.1
Types of Transitional Programs

Status of Clients:	Prisoners			:	Parolees
States:	NY	:	MI & PA	:	MN
Residence:	Prison	:	Community		

The reintegration language of the federal commissions provided the impetus for these and similar programs, and federal funds were essential to their implementation, except in New York. As these programs developed, their stated purposes and program descriptions tended to highlight those program aspects which were similar to the reintegration strategy of the national commissions. The differences among programs are equally important but likely to receive less attention. It was their connection to reintegration policy which helped to mobilize resources and increase perceived legitimacy. Their differences are often best explained in terms of the specific legal, political, and social characteristics faced by each program during implementation of the reintegration objectives. The following descriptions highlight these differences by focusing on six program dimensions: auspice, assumptions and objectives, staffing, client selection and characteristics, programming, and service linkages.

These descriptions concentrate on the operation of the programs during their heyday in the 1970s (see the endnote for a description of sources). To the author's knowledge, systematic evaluations of these programs have not been done since that time. Beginning roughly in the 1980s, increased prison commitments and prison overcrowding may have led to new operational patterns as the transition programs sought to accommodate the increased population pressures. The point here is not to describe current practice, which is in flux, but rather to demonstrate the wide variation in practice originating with very similar policy objectives.

Pre-release in New York

Auspice

The pre-release centers (PRCs) in New York began in the maximum security prison of Green Haven, in 1970. Inmates in Green Haven volunteered to administer a pre-release center for other inmates. Since that time, most centers in New York have been heavily influenced by their resident managers and counselors.

During the 1970s, the PRCs developed relatively independently of each other, although each had support from their respective prison administration and the central office of the Department of Correctional Services (DOCS). In 1980, DOCS and the Division of Parole (DOP) entered a series of agreements providing for joint administration of the PRCs and for some standardization of what the centers were to offer. Pre-release centers operated in about half of the DOCS facilities, in space ranging from one to several rooms. In 1980, DOCS and DOP determined that the program was important enough to extend PRC operations to all facilities except for a few minor camps.

Assumptions and Objectives

Because of the rigid distinction between institutional and non-institutional (parole) responsibilities in New York, many assumptions about pre-release highlight both the opportunities and the limitations of pre-release within a prison setting. DOCS evaluators reported the following assumptions. Pre-release center participation would: (1) increase knowledge about community resources and about the skills and behaviors necessary in the community, (2) improve the inmate's self esteem, (3) increase the inmate's degree of optimism about the impending release experience, and (4) reduce prison misbehavior. The departmental newspaper reported that a parole seminar in the Taconic facility stressed:

> the need for a positive outlook on the part of the inmates. [The] main points were to prepare mentally for the difficulties of reentry into society, to persist, and think success. (*Correctional Services News*, January, 1981:6)

The pre-release program descriptions indicated that preparation in a center prior to parole was intended to affect the performance of persons after they were paroled. The 1977 DOCS annual report argued that the 90 days after release were the most hazardous for recidivism and that the 90 days prior to release could be used to counteract the negative pressures of the transition period.

According to DOCS research staff, the first PRC at Green Haven began with the assumption that:

> If the inmate was connected to post release services prior to his Parole Board appearance, a suitable program could be established for Parole Board approval which could subsequently be implemented following release to the community (Morganbesser and Pollock, 1980:1).

While the emphases varied, the assumptions in the New York PRCs tended to have characteristics related to the rigid distinctions between parole and institutional life, and also to the paramount responsibility of satisfying the Parole Board about the inmate's parole plans. Because the inmates using the PRCs were generally relatively far from their home communities, programs focused on personal adjustments that could be made *in* the individual. These tasks were primarily knowledge acquisition and attitudinal change.

Staffing

An important characteristic of all but a few New York PRCs was the initiative and responsibility shown by the inmates who managed the centers and did much of the counseling. In 1981, a national survey of offender-led programs in the United States nominated the PRC at Walkill as "one of the best examples of offenders working in a correctional setting facility providing services to other offenders" (*Correctional Services News*, April, 1981:2). Almost all of the centers included as staff an inmate resident director and inmate peer counselors. The inmate staff played a significant role in shaping policy and deciding in the particular services to be offered at their PRC. When the DOCS and DOP affirmed their "commitment to enhance and expand the program" in 1980, the two agencies recognized the tripartite responsibility for standardizing and administering the existing PRCs: the superintendent's designate, the DOP designate, and the inmate resident director.

Inmate Selection and Characteristics

There was no statewide data on the characteristics of inmates who used the centers. With one exception, participation in center activities was voluntary. Some centers provided a note to the parole board about inmate participation. DOCS evaluators observed that more eligible inmates participated where this was the practice. The only known characteristics of the participants were that they were all within a few months of release (90 days at most facilities, 120 at Green Haven), had elected to use PRC services as a means of preparing for release, and were more likely to be exiting via parole than conditional release.

Programming

PRC program orientations varied from the heavily psychological at the two women's facilities to the heavily educational at one facility for young adult males. Most of the PRC programs fell between these two extremes, providing some emphasis on instruction and information-giving and some emphasis on mental and emotional preparation for release.

Frequently offered sessions included:

(1) an orientation session describing the services available to newly eligible inmates;
(2) parole board appearance practice sessions;
(3) a session on job development techniques;
(4) a mock employment interview;
(5) sessions dealing with coping/life skills techniques;
(6) a mock parole board hearing;
(7) a class dealing with the legal aspects of parole;
(8) a consumer affairs class;
(9) a reorientation to family life session;
(10) a session on field parole supervision;
(11) a summary session.

Each PRC remained free to offer or to develop additional seminars and discussion sessions as the local staff deemed appropriate.

Community Linkages

Because of the operating assumptions and constraints, the extent of community linkages would appear to have been weak at both the managerial and client service levels. There is evidence that PRC staff did what they could to establish communication, joint program development, and policy agreements with a variety of community groups and organizations.

The strongest interorganizational linkage was with parole. DOCS also had an arrangement with the New York Department of Labor to station employment specialists in correctional facilities to deal with job placement problems prior to release.

Each program also made more or less use of community resource people to offer some of the instructional and discussion sessions. The frequency of such participation depended on the orientations of the inmate directors and the staff supervisors. The centers at Woodburne and Eastern operated on the principle that:

> where field based experts exist, it is preferable to include them in a pre-release educational capacity rather than expect center pre-release staff to deliver [all] the educational seminars (Morganbesser and Pollock, 1980b:71).

One major function of the PRC's was to connect inmates nearing release with agencies that could provide some assurance of post-release employment. There is some evidence that PRC staff sought to make these meaningful relationships and to extract more than perfunctory promises of assistance from such agencies.

Pre-release in Michigan

Auspice

Like the pre-release program in New York, the pre-release program in Michigan is an effort of the state Department of Correction (DOC). The initial center was a joint undertaking with the Federal Bureau of Prisons. Five years later, in 1968, the Bureau took over the entire facility for its own expanding pre-release program and the DOC opened the Detroit Corrrections Center in a portion of the downtown YMCA.

By the late 1970s, the pre-release program in Michigan was one of the largest and most geographically dispersed in the country. Facilities ranged from individual rooms rented from private families, to space for less than a half dozen residents rented from another human service program, to large centers owned and operated directly by the DOC.

The Department's willingness to rent single rooms enabled inmates paroled to outlying districts the advantages of pre-release despite the fact that few parolees would be located in the same area. These single unit facilities were generally supervised by a parole agent, who in Michigan are members of the DOC. Having a unified department, with both parole and prison responsibilities, permitted Michigan more flexible, diverse and geographically dispersed programming than could be arranged in many other states.

The core of the pre-release system was the pre-release centers in the larger urban areas of the state. However, even within these areas, Michigan engaged in a wider range of facility management and resident supervision variations than was the case in many other states. The DOC rented portions of private facilities in smaller cities and supervised these units by designating a parole agent as a part-time center director.

Assumptions and Objectives

Like the other programs reviewed in this chapter, the Michigan DOC began its program espousing the familiar rehabilitative and reintegrationist objectives. But by 1975, the DOC had adopted decidedly incapacitative objectives in the development of its pre-release program. Ironically, perhaps, these concerns for safety and protection led the Michigan program to be less selective and more open to a greater proportion of Michigan inmates than was frequent in many departments which operated on assumptions about facilitating inmate change.

Under its Commissioner, Perry M. Johnson, the DOC developed a systematic set of policy statements directing not only the pre-release program but the entire plan of inmate classification and movement through all department facilities. One of the more representative statements of philosophy is a 1975 paper by Johnson and his director of planning and research, William Kime. They wrote (1975:10):

> there is at least one capacity of the system...which has never been adequately developed—the ability to identify the dangerous and retain them longer while allowing others to return to the community sooner.

They went on to argue (1975:11) that parole would not be rational:

> until it is linked with an institutional system which systematically evaluates and actively tests the readiness of each person under its jurisdiction to live free of crime in the community.

They called this correctional function "performance screening." Under this concept, inmates who performed well in the first stages of the correctional system were to be passed quickly on to less secure settings. Inmates who had trouble after any particular transition were returned to more secure settings. Within this system, the pre-release centers were to serve as the performance screen immediately prior to parole. As such, Johnson and Kime did not see the centers as changing inmate behavior. Instead (1975:13):

What we are looking for is not the ability of the program to change people...but for its ability to identify and distinguish between good and bad risks...the criterion of program success in achieving this aim is not the overall future success rate of persons going though the program, but the differential in success rates later on as between persons who succeed and those who fail in that program.

Relative to the pre-release phase, this idea meant to the DOC that as many inmates as possible should go through the pre-release program. Ideally, no inmate would be paroled who had not been tested first in pre-release. Consequently, the program was large and expanding, and not aimed at finding the inmates who "needed" it.

Staffing

The above change in policy had some implications for staffing. The performance screening system did not invest heavily in counseling personnel, since actively facilitating change was not a major goal. Nor was there a high staff-to-inmate ratio. There was an emphasis on record-keeping, particularly records reflecting the monitoring of resident behavior, in order to weed out the inmates who did not pass the performance screen.

Staffing patterns varied from center to center. The small centers, housing no more than twelve residents, were staffed part-time by correctional officials, usually parole officers, with additional duties. Somewhat larger centers were staffed by full-time supervisors, usually one caseworker, and in Detroit, employment specialists. The largest centers also employed up to four correctional officers. In most cases, the major staff responsibilities were maintenance of rules, including collection of rent, making referrals, and assisting residents to find jobs.

Resident Selection and Characteristics

The 1977 DOC annual report stressed the size and continuing growth of the pre-release program. In that year, the Department approved about 50 percent of the applications for center residence.

Certain offenses, including patterns of assault, predatory or assaultive sex offenses, narcotics trafficking and other crimes suggesting ties with organized crime, made inmates ineligible for pre-release placement. The selection for center placement was highly centralized. The central office used two risk prediction instruments (one for property and one for personal offenses). Offenders who scored low on both were scheduled for center transfer as much as two years prior to their earliest parole date, with riskier but eligible inmates transferred later in their sentences. According to some center staff, the centralized screening procedure caused center staff some problems. They reported that they could not always meet all program needs of the persons sent, even though the inmates met the formal screening criteria. Particularly troublesome, according to staff, were the high percentage of residents with alcohol and drug abuse histories.

About three-fourths of the residents had no prior prison commitments, and the vast majority were serving time for property offenses. Only 20 percent of the residents had minimums longer than three years. The median time served before transfer to the center was 17.1 months. The majority were male, and most were young, the majority being between 21 and 26 years old.

Programming

Programming, according to DOC documents, was neither complicated or extensive. Doing something to or with the residents was simply not a high priority. Far more important was moving out of the centers (as quickly as possible) residents who found jobs and obeyed the rules and returning to prison (as quickly as possible) those who did not. Most center residents became eligible for a parole-like status called "extended furlough" if they had found a job and had no rules violations for one month. When granted extended furlough, the resident could move to his own housing and report to center staff once a week. It is conceivable that some low-risk offenders were in a parole-like situation as much as 23 months prior to their first parole hearing. Important differences were that furloughed residents were still subject to prison escape charges and they could still be returned to prison without the level of evidence necessary for parole revocations.

Beyond its screening function, the program focused on employment. During the 1970s, the centers housed special employment programs run by the U.S. Department of Labor. By insisting that rent and sometimes board payments be made, the centers placed strong pressure on residents to find jobs and to pay their own way. Residents who were not employed within four weeks were returned to prison.

Community Linkages

While the centers were not staffed nor administered to emphasize service provision, all but a few centers had established ties to local agencies for provision of educational and vocational training and for psychological services. Some centers reported additional links for medical and legal services. In centers that were renting space from another program (such as a private halfway house) the center residents often had access to the agency linkages established by the host agency. These could be more extensive than those sought directly by the DOC.

Pre-release in Pennsylvania

Auspice

As in the previous two states, pre-release in Pennsylvania is run by the state. Like New York, Pennsylvania has a split system with separate bureaucracies for prisons (Bureau of Correction, or BOC) and parole (the Board of Probation and Parole, or BPP). When the pre-release program began in 1968, an interagency memorandum split the responsibilities for the pre-release centers between the BOC, which was to supply the facilities and the custodial staff, and the BPP, which was to select the residents and to supply the counseling through the assignment of parole officers to the centers. Although the two organizations disagreed about the reasons, they did agree that this arrangement did not last long. Within a year of program initiation, the BOC, not the BPP, was selecting residents for the program, most of whom had not yet been reviewed for parole. Counseling responsibilities were also assumed by the BOC, which developed an entirely new organizational plan and announced new Bureau positions to staff the centers.

By 1975, the Bureau administered 14 centers in nine cities. Two centers, one in Philadelphia and one in Pittsburgh, housed women. The rest housed men. The centers varied in capacity from 12 to 48 residents.

Most of the centers were located in single, two or three story houses rented from private landlords. Most of the centers were located in transient and commercial neighborhoods, although there were exceptions. The cities were selected for center development primarily in accordance with the proportion of parolees returning to the area, although the BOC also took strides to assure widespread geographic coverage.

Assumptions and Objectives

The BOC operated under no set of policy statements as systematic or as explicit about goals as those found in Michigan. Nevertheless, the following eleven assumptions have been gleaned from observations of program practice, program documents, and interviews with program staff.

When the program began, the centers were called Community Treatment Centers, a term borrowed from the Federal pre-release program, but also accurately portraying the initial program thrust. There was a heavy investment in the facilitation of change in center residents. It was assumed that treatment of some sort was important in aiding the offender's transition from prison to parole. This general assumption led to the following more specific premises:

(1) Placement in centers should be highly selective. Able to accommodate only 250 of the BOC's 6,000 inmates, an operating constraint, if not an assumption, was that not all offenders needed, or could have, a community pre-release experience.

(2) It was assumed that prison living was disruptive of the skills and routines necessary for living in the community. It was additionally assumed that the longer one spent in prison, the more trouble one would suffer. Parole, while seen as offering some supervision and support, was

viewed as inadequate for the types of offenders selected for the centers.

(3) It was assumed that pre-release should be an experiential testing process. Effective preparations for release could not occur in institutional settings.

(4) It was assumed, especially early in the program, that institutional staff—for both custody and treatment—did not have the requisite experience for community center work. It was also assumed that staff without prison experience were less likely to run centers like small prisons and would be more able to marshall community support and resources.

(5) It was assumed that community programs should acclimate the offender not to just any community but to the community in which parole would occur. It was an objective in most centers that residents would not need to change jobs or cities when they were paroled.

(6) Many of the centers operated under the assumption that center residents should be treated as community members, rather than as a separate group. In most centers, they were not encouraged to hang around the centers, to develop close ties to other residents, or to center staff.

(7) While it varied in degree, there was a visible assumption that linking the offender to parole was not as important as linking the offender to the community. Unlike staff in New York or Michigan, Pennsylvania staff often rejected the notion that the first program responsibility was for residents to achieve parole.

(8) It was assumed that residents who faced the transition to community before parole would fail parole less frequently than offenders who went directly to parole from prison.

(9) It was assumed that providing offenders with counseling and referral services would reduce recidivism.

(10) It was assumed that centers had size limits—that they should be small enough that they did not take on institutional characteristics and so that counselors could maintain daily contact with each resident.

Staffing

By 1976, all centers had a uniform staffing pattern of a director, two counselors, three full-time and three part-time house managers. Additional staff existed at three regional offices which each coordinated about five centers.

Staff education and training varied considerably, but with the exception of the house managers, the staff were human service professionals. Most directors and counselors had graduate degrees in fields such as vocational rehabilitation, counseling, psychology, social work, and public administration. During the 1970s, the BOC saw center work as distinct from prison work, did not foster lateral transfers between prisons and the centers, and was slow to enter center positions into the normal civil service examination series.

Resident Selection and Characteristics

The selection process in Pennsylvania stood in sharp contrast to the voluntary pattern in New York and the centralized system in Michigan. In the BOC, center staff had the greatest control over selection of residents. Offenders became eligible for center application when they had served half their term, had served nine consecutive months in prison and had had no major prison misconducts for six months. If the inmate met these minimum requirements, he could meet with his prison counselor to start the application process. The referral process followed the treatment chain of command from counselor to warden to center staff. The referred inmate was then reviewed. Often the inmate applying for center residency was given a furlough to visit the center for an interview. A major concern of center staff was how a prospective resident would get along with the present residents.

About one-third of center residents were black and two-thirds were white, while the racial proportion of inmates in the noneligible population was nearly the reverse of that. The disproportionality of whites in the centers was a reflection of the BOC attempt to establish centers in smaller cities, where most returning parolees were white. Center residents were also considerably older than most prison inmates. Five percent of center residents were under 25, while over 40 percent of the BOC general population was under 25. Center residents had often served longer prison sentences than inmates not referred. For example, 85 percent of non-center inmates had minimums of two years or less, while only 44 percent of center residents had minimum sentences that short. Most inmates who were eligible for parole in less than two years went directly to parole rather than to a center. The requirement that the inmates serve nine months in prison reinforced that pattern. Unlike the residents of many other pre-release systems, the residents in Pennsylvania were more likely than non-residents to be serving time for violent offenses. About 21 percent had been convicted of robbery and 26 percent of second-degree murder or voluntary manslaughter.

Programming

Treatment modalities were perhaps the most diversified aspect of the centers. Centers in Erie and Sharon used a token economy. The four Philadelphia centers used a social casework approach. In the Allentown and Scranton centers, treatment involved group dynamics, with residents participating in positive peer culture groups.

Compared to the Michigan program, counseling in Pennsylvania was relatively intense. Residents were expected to cooperate with some form of treatment program for six months or longer. While in its early years, the Pennsylvania program had an "out-residency" component similar to the Michigan extended furlough, this out-of-center placement did not occur until the resident had served much more time in the center. Even so, that program was cancelled during a gubernatorial campaign in 1974.

In 1975, the centers changed their name from Community Treatment to Community Service Centers. The change reflected a switch, in the staffs' view, from a rehabilitation to a reintegration stance toward the needs of the offenders in the program. This change meant many fewer revocations on treatment grounds and even greater use of community referrals rather than direct services by center staff. While the name change accurately reflected a switch in program orientation, by either name the treatment provided was more extensive than that provided in many other states.

Community Linkages

The centers in Pennsylvania appeared to develop stronger, more extensive ties with other human service agencies than was often the case in other states. The interorganizational relationships varied from center to center. In some areas, there was a much stronger resentment or mistrust of inmates and of correctional agencies than in other parts of the state. Some areas of the state, such as Pittsburgh and Philadelphia, were far richer in human resources than other areas of the state. When, for either reason, center staff could not find adequate service in their communities, they were more likely to develop services within the center, or to limit the kinds of residents that they could accept.

Some center linkages, such as with the local sheriff or police force and parole, were largely determined by policy. Other linkages were left to the discretion of local staff. Most of the staff had been in other human service jobs in the same region prior to the start of the center program, and they were effective in cultivating relationships with other organizations and officials in the community. For example, in the Pittsburgh region, the centers had gone so far as to develop contractual relationships with other service agencies involved in provision of services to center residents. In these agreements, the mutual responsibilities of the two agencies for the same client were spelled out.

Post-release in Minnesota

Auspice

The transition programs in Minnesota were not pre-release but post-release ventures. Most of these programs were operated by private, non-profit corporations rather than the state. However, the bulk of funding for the programs, especially in their first three years of operation was identical to the funding in Pennsylvania and Michigan: block grant funds from LEAA.

These private programs were prone to financial troubles, especially when the federal start-up funds were terminated after three years. One of the houses, for Native Americans, closed immediately when it was unable to secure continuation funds. Seven of the programs had contractual links to the state, one to the University of Minnesota, and one to the St. Paul Model cities program. An increasing number of the houses received funds from the Minnesota Community Corrections Act.

The majority of programs in Minnesota during the 1970's were concentrated in the Minneapolis-St. Paul area. This concentration was partly a function of the Corrections Act, which stipulated that, to receive funds, community programs had to be accessible to community resources. Additionally, the majority of offenders in Minnesota were from this urban area.

Assumptions and Objectives

According to a state evaluation team, all the centers were designed with therapeutic or rehabilitative intent. They were seen as aids in the transition process. It was assumed that something in addition to parole was essential to aid the transition of some offenders. All the programs shared four major goals:

(1) reduction in recidivism,
(2) increase in employment, educational level, and vocational skill level,
(3) rehabilitation, and
(4) using ex-offenders as staff members.

In order to meet these goals, specific objectives common to most, if not all, the programs were:

(1) to provide economic support in the form of room and board (there were no user fees as in Michigan and Pennsylvania),
(2) to provide counseling to prospective residents prior to their admission to the program,
(3) to provide employment, educational, and vocational counseling,
(4) to provide family counseling,
(5) to deal with chemical dependencies,
(6) to provide referrals,
(7) to involve the community in the activities of the programs,
(8) to hire ex-offenders,

(9) to provide follow-up after residence, and

(10) to utilize group counseling.

The heavy emphasis on group counseling, and the emphasis on the use of ex-offenders, made the orientation of the programs in Minnesota similar to the PRCs in the New York prisons. The Minnesota programs appeared designed with the belief that persons who have shared the same problems may be more effective in helping each other than are professionals in helping clients. The sharpest contrast would be with the Pennsylvania program which had invested heavily in professional staff.

Staffing

One of the more striking features of the Minnesota programs in the 1970s was the extremely high staff-to-resident ratios, ranging from 1:0.9 to 1:2.9. Staffing patterns varied considerably from program to program. Tables of organization tended to be complex, ranging from four to seventeen staff positions. Sixteen different staff positions were visible in just six halfway houses. The programs relied primarily on full-time staff, generally using one or two part-timers for nighttime coverage.

Minnesota evaluators argued that the administrative cadres were unusually large for such small programs. Administrative positions comprised as much as 50 percent and no less that 21 percent of all staff positions in these transition programs. It is ironic that these programs, the only ones of the four states that were not part of a state bureaucracy, and which were generally smaller in size than the houses in Pennsylvania and Michigan, also seemed the most overstaffed and most task-specialized.

One factor possibly influencing the large and differentiated staffs was the large investment in the hiring of paraprofessionals. In Minnesota, 87.5 percent of the staff in counseling positions were not college trained. Most of these were ex-offenders. In addition, three of the houses had directors who were ex-offenders. Could it be that a largely inexperienced staff mimicked what they thought would be good organizational practice by establishing many specialized positions?

A particular staffing problem noted in the Minnesota programs was high staff turnover. Three of the six centers experienced complete staff turnovers in their first three years of operation. In contrast, most of the initially hired staff in Pennsylvania are still in the program. Turnover did not necessarily mean that the para-professional staff were ill-equipped for their jobs, but it appeared to mean that the programs were ill-equipped to handle the desire for career mobility. Many of the paraprofessional staff left for better paying jobs that offered chances of advancement. Since the halfway houses were small, independent organizations, they offered little chance for career development.

In addition to the staff in the houses, many of the Minnesota programs paid other persons to provide pre-release counseling to inmates who were prospective residents and to make referrals of inmates to the programs. The programs continued the paraprofessional orientation in staffing these positions by employing inmates as pre-release counseling and referral staff.

Resident Selection and Characteristics

The target population for these houses was relatively restricted. All the houses sought residents who were 18 or older and who had two or more adult commitments. The majority of the parolees came directly from prison, although some were placed on regular parole first and then placed in the center as an alternative to recommitment. The centers placed priority on accepting residents for whom there were no other community alternatives. A number of these residents presumably would not have been paroled except for acceptance into the program.

The admissions process usually began with a referral or application directly by an offender. This contact would be followed by an initial screening for eligibility criteria, and pre-release counseling sessions, which often included a prison furlough for a visit to the program. Following this orientation, the staff would review the application and, if satisfied, they would proceed to the contract stage. The contract detailed responsibilities of the program and the resident and was signed by both parties. Where the residency was required as part of a parole plan, the parole agent would also be involved in the contract.

Thirty-six percent of the program referrals came from program staff (including the pre-release counselors). Twenty-three percent came directly from inmates, 11 percent from prison staff, and the remainder from courts, community agencies, or parole. This referral pattern would appear to indicate poor linkages and/or lack of legitimacy for these private programs with both the prison staff and the parole officials.

Characteristics of residents indicated a relatively high risk group. Eighty-five percent were male. The houses served a greater percentage of ethnic minorities than was proportionate to the general prison population. Forty-seven percent were white, 32 percent were black, and 19 percent were Native American. The residents were relatively old; the median age was 26.5 years. Eighty-seven percent had never had any vocational training and most had severe financial problems. The most frequent conviction offense (22.6 percent) was robbery. Equal numbers of residents had been convicted of personal and property crimes. Half the residents had served at least a full year in prison prior to their halfway house admission.

Programming

According to the state evaluation staff, the programs shared eight program elements:

(1) The programs were group-living experiences in which the group served special program functions. The programs tended to stress mutual responsibility and to foster commitment and cohesion of the residential group.

(2) All the houses employed house meetings for the discussion of house governance, grievances, and problem-solving.

(3) All the programs relied, to some degree, on surrounding social service agencies. Most referral resources concerned employment, education, vocational training, financial management, and substance abuse.

(4) All the programs used pre-release counseling as a selection device and as a preparation for the transfer to the house. Pre-release counselors assisted prospective parolees to develop parole plans and to prepare for living in the program.

(5) Most of the houses utilized program contracts with the residents as a means of formalizing the responsibilities of staff and residents.

(6) All programs emphasized counseling, both individual and group. Individual counseling stressed the implementation of the parole plan and addressed specific needs and adjustment problems. Group counseling varied in its orientation, from positive peer culture to reality therapy. Frequency of group sessions varied from several times a week to once a month.

(7) The programs shared a structured phase progression, moving most of the residents through five program phases: (a) pre-release, (b) an in-house orientation period, (c) parole plan implementation, (d) a residential plan completion and transition period, and (e) post-program follow-up.

(8) All programs used the post-program follow-up, with former residents returning to the house for continued counseling on a regular basis. There was also provision for short-term readmission for former residents having problems with regular parole supervision.

The emphasis on group commitment, and the emphasis on continued reliance on the program after release, stand in sharp contrast to Michigan and to most of the Pennsylvania centers, in which residents were encouraged to become independent of center associations and services before release from the center.

Community Linkages

The Minnesota evaluation staff was critical of the programs for not building the kinds of linkages deemed appropriate for supplementing and expanding in-house services and for establishing a network of support services which the residents would use when they left the programs. Some of the reasons for relatively weak linkages appeared to be structural. High staff turnover inhibits the kind of interagency continuity in communication required for strong interagency cooperation. Another part of the problem seemed related to the basic goals and assumptions for the programs. The emphasis on individual and group counseling appeared to turn residents toward staff and other residents for support, rather than toward other elements in the community.

Three types of linkages existed, representing the three kinds of agencies with which all the halfway house programs needed to deal on a routine basis. There were exchanges with the Minnesota prison system for pre-release counseling and for referrals. According to the evaluators, this link was always weak, partially by fault of program design. Since the programs employed their own pre-release staff, prison counselors never saw it as their responsibilty to make referrals. That the Minnesota prison system would permit the programs to hire inmates as pre-release counselors suggests that the prison system was liberal and not uncooperative on political or ideological grounds.

The second type of linkage was with parole. Since most of the residents were on parole, linkages with parole staff were somewhat better than with prison staff. The residents received parole supervision in addition to program services.

Thirdly, the programs had to establish access to services for residents. A variety of private and public agencies were used. The state evaluators recognized that, in some service types, community services did not exist and that, in others, community and in-program services were both necessary. Nevertheless, the evaluators criticized the programs for being haphazard in their development of community referral sources. The programs often referred to services to back up direct program services while simultaneously ignoring other offender needs altogether. The evaluators criticized an overreliance on direct and referred counseling services to the detriment of more practical economic assistance.

Variation in Transition Programming

In this chapter, we have reviewed four transition programs. Three of these were pre-release programs, and three of them were halfway house programs. They were selected partly on the basis of the differences they presented. If we enlarged our comparative base, most of the additional programs would probably fall within the extremes presented by the programs in New York and Minnesota. This is more likely true on some dimensions than others, however. One variable that did not vary greatly in this small sample was unit size. Detroit and Philadelphia centers, with capacities of just over 40 men, and the Sharon, Pa., center, with a capacity of 11, represented our size extremes. According to the Abt survey of prisons and jails (Mullen, 1980:70), in some states there are pre-release programs which house over 100 residents. Such units must be examined when considering the range of transition program options. Centers of the size reviewed here are more common, though, as many such centers are purposively kept small so that they remain residential in character, do not threaten neighbors, and allow for intensive services or monitoring.

The differences we have highlighted should caution students of community programming against many generalizations across programs. There are commonalities, to be sure; but we suspect that the differences may be equally significant to understanding operations and results. The programs in all four states claimed to facilitate, to some degree, the transition from prison to community living. But they attempted to do so in remarkably different ways. Even the transitional aid objective varied in priority when arrayed against other operational objectives. Some of these operational objectives were implicit and some were contrary to initial project proposals that were instrumental to center establishment in three states. For example, relative to its other objectives, it would appear that the New York PRCs functioned in the 1970s more to help an inmate obtain parole approval than to succeed once released. In Michigan, the centers operated more as a means to select inmates for parole than as an aid in the transition of specific clients.

The time allotted to aiding transition was remarkably brief in three of the states. Except in Pennsylvania, services were extended to clients for about 90 days. In Pennsylvania, the practice was to retain residents for six months to one year, although the initial plan had also been for a 90-day residency. The 90-day service regimen seems to be another of those magic correctional numbers, widely accepted without justification.

In addition to making generalizations about transition programming hazardous, the differences observed would tend to make very difficult any across-program comparisons of effectiveness. Programs varied in selection process and criteria, client characteristics, staffing patterns, locations, program assumptions and objectives, and the emphasis placed on in-the-house rather than in-the-community activity. It may be sensible to ask whether, in a particular state, a given program is advantageous compared to its alternatives. However, even within one state there appear to have been significant variations from center to center, even when the centers were administered by one central office.

Of particular note in the comparison of programs is the orientation toward service to residents and the level of resources devoted to service. Among these four programs, it would appear that only Pennsylvania had mounted a strong operational commitment to the facilitation of behavioral change. There are several reasons for this assertion. First, as stated above, the change objectives in New York and Michigan appeared secondary to other concerns (or severely limited by constraints). In Minnesota, the programs did seem intent on seeking residents with potential transition problems and then providing assistance. However, Pennsylvania's pre-parole program probably provided residents a running start at parole while Minnesota's post-parole efforts may have increased resident resentment. In addition, the Pennsylvania program permitted what seems a more reasonable period for transition. If leaving prison and adjusting to the community are difficult tasks (assertions which are not beyond dispute), then expecting residents to make the adjustments in a few weeks would seem overly optimistic. While recidivism comparisons are fraught with difficulties, the majority of Minnesota clients failed within six months of leaving the houses, while in Pennsylvania the vast majority of clients were trouble-free two years later, when compared to similar clients paroled directly from prison.

Compared to the other three programs, the Pennsylvania centers made the most frequent and intensive use of community resources, which would remain available to the residents when they had left the centers. This was definitely not the case in Minnesota, was not seen as very important in Michigan, and was not feasible in New York.

Examining only the issue of individual change potential, then, the Pennsylvania operation may have offered some advantages over the other types of transition programs. On some other dimensions, Pennsylvania fared less favorably. Michigan released by far the largest proportion of inmates to parole through pre-release. While the Michigan model, at least as amended by the emergent incapacitative aims of the mid-1970s, had limited individual change potential, it did appear to have system-change potential, in the sense that a large amount of the organization was affected by the program. The centers in New York and in Minnesota did best involving offenders and ex-offenders as change facilitators in the correctional process. One would suspect that the change wrought on the inmate staff through their participation in helping others may have been greater than that achieved by clients of this staff.

Administratively, the Michigan DOC would appear to have been the most flexible and imaginative of the initiating agencies. Compared to the other three states, including the private programs in Minnesota, Michigan developed the greatest variety of administrative forms and structures by which to advance its pre-release objectives. It is likely that the advantages of a combined prison/parole system are related to that show of administrative flexibility. Only in Michigan was coordination rather than conflict the most remarkable aspect of the relationship between prison and parole.

Finally, the importance of the legislative process to organizational innovation should be highlighted. In Michigan and Pennsylvania, liberal pre-release legislation, written expressly to enable the centers to open, removed from those two states constraints on transition organization that provided formidable obstacles in New York and Minnesota.

Reintegration policy on the justificatory and mobilizing level was important to the development of transition programs. Reintegration in practice would seem contingent on a number of other factors not always stressed in the policies themselves. In these four states, the administrative structure of the system, legal and funding constraints, the service strategy used, the adequacy of linkage between the service units and the intake referral units, and the experience and training of the program staff all had influences on what the programs became, or could not become.

Reference Note

The program descriptions on which this chapter is based are derived primarily from unpublished sources. In the cases of Minnesota, Michigan, and Pennsylvania, the principle documents are the state planning agency evaluations conducted when the programs were funded, in part, with LEAA money. These documents are probably still available from the planning agencies or their successors, and may be on file at the National Technical Information Service. The chief sources for the New York centers are a descriptive account and an evaluation proposal by research staff in the Department of Correctional Services. They are probably still available from that agency.

The references for Minnesota are Minnesota Governor's Commission on Crime Prevention and Control (1975 and 1976), with the 1975 report being the more richly descriptive. While the Minnesota reports were not widely circulated, they were highly regarded in other states by planning agency staff and were influential, as well as controversial, for recommending a moratorium on new transition center development until their apparent problems were addressed.

For the Michigan centers, the reports relied upon are Community Corrections Resource Programs, Inc. (1974), the most detailed account, Michigan Department of Corrections (1977), and Johnson and Kime (1975). In addition, Duffee conducted interviews with state planning agency staff, and DOC training and community center staff in 1977.

The best sources from the Pennsylvania evaluation are probably Duffee, Wright, and Maher (1974), and Duffee, Meyer and Warner (1977). There is an earlier evaluation by Informatics, Inc. (1973). Since then, some of the Pennsylvania research has been published. Relative to the issues covered in this chapter, one might consult Wright (1979); Duffee, Maher, and Lagoy (1977); and Duffee (1985).

The New York information comes directly from the agency operating the program rather than from a third party evaluation source. The reports issued by the Department of Correctional Services were written in preparation for mounting an evaluation, rather than as part of one. The intended evaluation project was not immediately funded. The PRCs are described in Morgenbesser and Pollock (1980a and 1980b). In addition, we have relied upon DOCS annual reports from 1977, 1978, and 1979, a number of PRC newsletters and DOCS news organs, and discussions conducted in 1988 with pre-release center peer-counseling staff at the Green Haven Correctional Facility.

Discussion Questions

1. How do the policy shifts of the 1960s described in Chapter 7 relate to the technologies described by Jester in Chapter 5? Do the probation technologies described by Jester appear to have analogs in the transition programs described in this chapter?

2. Although both Michigan and Pennsylvania centers were state-run or "community-placed," it is clear that these centers actually varied in their community field position. Why did the Pennsylvania centers stress a high degree of involvement on the horizontal dimensions of community while the Michigan centers generally did not do so? The Minnesota centers, in contrast, clearly demonstrate a more mixed resource and policy base than centers in Pennsylvania. However, many Pennsylvania centers, in fact, developed stronger interagency connections and greater use of out-of-center services for residents. Why?

3. What does rehabilitative or therapy orientation appear to do to interagency interaction in transition programs?

PART THREE
COMMUNITY CORRECTIONS IN CHANGE

Although the interaction of community and corrections is not a new phenomenon, there can be little doubt that contemporary community corrections has grown and been influenced by changes in correctional thought during the last two decades. As the U.S. prison population increases well beyond the half million mark, it is almost difficult to fathom that 15 to 20 years ago policy debate included serious discussion of prison abolition and a moratorium on prison construction (Mitford, 1973; Nagel, 1973). The deinstitutionalization, or destructuring (Cohen, 1985), movement provided the impetus for an expansion of community corrections programs. In many circles, these programs were seen as the answer to the prison problem. Small, community-based programs would replace the outdated and discredited prison, reformatory, and training school.

Today, abolitionists or moratorium proponents are likely to be seen as fringe elements and excluded from policy debate. Similarly, community corrections is not likely to be seen as replacing institutions, but rather as an additional component in the state's response to crime. Community corrections is now offered as a means of slowing the growth of prisons and easing the most extreme overcrowding.

This book is not offered as a forum for addressing the fundamental normative issues raised by this transformation of the role of community corrections vis-à-vis institutional corrections. However, any understanding of the structure of contemporary community corrections and the interaction of corrections and community would be incomplete without some attention to the effects of these policy shifts on community corrections. The initial chapter in this section explicitly deals with these policy shifts. The remaining two chapters present data on assessments of community corrections programs in this changing context.

In Chapter 8, Edmund McGarrell analyzes policy change in the New York State Division for Youth. This study demonstrates the necessity of simultaneously studying residential and non-residential corrections. McGarrell employs a snowball interview technique and an interest-group political theory to depict how vertical and horizontal forces inside and outside the Division for Youth combined to shift DFY from an institutional to a non-residential system and back again. The study illustrates the interaction of broad cultural shifts (as reflected in the deinstitutionalization and "get tough" movements) and state-level policymaking, and the resultant impact on a juvenile corrections system.

The next two chapters do not explicitly deal with change in community corrections, but do provide rather unique views of community corrections programs that have developed in recent years. Both present data on the perceptions of key actors within and outside the programs.

In Chapter 9, Michael Musheno, Dennis Palumbo, Steven Maynard-Moody, and James Levine present data from questionnaires administered to community corrections administrators and line-level staff in Colorado, Connecticut, and Oregon. This study clearly demonstrates the need to consider both goals and structure. All three states shared the goal of reducing commitments to the state prison system by developing community corrections. However, the structure of the states' community corrections programs differed along a number of the dimensions discussed throughout earlier chapters (e.g., centralization, judicial vs. executive control, privatization, professionalism, hierarchy). This variation leads to community corrections programs which, according to the model used in this book, differ in terms of their location on the vertical and horizontal dimensions of community structure. This variation, in turn, affects a number of program dimensions such as commitment, involvement, goal consensus, decision-making, coordination, and perceived external support. The authors' comparative analysis enables the reader to isolate several key dimensions of program structure that appear to relate to the ultimate commitment to these programs among the street-level service providers.

Paul Stageberg, in Chapter 10, presents similar data from what has been termed an exemplary program, the Polk County (Iowa)

Department of Correctional Services. Stageberg has the added advantage of being able to contrast data on perceptions with actual case processing data. Two interesting findings emerge. First, Polk County criminal justice officials developed rather inflated images of the positive impact of the program. Second, these perceptions varied from agency to agency and even from unit to unit within the same agency. The variation seemed to be the product of varied relationships with the new Department of Correctional Services.

Read in conjunction with the Musheno, et al. chapter, these studies suggest that the arrangement of sentiments and values, support and opposition, in a given community field, is likely to vary according to the location of the community corrections program on the vertical (see particularly Musheno, et al.) and horizontal (see particularly Stageberg) dimensions. This variation is particularly noteworthy when related to the findings presented in earlier chapters. Those findings consistently indicated that the extent of interaction between community corrections agencies and community organizations was not the product of general goal statements, but rather the product of the political, social, and legal forces shaping the program.

Chapter 8
Changing Characteristics of New York's Juvenile Corrections System: An Analysis of Policy Formation and Change

Edmund F. McGarrell

Some of the earliest writings in the area of crime and justice focus, to a large extent, on the preferred goals of the justice system (Beccaria, 1963; Bentham, 1973). Since the Progressive Movement at the beginning of the 20th century, the goals of rehabilitation and treatment have been dominant, at least at the correctional end of the system (Rothman, 1980). However, with the decline of the rehabilitative ideal, attention has once again focused on the proper goals of the justice system (van den Haag, 1975; von Hirsch, 1976; Cullen and Gilbert, 1982). While the goal-oriented debate has flourished, much less attention has been given to the question of how such goals are actually transformed into policy and the impact of such policy changes on the justice system.

The study of the dynamics of policy formation and change in the criminal and juvenile justice systems is crucial if we are to understand how and why specific policies are developed, and the effects of policy changes on these systems. Further, such understanding is essential for those wishing to influence policy. The analysis of policy formation stands as a bridge between the debates over preferred goals of the justice system and the more traditional emphasis in criminological research on evaluation of outcomes. The purpose of this chapter is to describe the changing characteristics of one state's juvenile corrections system and to analyze the key policy decisions that largely account for these changes.

Previous Literature

In their recent attempt to demonstrate the relationship of political science to the field of criminology, Nagel, Fairchild, and Champagne (1983) make the point that the dynamics of criminal justice policymaking have been relatively ignored in scholarly research. While a number of historical studies exist on the origins of particular criminal laws and on the development of the legal system,[1] the authors point out that our understanding of policy formation remains "spotty and in a formative stage." Despite this general assessment, there exist several studies which provide insight into the dynamics of criminal justice policy formation and change.

One of the most comprehensive studies of the process of change in a juvenile corrections system is provided in Miller, Ohlin, and Coates' (1977) analysis of change in the Massachusetts system. A key element of the study was that it involved analysis of change at both the policy level and the service delivery level. Miller, et al. provide both a theory of large scale change processes and a model for the analysis of such change. They found that the process of reform involved a struggle among interest groups and that change resulted from the impact of this struggle on a change resistant system. Miller, et al. urge that analysts adopt a "system model" which focuses not only on the youth corrections agency but on the political arena in which policy is established (Miller, Coates, and Ohlin, 1980). Having used this system model to structure the arena in which juvenile corrections policy is formulated and changed, Miller, et al. identify a set of empirical principles that seem to have accounted for the process of change in Massachusetts. Three of the key principles, which will be considered in the present analysis, include (Miller and Ohlin, 1985):

1. Sequencing. The process of change involves shifts in both aspired choices (what one wants to do) and available choices (what one can do). Change is most likely to occur when there is congruence between aspired choices and available choices.

2. Inertia and Crisis. A system such as the juvenile corrections system is characterized by bureaucratic iner-

tia. Change is most likely to occur during periods of crisis which open the system to the possibility of change.

3. Key swing groups. In conflicts between liberal and conservative interest groups, there are key swing groups, typically political actors, who are essential allies for either side to win. Shifts in position of these key swing groups can be important factors in change.

Miller, et al.'s theory of change draws support from other studies of criminal justice policy formation and change. The emphasis on the role of competing interest groups draws support from Ohlin's earlier work on corrections policy (1960) as well as from other studies of criminal justice policy formation (Roby 1969; Heinz, Gettleman, and Seeskin, 1969; Berk, Brackman, and Lesser, 1977). While these studies agree on the involvement of external interest groups, the degree of activity, influence, and actual impact remains unclear.

The literature on policy formation also provides some support for the three empirical principles. While more concerned with local level implementation than state-level policy, Handler and Zatz's (1982) study of deinstitutionalization of status offenders seems to illustrate the sequencing principle. They found that federal funds for deinstitutionalization (creating available choices) had the greatest impact where local officials already had favorable attitudes toward deinstitutionalization (aspired choices). The congruence between aspired and available choices led to change.

Lemert's (1970) analysis of the reform of the California juvenile code suggests the importance of crisis periods. Lemert argues that the legal system is characterized by inertia which is only overcome through the accumulation of anomalies. The accumulation of anomalies, defined as "facts left unexplained by extant paradigms (p. 7)," eventually creates sufficient pressure to overcome the system's resistance to change. While the notions of "crisis" and "accumulating anomalies" are loosely defined and difficult to measure, both Miller, et al.'s and Lemert's work suggest the importance of timing and accumulating pressures as necessary conditions for change.

Contradictory findings on the necessity of crisis are presented in Downs' (1976) study of deinstitutionalization of juvenile correctional facilities. Downs found that, while external interest groups played an important role in creating interest in an area such as juvenile justice, media criticism and investigations were unrelated to deinstitutionalization rates.

Finally, the role of political actors as key swing groups in the process of change and reform is suggested in Berk and Rossi's (1977) survey of correctional policymakers and interest groups in three states. Berk and Rossi found that the support of politicians and administrators was perceived to be essential for correctional reform and to be more influential than the support of interest groups. While these findings are based on ratings of influence, they seem to be at least suggestive of the role of politicians as key swing groups.

The following analysis of change in New York's juvenile corrections system will follow the general approach of the Miller, et al. model and will examine the applicability of the empirical principles in the New York case.

Profile of a Changing Juvenile Corrections System[2]

In 1970, the New York state juvenile corrections system consisted of 14 training schools and centers housing approximately 2,000 youths. These 14 training schools ranged from small 17 and 18 bed facilities to large congregate institutions housing over 300 youths. Two of the training schools, one housing approximately 90 boys and a smaller facility for girls, were considered secure facilities. In addition, approximately 600 juveniles were held in rural camps, urban homes, and small treatment centers. Although many of the training schools and rural camps engaged youths in the local community, only the urban homes and newly created Youth Development Centers could be considered community-based. In these latter programs, youths remained in their home communities and participated daily in community activities such as school and work. Youths confined in the training schools, camps, treatment centers, and community-based facilities included both adjudicated juvenile delinquents and persons found to be in need of supervision (PINS). Juveniles were committed to these facilities for an initial period of 18 months, though placement could be extended on a year-to-year basis until age 18.[3] The state agency responsible for the facilities had absolute discretion on when to release. Available data indicate youths typically were released after nine months of confinement.

By early 1978, a number of training schools and centers had been closed and the population of the training schools had been drastically reduced to less than 500 youths. In addition, the size of the remaining training schools had been reduced so that none of the facilities held more than 120 youths. The number of juveniles placed in secure settings rose to around 140 with the addition of two small secure centers. The population within the secure centers and training schools also changed as PINS youths were no longer placed in these facilities. In conjunction with the decline in the training school population, there was an increase in community-based placements from approximately 200 in 1970 to over 900 in 1978. One further change that had developed by 1978 had to do with length of placements. Youths found to have committed one of a select number of serious offenses, could be given a restrictive placement of 3 or 5 years with limits placed on the Division for Youth's discretion to release.

By 1983 the juvenile corrections system had undergone more change. The number of youths in non-community-based programs, (training schools, camps and other residential programs) excluding the secure facilities, had increased from slightly over 700 in 1978 to approximately 850. The number in community-based programs declined from over 900 in early 1978 to approximately 650 in 1983. Perhaps the most dramatic change was in the rise in the number of youths in secure facilities. In 1983, over 500 youths were confined in secure facilities compared to 140 in 1978. Related to the increase in secure placements were changes in sentencing practices. Youths committing serious offenses now faced possible sentences of 7, 10, 15 years and even life. Facility size remained fairly stable, with the largest facility housing 160 youths, two facilities with just over 100 youths, and the rest with less than 100 youths.

Thus, over the course of the last 13 or 14 years, New York's juvenile corrections system has undergone significant change. The number of youths removed from their communities and placed in public residential facilities has significantly decreased. Additionally, the size of facilities has been reduced. Juveniles adjudicated as persons in need of supervision have been removed from the training schools. The number of youths placed in community-based settings has also increased since 1970. On the other hand, there has been a significant increase in the number of secure facilities and the number of youths confined in secure facilities since 1978. At the same time there has been a decrease in the number of youths placed in community-based settings from the levels of the mid-1970s. Finally, a number of youths find themselves serving longer periods of confinement than would have been possible in the early 1970s.

The purpose of this chapter is to further examine this process of change. Of particular interest, are those key policy decisions that, to a large extent, account for this changing profile of New York's juvenile corrections system.

Methodology and Data

The data for this chapter come primarily from interviews with key actors involved in influencing or formulating juvenile corrections policy in New York state during the period from the late 1960s to 1984. Initial respondents were identified by having been in obvious policymaking positions during various periods of the overall time frame. The interviewing then progressed through a snowball procedure in which each respondent was asked to identify key individuals and groups active in various policy issues. This chapter is based on interviews with 49 respondents. While this sample does not represent all individuals who have been named in the snowball procedure, it does include at least one key actor from each of the groups identified as active in the policymaking process. Respondents include key actors from the Governor's office, legislators and their staff, administrators of relevant state agencies, practitioners from the juvenile justice system and representatives of citizen advocacy groups.

Interviews were semi-structured around four basic questions:

1. *Who* was actively concerned about these issues?

2. *Whom* were they trying to influence?

3. *What* were their goals?

4. *How* did they try to achieve these goals, and with what success?

Additional questions asked respondents to identify other factors influencing policy and their assessment of the impact of policy changes on the juvenile corrections system.

A key threat to the validity of the findings is the retrospective nature of the interviews. As a way of addressing this threat, findings are only presented that have been corroborated by two or more respondents. Where discrepancies arose, follow-up phone calls were used for clarification. Additionally, the study involved an extensive review of archival materials. Wherever possible, archival materials were checked for consistency with respondent's reports.

Change in New York's Juvenile Corrections System

The following analysis attempts to examine the key policy decisions that have accounted for the previously described changes in New York's juvenile corrections system. The term *key policy decision* is used to refer to those "critical decisions" (Selznick, 1957) that have shaped the institutional development and overall mission of the New York system. The term is used to include both discrete decisions, such as a legislative act, and more general policy decisions, such as the goal of deinstitutionalization.

In looking at the New York system, it appears that the key policy decisions that have affected the shape of the system fall into three basic areas: deinstitutionalization generally, removal of status offenders from the training schools, and responses to the serious juvenile offender.

Background

In 1970, New York found itself with two separate public agencies responsible for running facilities for court-related youth. The larger and older of these was the Department of Social Services which was responsible for administration of the state's 14 training schools and centers. Along with the training school system, delinquents and status offenders could be placed with the New York State Division for Youth (DFY). The origins of the DFY developed with the creation of the Temporary State Youth Commission in 1945 that was to provide technical and financial support for youth programs in communities. In 1960, the Commission became the Division for Youth and was given the added responsibility of creating alternative, experimental residential programs. From 1960 to 1971 the Division created a number of programs for court-related youth aged 15 to 17 who entered at the discretion of the DFY. These programs provided less secure settings than the traditional training schools and included rural camps, residential centers, group homes and day services programs.

Mandate for Change

Throughout the latter 1960s and early 1970s a number of factors seemed to coalesce and lead to change in New York's juvenile justice system. These factors included developments at the national, state, and local levels.

At the national level, the series of Supreme Court cases (Kent, Gault, Winship[4]) dealing with the juvenile justice system called into question the lack of procedural safeguards for juveniles and signaled the need to critically examine the juvenile justice system. The President's Commission on Law Enforcement and Administration of Justice (1967) further chronicled the failings of the traditional juvenile justice system and called for a number of reforms of the system.

At the state level, several citizen's advocacy groups studied the state's training school system and issued critical reports of the training schools and the Department of Social Service's administration of the schools. The reports cited instances of brutality and abuse and concluded that the training schools were excessively costly and failing to rehabilitate. Additionally, the Department of Social Services found itself the subject of several lawsuits brought by the New York City Legal Aid Society alleging excessive use of solitary room confinement in the training schools.

At the local level, these criticisms of institutionalization in general, and New York's training schools in particular, seemed to have an effect on placement practices within Family Court. While no systematic data on judicial attitudes exist, both legislative studies and respondents reported that Family Court judges began to view the training schools as a place of last resort. At the same time, the growth of the Division for Youth from a capacity of 40 beds in 1960 to over 600 in 1971, and the development of locally run community-based programs, led to a number of alternative placement options for Family Court judges. Admissions to the training schools declined from over 2,200 in 1966 to just over 1,300 in 1971. To the extent that respondents have correctly identified judicial changes in placement preferences, the decrease in placements seems to be an instance of what Miller and Ohlin (1985) term "sequencing." Change in aspired choices, i.e., judges' preferences to place in alternatives to the training schools, coupled with changes in available choices, the increase in alternative placement options, led to change in actual placement practices.

The initial drop in training school placements set up a circular process which became a significant policy input in the early 1970s. Because the training schools had large physical plants, there were significant fixed costs involved in keeping the facilities open despite the reduced number of youths. With reduced populations but constant costs, the rate for maintaining an individual youth in a training school drastically increased. Since the state and localities split costs for maintaining a youth in a training school on a 50/50 basis, the per diem rate charged back to the localities increased from $21 in 1966 to over $52 in 1971. The increasing per diem rate created a further disincentive for localities to place youths in the training schools. This, in turn, further reduced placements and further increased the per diem rate. The training schools became seen as an excessively expensive placement option.

The decreasing populations and increasing costs of the training schools became particularly important in 1971 as the state experienced the first major fiscal crisis in modern times. At a time when all state agencies were asked to take cuts, the training schools became a logical place to look for budget reductions. As a result, the Governor's office ordered the Department of Social Services to close two training schools. The closing of the 330-bed New Hampton school for boys, and the 80-bed Wynantskill school for girls became the first in what was to be a series of reductions in the state's training school capacity over the next several years.

Transfer and Reductions in the
Training School Population

The closing of these two training schools was not to be the only significant event in the juvenile corrections system during 1971. The criticism of the training schools proved to be only one of a larger number of criticisms of the Department of Social Services (DSS) and the social welfare system in general. The result of this crisis in the social welfare system led Governor Rockefeller to propose a complete reorganization of the state's social welfare system. One part of this reorganization involved the transfer of the training schools from DSS to DFY.[5]

A number of factors influenced the decision to transfer the training schools. First, the training schools were always considered an appendage of DSS, in no way central to the core mission of the Department. As one DSS administrator stated, the training schools were "like the tail on the dog." Second, the criticisms of the training schools by the advocacy groups, and the lawsuits brought by the Legal Aid Society, created a desire within the Governor's office to "do something" with the training schools. This feeling was exacerbated by the crisis in the overall social welfare system. One official put it, "DSS had headaches on headaches, removing the training schools was a way of removing one of the headaches." The decision was made more attractive by the availability of DFY. The Division, because of its emphasis on prevention programs, small open facilities, and community-based programs, enjoyed a much more favorable reputation among the advocacy groups and juvenile justice professionals than did the training schools. By placing the training schools in DFY, the Governor was not only relieving DSS of its unwanted burden, but gaining political credit for placing the training schools within this "enlightened" administration. Respondents were in virtual agreement that the transfer decision was not so much based on substance as it was on the desire to remove a liability from DSS and gain some credit by putting the schools in DFY. As one official noted, "the transfer did not have anything to do with what's best for kids." The transfer decision appears to again demonstrate the sequencing principle. Investigations and criticism of the training schools led to the aspired choice of doing something with the training schools. The presence of DFY created the available choice of what to do.

The transfer of 12 training schools housing 1,900 youths from a large state agency to a small experimental agency was an important change in and of itself, but what was most important was that this structural change opened the way for subsequent reform.

The training schools under DSS had developed as essentially independent facilities which looked to the Department's administrators within the Bureau of Children's Institutional Services primarily to provide support services. The independence of the training schools was sustained by the fact that each was formally supervised by a governing board of visitors who reported directly to the Governor (bypassing DSS). The superintendent of each facility in turn controlled the Board of Visitors. DSS Central Office administrators reported that they were never clear what, if any, legal power they had over training school superintendents. In practice, DSS Central Office adopted a stance whereby they could "advise," but never tell, the superintendents what to do.

The Governor's office, which had decided to transfer the training schools without consultation of DFY or the DSS Bureau of Children's Institutions Services, approached DFY and told Division administrators that they were to assume responsibility for the training schools and that the Division had five days to draft enabling legislation. The Division's response was to attempt to draft legislation that would give DFY some control over the training schools. The Division did this by including two key provisions in the legislation. The first gave the Director of DFY control over the appointment and removal of training school superintendents. The second gave DFY control over intake of youths. Previously, Family Court judges would place juveniles in a particular training school. Now placement would be to DFY, with Central Office actually making the specific placement decision. These provisions were essential to providing the administrative structure necessary to gain any type of Central Office control over system-wide policy.

The Director of DFY, Milton Luger, was openly committed to smaller facilities and opposed to the large, congregate training school model. This administrative commitment was coupled with the continued fiscal directive of the legislature to "close and consolidate" the large expensive training schools. In 1972, this legislative pressure was clearly articulated as the Joint Legislative Fiscal

Committee decreased appropriations to the training schools by $1.9 million while increasing appropriations to DFY community-based settings by $1 million. In its press release, the Joint Fiscal Committee stated:

> This reorganization of the training schools represents a positive step toward the elimination of large congregate institutions in the treatment of youth delinquency and will permit DFY to decentralize the cottage components at the training schools and gain the advantages inherent in small institutional rehabilitative environments. ("Costs of Institutional Care," 1973, p. 9.)

The combination of Luger's commitment to small facilities and community-based settings, and the fiscally driven support of the Governor's office and the legislature led to the closings of several more training schools, reduced populations in the remaining schools, and increased community-based settings during the years 1971-1975. Training school populations were reduced somewhere in the vicinity of 1,000 during these years, while community-based programs increased from approximately 240 to 390. The transfer of the training schools placed the schools under the administration of a director who aspired to reduce the level of the training school population and the size of individual facilities. Further, the transfer included provisions which gave Luger some control over the training schools, thus providing Luger with available choices. The support of the legislature for training school reductions reinforced this aspired policy choice and created available choices by providing appropriations for community-based alternative settings.

PINS Removal and Increased Community-Based Settings

With the change from a Republican to Democratic governor in 1974, Peter Edelman was brought in to replace Luger as Director of DFY in 1975. This change did not signal the end of the move away from large institutions; rather, Edelman continued and even accelerated the move from institutions to community-based settings. Edelman, who came from the University of Massachusetts and was familiar with Jerome Miller's efforts to close the training schools in

Massachusetts, entered with the "fundamental premise that young people are overinstitutionalized." While the Edelman administration believed that, for both substantive (larger population and more serious juvenile offending) and political (stronger conservative element in the legislature) reasons, New York would not be able to go as far in closing facilities as was the case in Massachusetts, reductions in the number of youths in training schools was a clear priority. Indeed, before Edelman officially arrived in New York, he ratified a prior decision to close the Hudson training school for girls. Edelman's effort to reduce the number of non-community-based institutionalized juveniles involved two basic steps. The first was the total removal of PINS youths from the training schools. The second involved the development of additional community-based programs for both PINS and juvenile delinquents traditionally held in the training schools.

The issue of PINS placement in the training schools arose in a 1973 court case, in which the New York Court of Appeals prohibited the placement of PINS in training schools that also housed juvenile delinquents.[6] The Division's response to this ruling was to prohibit the commingling of PINS and juvenile delinquents by dividing the training schools into facilities housing PINS and facilities housing juvenile delinquents. While the Luger administration was committed to reductions in the training school populations, they still maintained that such placements were necessary in certain cases. Further, the question of whether to place a youngster in the training schools was to be based on the youths needs, not on what was seen to be an artificial legal distinction between PINS and juvenile delinquents.

With the arrival of Edelman in 1975, the Division's policy on placement of PINS changed. One of Edelman's first administrative efforts was the removal of PINS youths from the training schools. This administrative effort was codified by the legislature in 1976 which passed a law prohibiting the placement of PINS in training schools.[7] The bill was part of the Division's legislative agenda and was supported by the Governor's office, the Child Care Committee of the Assembly, and the Senate Controlled Temporary Commission on Child Welfare. The legislation was sold on the basis that it merely codified existing DFY practice and that it was necessary to secure federal funds under the Juvenile Justice and Delinquency

Prevention Act of 1974. The bill was passed with very little opposition. The results of Edelman's administrative policy and the subsequent legislation were dramatic. In 1973, at the time of the court decision on PINS placement, approximately 400 PINS youths were held in the training schools. By 1978 there were no PINS in the training schools and only 57 in DFY non-community-based facilities.

In addition to the PINS efforts, Edelman sought to further the goal of reduced institutionalization by closing several of the old training schools and increasing community-based placements. The early years of the Edelman administration were also the years of the New York City fiscal crisis which, in turn, created fiscal pressures on the state. Because of these fiscal pressures, DFY was asked to take budget cuts. Edelman responded by cutting appropriations for the training schools. In addition to his ratification of the closing of Hudson, the Overbrook, Highland, and Warwick facilities were closed. At the same time, the Division was able to secure federal funds through the state's Division of Criminal Justice Services (LEAA funds) and the State Division of Budget (federal countercyclical funds). These federal dollars were used to fund a variety of alternative programs, the majority of which were community-based. Among these efforts were the expansion of group homes, youth development centers, and foster care, and the development of new programs including day services and independent living programs. In addition to these federal funds, the move to increase community-based programs was enhanced by legislation passed in conjunction with the bill prohibiting PINS placement in training schools. These additional provisions gave the Division statutory authority to increase community-based programs, authority to contract with private non-profit agencies for services to DFY youth, and provisions to make DFY youth placed in foster care eligible for federal reimbursement under the Aid to Dependent Children program. The result of these policy choices was that, by 1978, training school populations were further reduced to under 500 youths while the number in community-based settings rose to over 900. Further, no PINS youths were in training schools and no institution housed over 120 youths.

The factors involved in Edelman's efforts to remove PINS from training schools, and the general effort to move from an institutionally oriented system to a community-based system, lend support to several of Miller and Ohlin's empirical principles. In the PINS effort, the importance of what Miller and Ohlin call the key swing group, in this case the key swing actor, is illustrated. During the Luger years, pressure by the Legal Aid Society and federal initiatives under the Juvenile Justice Delinquency Prevention Act to remove PINS from training schools were met by resistance from the Luger administration. With the arrival of Edelman, the Division's posture changed from resistance to immediate efforts to remove PINS from the training schools. Edelman's emphasis was enhanced by the support of the Governor's office and the key interest groups within the legislature. The assertion that Edelman played the key swing role is supported by Downs' (1976) finding that executive director ideology was an important predictor of deinstitutionalization in juvenile corrections. Whether Luger would have been able or would have desired to continue to resist pressure to remove PINS in light of the national movement to do so (Handler and Zatz, 1982) cannot be answered. What is clear is that, with the change in philosophy that resulted from change in leadership, PINS were quickly removed from training schools.

The PINS removal and the general reduction in training school populations and increases in community-based programs also reflect the sequencing principle. Edelman clearly aspired to decrease institutionalization and increase community-based programs. Fiscal pressures and federal initiatives tended to make this policy direction an aspired choice among key decisionmakers within the legislature and the Governor's office. The work of DFY under Edelman to develop alternative community-based programs and the availability of federal funds to pay for such programs, made this an available policy option. Hence, again we see the combination of aspired and available choices leading to significant change.

Dealing with the Serious Juvenile Offender[8]

Sometime around 1974, interest in the issue of how to handle the serious juvenile offender arose. Over the course of the next four years, this question became a pre-eminent political issue in the state.

Initial interest in the serious juvenile offender was stimulated by the investigations and findings of two legislative committees in 1974. The first of these was conducted by an Assembly Subcommittee on the Family Court and examined the perceived rise of gang delinquency and violence in New York City. The theme of the Committee's reports, as suggested by the title of one of the reports *(Armies of the Streets)*, was that New York City had witnessed a resurgence of gang activity, that gang members were frequently armed and were engaging in more violence, and that the Family Court was failing to adequately respond to the problem.

The second Committee, the New York State Select Committee on Crime, chaired by a conservative Senator who also chaired the Senate Committee on Crime and Correction, focused on many of the same themes. After looking at robbery arrest statistics for New York City juveniles, the Committee noted a tremendous increase in juvenile robbery since 1960 and criticized the Family Court for failing to adequately respond.

Legislative attention to juvenile crime continued in 1975. In addition to the continuing work of the Select Committee on Crime, the Senate-controlled Temporary State Commission on Child Welfare's Subcommittee on Juvenile Justice issued its first report, and the newly created Assembly Child Care Committee embarked on what was to be a 16-month investigation of juvenile crime and the juvenile justice system. The findings of both of these Committees echoed many of those just described—an increase in juvenile crime and a Family Court system that fails to adequately respond to these juvenile lawbreakers. Additional criticism focused on the unfettered discretion of the Division for Youth. DFY was said to employ a "rapid release policy" and the Division was criticized for having a large number of runaways. Consistent in the reports of these Committees was the theme that the juvenile justice system in New York was neither helping the youths nor protecting the community.

In addition to the legislative committee activity, and perhaps in response to such activity, the media apparently began to focus on the topic of juvenile crime, and juvenile violence in particular. Whether respondents are noting a real increase in media attention or a perceived increase due to their own heightened sensitivity to the issue remains an empirical question awaiting systematic investigation.[9] However, whether real or perceived, the importance of the press ran through all of the interviews. Respondents unanimously spoke of the importance of this heightened media attention in the subsequent legislative changes enacted from 1976 to 1978. The media attention, particularly among prominent New York City newspapers, was seen as key to keeping the juvenile violence issue alive and in expressing public pressure for a "toughened" system.

In response to the criticisms of the juvenile justice system, a number of bills were introduced during the 1975 legislative session, including several that provided for major reform of the traditional juvenile justice system. Among these reform bills, there arose two distinct approaches that became the focus of a political battle that was to be waged over the next three years. The first approach was embodied in a bill sponsored by the Senate Chair of the Select Committee on Crime (and Senate Committee on Crime and Correction) and provided for waiver of juveniles accused of serious offenses into the adult criminal court. The Senate sponsor was joined in support of this bill by the Assembly Chair of the Ways and Means Committee, one of the most powerful committees in the Assembly. The second approach, incorporated in a bill introduced by the Chair of the Assembly Child Care Committee, rejected waiver but provided measures to strengthen the Family Court. This second approach, supported by both the Assembly and Senate leadership, was passed. The bill was vetoed, however, by Governor Carey. The Governor argued that he had just hired Peter Edelman as Director of the Division for Youth and, as such, Edelman should have a voice in such a significant policy change. Additionally, the Governor announced that he was appointing a blue-ribbon panel to study the problem of juvenile violence and to recommend policy changes for the state's juvenile justice system.

Juvenile Justice Reform Act of 1976

The stage was thus set for policy debate in 1976. Conservative forces were advocating a waiver-up position. Many traditional liberals agreed that reform of the juvenile justice system was needed, but did not want to go as far as a waiver-up system. The Governor, on record as opposing waiver, awaited the findings of his blue-ribbon panel.

The Governor's panel, known as the Cahill Commission, was comprised of a number of prominent citizens from across the State. Within the panel, Peter Edelman took a key leadership role. Like the Governor, Edelman opposed the waiver-up approach. He took the position that there were problems in the juvenile justice system and advocated an approach similar to that of the Assembly Child Care Committee. Edelman urged to retain Family Court jurisdiction but to provide for procedures which would allow differential treatment of juveniles committing serious offenses. In taking this position, Edelman found himself between the traditional child advocacy groups who opposed any increase in sanctions for juveniles, and the supporters of waiver to criminal court. This mid-road approach was sold to liberals as less punitive than a waiver-up approach (for which there was considerable legislative support), and to conservatives as a way of dealing with serious offenders that would also be politically feasible (in light of the Governor's threatened veto of waiver bills). Eventually, this approach prevailed and the Panel issued its report with the recommendation that Family Court retain exclusive jurisdiction over all juveniles but be provided with placement options to increase sanctions for the serious juvenile offender.

Following release of the panel's recommendations, Gubernatorial and DFY staff began drafting a Governor's bill that incorporated the panel's key themes. At the same time, supporters of the waiver-up approach had introduced bills providing for waiver. Once the Governor's package was developed, the key parties entered negotiations. This involved the Senate and Assembly leadership, the Senate Crime and Correction Chair, the Assembly Child Care Chair, as well as the Governor's staff and DFY staff. Among these key actors only the Chair of the Senate Crime and Correction Committee was opposed to the premise of retaining Family Court jurisdiction. The support of the Assembly and Senate leadership was key, particularly in light of expressions that the rank-and-file legislature preferred the "tougher" waiver-up proposals. While disagreements existed over specific provisions, these were resolved through negotiation, and an "agreed upon" bill was presented to and passed overwhelmingly by the legislature.

The law, known as the Juvenile Justice Reform Act of 1976, retained Family Court jurisdiction over all juveniles but provided for differential procedures for dealing with juveniles accused of serious offenses.[10] For juveniles given a restrictive placement, the Act provided a three- or five-year sentence depending on the class felony (as opposed to the traditional 18-month placement) and mandated that DFY keep the youth in secure confinement for a minimum of 6 or 12 months.

The Juvenile Justice Reform Act of 1976 represented a historic change in the New York juvenile justice system. For the first time the law made offense-based distinctions in procedure and sentencing. Judges were told to consider community protection in addition to the traditional focus on the children's needs. Finally, the law placed limits on DFY's release discretion and mandated that a portion of the placement be in a secure facility.

Juvenile Offender Law of 1978

The apparent consensus on the approach embodied in the Juvenile Justice Reform Act lasted only 18 months and, indeed, signs of discontent with retaining Family Court jurisdiction were immediately apparent. At the press conference announcing passage of the bill, the Republican Chair of the Senate Crime and Correction Committee, formally a co-sponsor of the Act, announced that the Act did not go far enough to address the problem of serious juvenile crime and would not defuse the public clamor for tougher measures.

During 1977, several additional reports were issued critical of the juvenile justice system. The Senate Research Service issued a report that once again emphasized the theme that the juvenile justice system neither deterred nor rehabilitated. The Senate Crime and Correction Committee and the Select Committee on Crime issued joint findings from public hearings that portrayed the juvenile justice system as overburdened by the large number of cases and unwilling to impose sufficiently harsh sentences. Although some amendments were passed to the 1976 Act, and despite the fact that the Senate Crime and Correction Chair continued to introduce waiver-up bills, the 1977 and the 1978 legislative sessions ended without significant changes in the juvenile justice system. However, the issue of juvenile crime proved resilient and emerged once again as a key issue during the summer of 1978.

Crucial to keeping juvenile crime a "hot" topic were the actions of the Senate Committee on Crime and Correction (and corresponding Select Committee on Crime), which continued to hold hearings and issue reports and press releases critical of the Family Court and DFY. The Committee also began to explore the idea of placing original jurisdiction of targeted offenses in adult criminal court and allowing for a reverse, or waiver-down procedure. Additionally, the media continued to focus on the topic of juvenile crime, particularly on several sensational cases involving youths under DFY care. Respondents reported "unrelenting media coverage of juvenile crime" and that the media continued its "virulent campaign on juvenile violence" during 1978. Together, the action of the Senate Committee on Crime and Correction and the media attention ensured that the juvenile violence issue would not easily or quietly disappear.

Of particular importance in subsequent policy development was the fact that 1978 was an election year. As one respondent put it, "everyone saw themselves as vulnerable on the juvenile crime issue." This was particularly so for the Democrats who were accused of blocking the tough waiver proposals of the Senate Crime and Correction Committee. Further, the topic of crime became a key issue in the gubernatorial race. Perry Duryea, the Republican candidate for Governor, portrayed Governor Carey as being soft on crime, and made the Governor's opposition to the death penalty a key campaign issue. Respondents associated with the Democratic Assembly indicated that the crime issue was seen as not only making Carey vulnerable, but as putting some Democratic seats at risk. This concern, that the anti-capital punishment and anti-juvenile waiver stands were hurting the Democrats, was expressed to the Governor by members of the Assembly.

The culmination of these pressures appeared to erupt while the Governor was on a campaign flight. The Governor was handed a newspaper which headlined a story about a recently released DFY youth who had murdered two subway passengers. This was a particularly brutal and senseless murder, which caused some of the staunchest opponents of juvenile waiver to question their stand. Upon learning that the 15-year-old repeat offender could only be held until his 21st birthday, the Governor announced that he was going to submit legislation that would place this kind of youth in adult court and provide sentences that would keep such a youth off the streets.

The Governor's abrupt change in position, done without consultation of his key aides or of Peter Edelman, the Director of DFY, moved Carey from the position of key opponent to that of key proponent of adult court jurisdiction for serious juvenile offenders. The Governor's change in position also dissolved the coalition that had formed in support of the Juvenile Justice Reform Act of 1976. The Senate leadership (Republican) which had opposed waiver-up provisions, now moved in line with the Senate rank-and-file and the Crime and Correction Committee in favor of placing original jurisdiction of serious juvenile offenders in criminal court. Likewise, the Assembly leadership (Democratic) moved to support the Governor. Attempts by the Chair of the Assembly Codes Committee, the Chair of the Assembly Child Care Committee, Edelman, and some of the Governor's own staff to move to a less drastic stance, such as limited waiver-up, were fruitless because the political costs of the Governor backing down from his campaign pronouncement were judged too high. As one key Assemblyman stated, "you can bury proposals in Committee, and you can fight the Senate, but you can't fight your own Governor."

When key actors from the Senate, Assembly, Governor's office, and DFY met to negotiate the specifics of the bill, it was clear that since the Governor had already committed to the position favoring original criminal court jurisdiction for serious juvenile offenders, there was little for those seeking a less drastic approach to bargain with. The conservatives knew the Governor wanted to get credit for a strong bill, and they were not going to back down.

The law was drafted in a matter of a few days and was presented to the legislature as part of an omnibus crime control bill during an "extraordinary session" of the legislature. The bill, which became known as the Juvenile Offender Law, was distributed to the legislators on their way into session and voted upon in the same session. Because of the short period of time from drafting to passage, there was no time to examine the effects of the 18-month-old Juvenile Justice Reform Act, no chance to consider less drastic proposals, and no chance for advocacy groups to mobilize against the bill. As one member of the Governor's staff said, "it was an absolutely insane atmosphere for making policy." What the legis-

lators wanted to know was whether the law got tougher. Assured
that the law did indeed get tougher, the bill was passed with over-
whelming support.

The basic and fundamental provision of the Juvenile Offender
Law is that it placed original jurisdiction of 13-year-olds committing murder, and 14- and 15-year-olds committing one of a list of
the most serious offenses, in the adult criminal courts.[11] While the
district attorney, grand jury or judge can waive a juvenile to Family
Court, if convicted in adult court, the youth potentially faces
among the most severe penalties for juveniles in the United
States.[12] Further, the law mandates that a youth convicted as a
juvenile offender be confined in a secure DFY facility until release
or transfer to the adult Department of Corrections at age 21
(although transfer may occur prior to age 21). The provision
requiring mandatory confinement in a secure facility is even more
stringent than that for adult felons, where the Department of Corrections has discretion to move prisoners among different levels of
security. Release decisions are placed with the Parole Board rather
than DFY.

In addition to the symbolic move away from the traditional
juvenile approach, the Juvenile Offender Law has had a major
practical impact on DFY. The fact that the Law mandates placement in secure facilities during the entire stay in DFY facilities (as
opposed to the mandatory 6- or 12-month stay in secure facilities
under the Juvenile Justice Reform Act) has created tremendous
demand for DFY secure beds. This forced DFY to place a major
priority during the years 1979 to 1983 on developing additional
secure beds. New secure facilities were opened and old facilities
converted into secure settings. This increased demand for secure
beds accounts for the increase in the number of youths confined in
secure facilities from 140 in 1978 to approximately 450 at the end of
1983. The majority of these youths are juveniles sentenced in adult
court under the Juvenile Offender Law.[13]

Summary of Findings

The findings of this study provide insight into both the dynamics of criminal justice policy formation and the more general
process of change.

First, juvenile corrections policy is affected by a wide range of factors. These include developments at the national, state, and local levels, and both direct (e.g., interest group activity) and indirect (e.g., Supreme Court decisions, fiscal policies) influences. Further, the juvenile corrections system is affected by both internal policy decisions, i.e., policy decisions of the agency's Director (e.g., PINS removal), and externally imposed decisions, i.e., Governor's executive order or legislative act (Juvenile Offender Law). However, even in apparent internal decisions, the role of external influences appear crucial (e.g., support of politicians, available funding). The wide variety of actors and wide variety of factors influencing juvenile corrections policy supports Miller et al.'s call for a "system model," and supports those who have urged an open, systems perspective that considers the sociopolitical arena in which the juvenile corrections system, and criminal justice in general, function (Cole, 1973; Duffee, 1980; Wright, 1981).

Fairchild's (1981) note that criminal justice legislation is typically the product of a small number of key politicians, and is usually enacted on a consensual basis, was supported in the present project. Key actors in formulating juvenile corrections legislation included the Governor's staff, the Director of DFY, legislative committee chairs responsible for juvenile justice issues, and (at times) the Assembly and Senate leadership. The degree of involvement of these actors varied from issue to issue. Once an issue was formulated, these key actors would enter into negotiations and typically agree on an approach. By the time a bill reached the floor for a vote, support was assured.[14]

In the terms of Miller and Ohlin's (1985) theory of change, this study provides support for several of the principles of change, while also pointing to the need for further clarification and specification.

The sequencing principle, that is, the idea that changes in both *aspired* choices and *available* choices (and the correspondence between the two) are necessary for change, was supported in this study. In the general deinstitutionalization movement of DFY under both Luger and Edelman, the constellation of aspired and available choices led to change. Putting the training schools under Luger and the hiring of Edelman, ensured that DFY would pursue an aspired policy of reduced institutional populations. Fiscal concerns ensured the support of the legislature and the Governor's office, thus favoring the aspired choice and also giving DFY the freedom, i.e., the available choice, to pursue these policies. The availability of state, and particularly federal funds, to expand community-based programs made deinstitutionalization an available choice. In the more specific area of PINS deinstitutionalization, the change from Luger to Edelman made PINS removal an aspired choice for DFY, and one which was possible (available) due to lack of political opposition and the availability of federal funds. The sequencing principle was also supported in the more conservative reform of the mid-1970s, when the politicalization of juvenile violence made the choice of "tougher" juvenile laws the aspired choice of the politicians, a policy decision that would seem to have always been available to the Governor and legislature under the structure of political decision-making.

Miller and Ohlin's second principle, the crisis principle, maintains that crisis is a necessary condition of change due to the inertia of large bureaucratic systems such as correctional systems. The crisis principle was generally supported, but questions can be raised as to the necessity of crisis for change. The transfer of the training schools in 1971 followed criticism of the training schools, and the Department of Social Services administration of the schools. However, respondents pointed out that it was not perceived a matter of widespread abuse and scandal, as was the case in Massachusetts (Miller, Ohlin, and Coates, 1977). On the other hand, the criticism did coincide with a crisis in the overall social welfare system and the transfer was part of a larger reorganization of the Department of Social Services.

The enactment of the Juvenile Offender Law of 1978, which led to significant increases in time served for particular juveniles and significant increases in DFY secure institutions and populations, seems to have been a product of crisis. The years 1975 to 1978 saw juvenile crime, particularly violent crime, become one of the key political issues in the state. A number of legislative committees seized upon the issue and it became central in the 1978 gubernatorial campaign. While the question of media attention awaits systematic investigation, respondents were unanimous in describing the perception that the media was inordinately highlighting the juvenile violence issue. The crisis atmosphere is also suggested by the process in which the law was enacted. Key professionals, such as the Director of the Division for Youth were not even consulted, and legislators were described as being unconcerned with anything but the question of whether this bill "got tough."

On the other hand, the removal of PINS from the training schools does not appear to be the product of an immediate crisis situation. Edelman administratively removed PINS, and the legislature formally codified the decision with little or no controversy or opposition. One interpretation of this finding is that while crisis may lead to change in certain situations, it is not a necessary condition of reform or change. An alternative interpretation is that the entire deinstitutionalization of status offenders movement was a product of the crisis in juvenile justice that surfaced with the questioning of the juvenile justice system in the U.S. Supreme Court cases and the Presidential Commission reports. Without this crisis, the Edelman-type philosophy as well as the federal initiatives under the Juvenile Justice and Delinquency Prevention Act, may not have developed. This second interpretation draws support from Lemert's (1970) contention that significant legal change is often the product of the accumulation of anomalies which call into question the traditional way of doing things. Just as the accumulation of anomalies led to the development of a juvenile code in California (Lemert, 1970), the anomalies led to a nationwide questioning of the traditional handling of status offenders. This questioning eventually translated into change at the state level. This second interpretation expands the notion of "crisis" beyond that of crisis in a particular service system to include these larger, nationwide shifts in preferred social policies. These alternative interpretations point to the need for additional study, and also to the need for further clarification and definition of the crisis principle.

The third principle, the importance of key swing groups, is also supported in this study. This principle holds that, in many issues, the support of a key swing group is often essential for change. In the early 1970s pressure for removing PINS from the training schools was blocked by Milton Luger, the Director of the Division for Youth. When Luger was replaced by Peter Edelman, who favored removal of PINS, status offenders were administratively removed from the training schools. The appointment of Edelman swung the balance of forces to the position favoring PINS deinstitutionalization. In the adoption of the Juvenile Offender Law, liberal and conservative forces were opposed on the issue of retaining exclusive Family Court jurisdiction for juveniles. Governor Carey's promised veto of any bill that would place juveniles in adult court was considered a key to the passage of the Juvenile Justice Reform Act of 1976. The Governor's abrupt change of position in 1978 was a clear example of a key swing actor, as his change in position dissolved the liberal interest coalition and precluded any effective opposition to the passage of what became the Juvenile Offender Law.

Limitations

While this study does tend to support the principles identified by Miller and Ohlin (1985), several precautions should be noted. First, by examining only those issues that actually were formulated into policy decisions, and then relating these findings to the principles developed by Miller and Ohlin, the findings are subject to the problem of selective observation (Campbell, 1979). In further stages of the project, comparisons of initiatives that became policy with those that were not acted upon may provide a more adequate test of whether these findings support Miller and Ohlin's theory of change. A related limitation has to do with the concern for generalizability inherent in any case study.

A more general concern has to do with interpretation of these findings. Studies of implementation demonstrate the frequent lack of association between enunciated policy and actual practice (Pressman and Wildavsky, 1973; Rose, 1972). In light of these findings, one must be careful not to draw overly broad inferences on change at the service delivery level based on changes in policy and the broad level changes emphasized in this study (Duffee and Klofas, 1983). For example, in the case of PINS deinstitutionalization, this study shows that PINS have indeed been removed from the training schools. There is no indication of whether these youths are engaged in programs that actually increase community linkages, whether additional services have been provided, or whether alternative forms of social control have arisen (see Spergel, 1976; Coates, Miller, and Ohlin, 1978). Similarly, while juveniles sentenced under the Juvenile Offender Law face longer sentences and mandatory secure confinement, they are also housed in smaller facilities than their counterparts of the 1960s and have access to legal protections through an active ombudsman program. The point is that inferences about programmatic change based on policy change are problematic. While policy sets constraints on the system and makes real differences in the lives of juveniles, i.e., a policy keeping a child within his/her community versus a rural institution, or a policy which provides a 14-year-old with a 10-year sentence, as opposed to an 18-month sentence, certainly make a difference to the youth, the issue of the impact of policy change at the service delivery level remains an empirical question.

Conclusion

The New York State juvenile corrections system has undergone significant change during the years of the late 1960s to 1983. Following a period of reductions in institutional populations and increases in community-based programs, the state experienced a significant growth in the number of secure facilities and the numbers of youths housed in secure settings. Rather than reflect simple reversals of policy, these changes seem to be tied to nationwide trends to discriminate levels of custodial control for different types of youths (Duffee and Klofas, 1983). While aware of these nationwide trends, this paper has focused on the key policy decisions accounting for the specific changes that have occurred in the New York system. Consideration of present findings in light of previous studies led to several points about the structure of policy formation and the dynamics of change. Since these findings, and several limitations of the study, were previously summarized, they need not be addressed here. However, consideration of the findings and limitations points to several concerns about future research needs. First, the wide range of policy inputs and the development of policy issues over time point to the need for intensive, longitudinal analysis. The Massachusetts (Miller, Ohlin, and Coates, 1977; Miller and Ohlin, 1985) and New York case studies provide such analysis. Unfortunately, questions of generalizability arise. As with many social science issues, there seems to be a need for a combination of strategies which include intensive, longitudinal analysis with comparative analyses of different state systems. Such efforts are crucial if we are to further understand the dynamics of policy formation and the impact of policy decisions on the juvenile and criminal justice systems.

Notes

[1] For origins of particular types of laws, see, Hall, 1952; Becker, 1963; Chambliss, 1964. Of particular interest in relation to this paper are studies of the origins of the juvenile justice system, see Platt, 1969; Mennel, 1973.

[2] Population and related data referred to in this section were compiled from a variety of reports provided by the New York State Division for Youth. Population counts are presented as "approximate" due to changes in reporting practices over the years. While such figures are approximate, the consistency between different DFY documents lends confidence in the accuracy of the general profile presented.

An important point about New York's juvenile justice system is the low age of majority. All individuals 16 years of age and older are considered adults and are excluded from New York's family court (family court being New York's juvenile court).

[3] An exception to the 18-month placement were provisions allowing 15-year-olds charged with class A or B felonies to be placed in the adult reception center at Elmira (for offenders 16 to 21 years old) for a period up to three years. N.Y. Family Court Act, sec. 758 (McKinney 1975) (repealed 1976).

[4] *Kent v. United States*, 383 U.S. 541 (1966); *In Re Gault*, 387 U.S. 1 (1967); *In Re Winship* 397 U.S. 358 (1970).

[5] N.Y. Laws 1971, c. 947.

[6] *Ellery C. v. Redlich*, 32 N.Y.2d 588 (1973).

[7] N.Y. Laws 1976, c. 515, 516.

[8] In the following sections dealing with legislative changes, it is instructive to note that New York has a two-house legislature. During the years 1974-78, the Assembly was controlled by the Democrats and the Senate by the Republicans. Governor Carey was a Democrat.

[9] Subsequent analysis indicates there was an increased level of reporting in the *New York Times*, see McGarrell (1988).

[10] N.Y. Laws 1976, c. 878.

[11] N.Y. Laws 1978, c. 481. The original list of targeted offenses included: murder 2, kidnapping 1, arson 1 and 2, manslaughter 1, rape 1, sodomy 1, burglary 1 and 2, robbery 1 and 2, attempted murder 2, attempted kidnapping 1, assault 1.

[12] For example, for murder 2, a maximum sentence of life and a minimum sentence of 5-9 years; for kidnapping 1 and arson 1, a maximum 12-15 years

and a minimum 4-6 years. For class B felonies (manslaughter 1, rape 1, sodomy 1, burglary 1, robbery 1, arson 2, attempted murder 2, and attempted kidnapping 1) a maximum 3-10 years, minimum one-third of maximum. For class C felonies (assault 1, robbery 2, and burglary 2) a maximum 3-7 years, minimum one-third of maximum. (N.Y. Penal Law 70.05 (McKinney Supp. 1983)).

[13]Eighty-eight percent of the placements to DFY secure facilities in 1983 were youths sentenced in criminal court under the Juvenile Offender Law (data provided by New York State Division for Youth).

[14]For example, the bill which enacted the Juvenile Justice Reform Act of 1976 was passed by votes of 136-8 in the Assembly and 55-2 in the Senate. The bill which enacted the Juvenile Offender Law of 1978 was passed by a vote of 125-10 in the Assembly and 46-2 in the Senate. The fact that these two bills, embodying distinct approaches to serious juvenile crime and enacted within two years of each other, could gather such support, reflects this process in which a small group of key actors decide on a specific approach and then enlist the support of the rest of the legislature.

Discussion Questions

1. McGarrell's study of the New York State Division for Youth would indicate that horizontal interactions occur not only at the local level (e.g., referrals across service agencies) but also at power and policy centers. According to this description, when were policy actors in different units of state government most likely to interact?

2. This study describes fluctuations in policy from conservative to liberal positions and back again. Did the liberal period, with significant reduction in training school populations, involve more or less control by local actors? For example, what happened in this period to the sentencing discretion of Family Court judges?

3. It would appear that the structure of state government can give representatives of one locality considerable power over policies affecting other localities (e.g., the power of the chair of the Senate Crime and Corrections Committee). Are there other ways in which state officials and localities can interact that would provide each locality with greater control over correctional policy for its own people? What kind of problems might this local discretion create?

Chapter 9
Evaluating the Implementation of Community Corrections*

Michael Musheno
Dennis Palumbo
Steven Maynard-Moody
James Levine

This study is an evaluation of the implementation of community corrections in Oregon, Colorado and Connecticut. The goal of this study is to discover what factors contribute to the process of putting in place a program of community corrections which works. One strand of the literature on implementation focuses on how faithfully statutory goals are adopted or on the intensity of efforts to achieve these goals (Edwards, 1980; Brewer, 1974; Levine, 1972). A second strand of implementation research presumes that implementing also requires adapting intentions and actions to new and local situations (Hall and Loucks, 1977; Musheno et al., 1976; Majone and Wildavsky, 1977; Levine, Musheno and Palumbo, 1980; Morash, 1982).

The guiding theory of this study is that successful implementation of policies, like community corrections, requires a delicate balance between the essential but somewhat contradictory processes of faithful adoption and constructive adaptation (see Palumbo, et al., 1984). We do agree that where policy goals are clear, conflict is not aroused, the social technology for achieving consensus goals is available, and relatively few administrative decision

*This research was funded by the National Institute of Justice (Grant #82-15-CV-K015). The views expressed in this chapter, however, are solely those of the authors and not those of the Institute. An earlier version of the chapter was presented at the Annual Meeting of the Academy of Criminal Justice Sciences, St. Louis, Missouri, March 15-19, 1987.

points have to be overcome, successful implementation can be achieved with little modification or adaptation to local conditions (see Sabatier and Mazmanian, 1979). However, seldom do these political and organizational conditions exist for social policies and clearly, they are not present with regard to community corrections in the states we observed. At the same time, adaptation can lead to gross distortion of policy. For example, when community corrections is reduced to placing offenders in local jails instead of a state prison, the policy is unfulfilled or bled empty through maladaptive practice.

Policy and Settings

Like many social policies directed at human services delivery, "community corrections" normative premises are sufficiently ambiguous so as to attract a broad range of political support and a host of program applications. For some, community corrections is an extension of positivist reform principles which presume that the causes of criminality can be isolated and treated, but only in humane settings where clients are gradually reintegrated into patterns of everyday life.

Others view community corrections as a policy departure from positivist premises of criminality and locate it within a larger trend of the 1960s to engage the community in human services' decision making and delivery. The "community control" movement sought to reduce the influence of large-scale governmental bureaucracies on human services and to increase the participation and influence of community residents and service clients (see Fantini and Gittell, 1973; Lipsky and Lounds, 1976). A "new criminology" emerged from this larger movement and was applied to corrections by members of President Johnson's 1967 Commission on Law Enforcement and the Administration of Justice:

> The general underlying premise for the new directions in corrections is that crime and delinquency are symptoms of failures and disorganization of the community as well as of individual offenders... The task of corrections, therefore, includes building solid ties between offenders and the community, integrating and reintegrating the

offender into community life—restoring family ties, obtaining employment and education, securing in the larger sense a place for the offender in the routine functioning of society (quoted from Irwin, 1980:159).

Most recently, fiscal conservatives have been drawn to the utility principles of community corrections which claim that this policy provides a cost effective sentencing alternative to prisons, including no additional "costs" to community safety (Palumbo, 1986). While the utility, community involvement and treatment claims of community corrections have been challenged (see Scull, 1977; Scull, 1982; Austin and Krisberg, 1982), a number of states have adopted community corrections policies based on one or more of these normative premises.

Focusing largely on nonviolent offenders, these policies provide funding for pretrial release programs, sentencing alternatives to state prisons, and transitional programs for those within a year of release from prison. The services provided through these programs are *human services* in that *actions* of the street-level employees of these programs represent the *core resource* delivered through this policy (see Lipsky, 1980:3). These services include vocational training, job skills, drug and alcohol treatment and family counseling.

The community corrections' policies of Oregon and Colorado are similar in that state funds are invested in sentencing alternatives and human services for nonviolent felony offenders. However, the organizational structures for administering alternatives and providing services vary markedly between the two states. Both structures include elements of decentralization, but the Oregon process is more bureaucratized.

The Oregon state Department of Corrections invests financial resources in county departments of community corrections, based on the abilities of counties to divert nonviolent felony offenders from the overcrowded state prison system. Each local department of community corrections is integrated into the chain of command of its county government with management personnel of the county overseeing management personnel of the local unit. Probation officers, certified by county and state governments, staff the halfway houses and offer intensified client services.

In many counties, the State's Community Corrections Act has allowed officials to further rationalize the organization of correctional services in place prior to its passage. Counties have increased "professional supervision" over referral and volunteer services and increased the number of probation officers as service providers, displacing part-time and voluntary workers. Unit heads have been hired to manage discrete service areas (e.g., residential services, mental health services, clerical and fiscal services) with unit heads reporting to a director of community corrections who, in turn, reports to a county administrator.

In Colorado, the State Judicial Department contracts with its 22 judicial districts which have formed advisory boards to identify and fund private agencies willing to provide community corrections' services. District court judges are granted authority to sentence nonviolent offenders to community corrections rather than state correctional facilities.

In most districts, the private agencies are nonprofit, multiservice community agencies which offer residential and nonresidential services for a variety of clients. These multiservice agencies are staffed by volunteers and paraprofessionals, including ex-convicts. The advisory boards play the critical role of coordinating the community corrections' services of contracted agencies. Consisting of elected officials, criminal justice administrators and line personnel and influential citizens, these boards serve also as local advocates of community corrections.

While probation officers serve on local boards and have supervisory authority over certain clients of the community agencies, many of the direct service providers are employees of the nonprofit agencies. These agencies, usually small collectives, invest ultimate authority in committees and "directors" of these agencies are frequently service providers as well. Coordination and supervision of responsibilities are secured through personal relations rather than role differentiation and hierarchy.

The community corrections' policy of Connecticut diverges from those of Oregon and Colorado, both with regard to the nature of services and organizational structure. Specifically, it concentrates on transitional services for nonviolent felony offenders and their families. Also, the policy provides for public information services or what is formally called "constituency building"—developing a political constituency in the private sector for improving criminal justice policies, establishing public support for community services relevant to corrections, and improving coordination among public and private agencies involved in correctional service delivery.

Organizationally, the Connecticut process is a hybrid of the Oregon and Colorado systems. That is, like Oregon, it is administered by the State Department of Corrections through its Community Services Division. However, like the Colorado process, Connecticut's state department of corrections contracts with a network of private agencies to provide transitional services for inmates, offers support services for families of inmates and executes the mandate of constituency building.

Methodology

The principal proposition of this study is that community corrections becomes more embedded in its larger sociopolitical environment and impacts society more favorably as it (1) enjoys greater commitment among those engaged in its diffusion; (2) invokes greater agreement among implementors as to what policy should accomplish; (3) maximizes adaptation at the local level; (4) expands access to decision-making among participants; and (5) gains support among critical professional and community groups.

The implementation, environmental, embeddedness, and impact factors were operationalized through the construction, administration and analysis of close-ended questionnaires. However, the research began in each state with unstructured, open-ended interviews by six researchers who spent two weeks in Oregon and a week each on Colorado and Connecticut. We conducted research in each state in turn, finishing one before moving on to the next. This strategy enabled us to maintain consistency in our investigation across states while adapting our research to the unique conditions surrounding community corrections in each state. All face-to-face interviews were tape-recorded and transcribed by the field research teams.

After the field research was completed and data analyzed in each state, we constructed and administered close-ended questionnaires and mailed these to the *total population* of key participants in community corrections. The participants were divided into two groups, upper-level implementors and street-level implementors (see Lipsky, 1980). Upper-level implementors are all those participants who do not have daily contact with clients and who occupy executive, managerial and advisory positions in their community corrections' network. They include advisory board members, program directors and managers, judges, prosecutors, and sheriffs. The street-level implementors are those who have day-to-day contact with clients and include probation officers, institutional counselors, volunteers, program staff, parole officers, residential facility counselors and other treatment staff.

In each state, the response rates were over fifty percent for both categories of implementors. For each category, those who did respond were representative of the range of participants and for each type of participant (e.g., probation officers), those who did respond were representative of their job classification.

With regard to the implementation dimensions, the degree of commitment that participants have to community corrections is measured by two questions: (1) the extent to which they believe community corrections is an effective way of handling offenders; and (2) how much they support community corrections. The remaining implementation dimensions were operationalized as single indicator variables, based on direct questions from the questionnaire.

For the impact dimension, we used two indicators of success, each measured by a discrete question from the survey instrument. Specifically, we analyzed their perception of how successful community corrections has been in their respective states and whether they agreed that their state's administrative structures have been successful in its implementation of community corrections. Finally, to determine the extent to which respondents perceive that community corrections has become embedded in the larger sociopolitical environment of their respective states, we asked them to assess the degree of improvement in various conditions (e.g., coordination among criminal justice agencies) and how they perceive that their state's community corrections program has affected cooperation among groups who see the policy as salient.

Findings

This section compares responses across states, combining in each state the responses of street-level and upper-level implementors. After demonstrating that Colorado scores highest among the states on most dimensions, we conclude the paper by noting qualitative differences among the states, including some discussion of Colorado's organizational style of implementing community corrections and how this style of implementation results in a higher investment in community corrections among street-level participants, particularly when compared to the Oregon system.

Implementation—Dimension

There is fairly wide variation in the degree of commitment to the program. As Table 9.1 shows, Colorado and Connecticut are considerably higher than Oregon. Both have a far higher percent who believe in the effectiveness of community corrections and who support it; in fact, a high percent, around 90 percent in Colorado and 70 to 80 percent in Connecticut, both believe in and support the programs. Even in Oregon, around 50 percent of the implementors believe in the effectiveness of community corrections and almost 56 percent support it; thus, there is a fairly high level of commitment to community corrections in all three states.

Colorado's respondents have a significantly higher percentage who say there is agreement among participants in community corrections about what the program should accomplish (see Table 9.2).

Table 9.1

Level of Commitment to Community Corrections

	Oregon		Colorado		Connecticut	
	%	N	%	N	%	N
1. Belief in community corrections as an effective way to handle felons:						
Percent who...						
Agree	48.9	132	88.9	279	71.3	300
Are neutral	22.2	60	7.0	22	19.2	81
Disagree	28.9	78	4.1	13	9.5	40
		270		314		421
2. Support for community corrections:						
Great deal	25.6	69	59.0	182	48.3	205
Moderately high	30.0	81	32.5	100	35.1	149
Moderately little	24.8	67	7.5	24	14.9	63
Not at all	19.6	53	1.0	2	1.7	7
		270		308		424

Table 9.2

Agreement Among Participants in Community Corrections About What the Program Should Accomplish

Percent who...	Oregon	Colorado	Connecticut
Agree or strongly agree	57.2	73.0	49.5
Are neutral	22.9	14.0	32.5
Disagree or strong disagree	20.9	14.0	18.0
N =	271	285	406

Colorado also has a significantly higher percentage who believe there have been changes in the program since its inception (Table 9.3) and more than three-quarters of these respondents believe the changes that have been made have been constructive in adapting the program to local needs.

Table 9.3

Extent to Which Community Corrections Programs Have Changed Since their Adoption

Percent who say it has changed...	Oregon	Colorado	Connecticut
A great deal or quite a bit (yes)	36.0	55.0	38.0
Some		31.0	43.1
Little or none (no)	64.0	13.0	18.8
N=	253	287	415

Colorado also tends to be the highest in the percentage who believe they have a great deal or a fairly large amount of access to decision-making in community corrections (see Table 9.4). However, there is a small percentage in each state who feel they have some access.

Connecticut has yet to empower or give a political stake to a wide range of participants and it is evidenced by the fact that only 7.1 percent of the respondents in that state feel they have access to statewide decision-making and three-quarters feel they have almost none (see Table 9.4).

Table 9.4

Access to Decision-Making in Community Corrections

	Oregon	Colorado	Connecticut In-area	Statewide
Percent who have...				
A great deal or fairly large amount	32.5	34.0	15.6	7.1
Moderate amount	15.9	23.0	25.0	18.6
Relatively little or none	51.6	43.0	59.4	74.4
N=	157	295	436	

Colorado also has the highest percentage who feel there is much or some support for the program by elected officials, service providers, probation officers, and the community (see Table 9.5). However, all three states see relatively little support from the community. Community antagonism, particularly about where half-way houses should be located, is a problem for community corrections all over. Surprisingly, this opposition of the community does not get translated into opposition by elected officials; thus, a majority of elected officials in all three states support the programs. It appears elected officials can both support community corrections and have a "get tough" approach to criminals. In fact, our field research revealed that in both Colorado and Connecticut determinate sentencing laws were passed that had the effect of greatly increasing the number of individuals who were prosecuted and sentenced to state prisons at the very same time these states were expanding their community corrections programs.

It is noteworthy, also, that Colorado has the highest percentage of probation officers who are perceived to support community corrections (91%—see Table 9.5), and Oregon has the smallest percent (31%). Our field interviews revealed that Oregon's probation officers' low degree of support stems from opposition by the

Table 9.5

Perceptions of the Extent of Support for Community Corrections

Percent who say there is among		Oregon	Colorado	Connecticut
Elected Officials...				
Much or some support		61.1	73.0	57.5
Undecided		20.2	18.0	24.9
Much or some resistance		18.7	8.0	17.6
	N =	267	282	409
Service Providers...				
Much or some support		67.3	92.0	83.0
Undecided		16.9	7.0	12.5
Much or some resistance		15.8	2.0	4.5
	N =	266	286	400
Community...				
Much or some support		37.4	38.0	37.5
Undecided		49.2	40.0	28.2
Much or some resistance		13.2	21.0	34.4
	N =	262	287	408
Probation Officers...				
Much or some support		30.8[1]	91.0	70.6
Undecided		12.3	5.0	21.5
Much or some resistance		56.9	5.0	8.0
	N =	130	288	391
Parole Officers...				
Much or some support			76.0	71.0
Undecided			18.0	21.0
Much or some resistance			5.0	7.9
	N =		269	390

[1]Probation and parole officers were combined in the Oregon questionnaire. These percentages represent the probation and parole officers who said they supported community corrections. The "undecided" category was not among the response choices.

probation officers' union. This opposition exists because the probation officers must become county employees under the Community Corrections Act if their county chooses to participate in the program. The move from state to county employee jeopardizes the probation officers' job security and their union.

Another aspect influencing probation officers' support is one of a "turf" problem. In all three states, disagreement exists about whether community corrections should be located in the judicial branch rather than the corrections department. In order to be successful, the program needs the cooperation of the judiciary. However, when the program is administratively housed under corrections' authority the judicial branch (which includes probation officers) supports community corrections less. This is the situation in both Oregon and Connecticut. In Colorado, on the other hand, the program is in the judiciary branch and probation officers there are far more supportive.

Environmental Embeddedness

There is considerable agreement among the states' participants about what improvements have been made in various conditions since the adoption of community corrections (see Table 9.6). Direct services to offenders ranks first among the conditions listed on the questionnaires of all three states—although this item was not on the Connecticut questionnaire, our interviews and other questions asked indicate Connecticut respondents feel direct services have been greatly improved. All three agree that coordination among agencies of the criminal justice system has substantially improved. This fits in with the notion that community corrections is not really a new set of programs and goals, but the traditional goals of treatment services organized in a new administrative structure that draws upon and integrates services in a much more effective and efficient manner. Of the various conditions, crowding in jails has improved the least.

Overall, Colorado ranked highest in conditional improvements, with participants rating their states' conditions improving on four dimensions: crowding, direct services, coordination among criminal justice agencies, and coordination between public and private agencies. The results in Oregon and Connecticut are less consistent with Oregon's respondents the most mixed in their judgments about how well community corrections has affected related conditions.

Table 9.6

Degree of Improvement in Various Conditions Since the Adoption of Community Corrections

	Oregon		Colorado		Connecticut	
	%	Rank †	%	Rank †	%	Rank †
Correctional crowding:						
Slightly or much better	24.4	5	44.0	5	34.8	4
No change	27.6		34.0		32.3	
Slightly or much worse	48.0		22.0		32.8	
Direct services to offenders:						
Slightly or much better	65.4	1	80.0	1	*	
No change	17.7		15.0			
Slightly or much worse	17.0		4.0			
Community safety:						
Slightly or much better	39.5	4	32.0	6	38.8	3
No change	40.3		55.0		50.5	
Slightly or much worse	20.2		14.0		10.7	
Coordination among criminal justice agencies:						
Slightly or much better	65.4	1	64.0	2	54.2	2
No change	23.4		33.0		42.5	
Slightly or much worse	11.2		4.0		3.3	
Coordination among criminal justice agencies and private agencies:						
Slightly or much better	58.4	3	62.0	3	56.4	1
No change	26.4		33.0		39.7	
Slightly or much worse	15.2		5.0		3.8	
Probation and parole services:						
Slightly or much better	60.2	2	49.0	4	*	
No change	24.4		44.0			
Slightly or much worse	15.4		8.0			

*These items were not included on the Connecticut questionnaire.
†Rank ordering among states on perceived improvement in conditions, by indicator. Rankings determined by highest score after differencing first and third categories of responses.

When specifically asked about how the state's community corrections program has affected cooperation among various groups,
the majority of respondents in all three states said that cooperation
had increased. But, consistent with the direction of implementation variables, Colorado has the highest percent of the three states
who see an increase in cooperation (see Table 9.7).

Table 9.7

**How the State's Community Corrections Program has Affected
Cooperation**

	Oregon	Colorado	Connecticut
Increased	56.2	74.0	68.3
Neither	34.2	24.0	30.3
Decreased	9.6	2.0	1.5
N =	260	287	347

Impact

Likewise, the program perceived to be the most successful by
those who implement it is the one in Colorado. Table 9.8 shows
that 70 percent of the Colorado implementors believe the program
has been moderately or very successful, 67.6 percent of the Connecticut respondents and 61.2 percent of the Oregon respondents
believe this.

Table 9.8

Perceptions of Success

	Oregon	Colorado	Connecticut
A. Community corrections has been:			
Very successful	23.6	24.0	13.1[1]
Moderately successful	37.6	55.0	56.1
Neutral	14.1	15.0	0
Moderately unsuccessful	10.3	5.0	26.4
Very successful	14.4	1.0	4.4
N =	263	296	367
B. The state's existing corrections administration has been successful in its implementation of community corrections:			
Percent who…			
Agree	39.1	59.0	47.6
Neutral	29.9	26.0	33.9
Disagree	31.0	15.0	18.5
N =	261	309	410

[1]These figures are the average percent who rated the Connecticut program on six different dimensions. The total N ranged from 390 to 410. For Oregon and Colorado, the percents are the responses to a single question.

Conclusions and Implications

The direction of all indicators is consistent in Colorado and points toward a site where community corrections is being successfully implemented. However, one could argue that this evidence suggests only that community corrections serves more interests, more effectively in Colorado than in the other sites under investigation. According to this argument, community corrections may be appealing to a range of interests and become embedded in the organizational environment of criminal justice; but it remains a dangerous reform because it allows for a widening of the net of social control (see Scull, 1982).

Colorado represents an appropriate site for inquiring about negative impact and probing more deeply for those factors which set this site apart as an "extreme case" of implementation. In her outline of a strategy for conducting research on public sector performance, Trudi Miller (1984: 251-266) calls for less focus on many settings and central tendency and more inquiry of those few settings where the commitment to support (and resist) a particular reform is highly visible. Such inquiry reveals more about the potential for the diffusion and transferability of programs associated with a given social policy. While our investigation of three sites revealed no extreme case of resistance to community corrections' programs, Colorado does provide an opportunity for further probing of the organizational dimensions which may contribute to the successful implementation of community corrections.

Net-Widening

But first, does Colorado produce the negative effect of net-widening? To probe this issue, we used a regression equation to predict the number of expected commitments to state correctional institutions for each year following the enactment of the Colorado Community Corrections Act in 1976. We found reductions below the expected levels for every fiscal year under investigation—1977-78 through 1982-83 (for details on calculations and findings, see Palumbo, Musheno and Maynard-Moody, 1985:194-196).

Reductions in commitments improved every year from 1977-78 through 1980-81. While reductions continued after 1980-81, the rate of difference between expected and actual commitments slowed in 1981-82 and 1982-83. The lower rate of difference between expected and actual commitments is most likely due to stiffer mandatory sentencing legislation passed in 1980. This legislation increased the number of individuals being sent to state penal institutions and community corrections' placements failed to offset fully the impact of this legislation on incarceration rates.

The Colorado Judicial Department contracted with an outside party to investigate the net-widening issue as well. The consultant used discriminant analysis to predict where, among three options (i.e., probation, community corrections, prison), community corrections' clients would be sentenced based on law-related variables that best differentiate these individuals (see Winterfield, 1983). The analysis revealed that 20 percent of community corrections' clients would have been sentenced to probation, 74 percent would have been given community corrections, and six percent would have been sent to prison. Therefore, the overlap between community corrections and probation clients is approximately 20 percent, suggesting that a modest amount of net-widening is occurring.

Transferability

Our probing of conditions operating in Colorado reveals a high belief in the efficacy of community corrections as a way of handling nonviolent felons among *both* street-level and upper-level implementors (Palumbo, et al., 1985:166). Oregon, which has consistently lower scores across all dimensions in comparison to Colorado, shows that efficacy is high only among the upper-level implementors (Palumbo, et al., 1985: 54). Moreover, street-level workers in Colorado report high levels of involvement and access to decision-making consistent with upper-level participants. Thus, all strata of workers are empowered in the Colorado system; but such empowerment does not extend to the street-level participants in Oregon (see Palumbo, et al., 1985: 167-173, 54-58).

What is it about the organizational environment of Colorado which tends to promote broader involvement and greater access to decision-making? As we pointed out above in the description of the organizational styles of each state's program, Colorado is less bureaucratic than the others, relying on a network of nonprofit community agencies which invest ultimate authority in committees of workers. Similar to others who have investigated nonprofit community agencies (see Rothschild and Whitt, 1986; Musheno, 1982), our research suggests that such an organizational style of implementation has potential to maximize commitment among the full range of participants engaged in the diffusion of a social program and expand access to decision-making to include street-level workers (see, for example, Maynard-Moody, et al., 1987).

Private, nonprofit agencies have long been involved in providing community and transitional services for nonviolent adult and juvenile offenders. Our research and that of others indicate that private service providers have achieved mixed results, at best, in seeking broad, community support for their activities (see, for example, Miller, Ohlin and Coates, 1977). However, due to the internal organizational cultures of the private, nonprofit agencies we observed in Colorado, we do find find that reliance on such agencies may offer potential solutions to one, critical implementation problem. Namely, such agencies, unlike the county bureaucracies we observed in Oregon, may provide a more appropriate, internal environment for gaining the support and full involvement of those who represent the "core" technology or people power of community corrections—the street-level, or human services worker.

Discussion Questions

1. According to Musheno and his colleagues, the community corrections officials in these three states found "low support" for community corrections among communities, with the exception of elected leaders. Yet it is clear that most of these community corrections officials supported such programs. Are they not also members of these communities? Since these programs were being implemented, in what sense were "communities" not supportive?

2. How does this chapter demonstrate the importance of the vertical dimension of community structure?

3. Musheno et al. suggest that reliance on private agencies in Colorado may have been important to the degree of commitment to community corrections found in that state. Why might this happen? Would you think private involvement is necessary? (Re-examine the description of the Pennsylvania system in Chapter 7).

Chapter 10

An Examination of Officials' Perceptions of the Operation of the Polk County Department of Correctional Services

Paul Stageberg

Introduction

In 1973, the Law Enforcement Assistance Administration selected the Polk County (Iowa) Department of Court Services—frequently called the "Des Moines Project"—as its first Exemplary Project. In selecting the Department (henceforth referred to frequently as "the Department" or "the DCS"), the National Institute of Law Enforcement and Criminal Justice (NILECJ) cited it as unique both in having been evaluated by an independent research team and in providing an array of correctional services coordinated under a single administrative unit. Although the Department maintained some programs that were common (i.e., Vera-Manhattan style pre-trial release and county probation), the Institute regarded the coordination of these programs with two more innovative projects (supervised pre-trial release and a non-secure residential facility) as unique and worthy of replication. The Institute later provided funds for replication of the Department's programs in eight other jurisdictions.

According to the Exemplary Project announcement:

> Each of the [Department's] components appears to have brought about significant improvements in the Polk County criminal justice system. The combined effort, operating from a single administrative unit, provides an outstanding array of well-coordinated correctional services. The continuum of services provided is in sharp

contrast to the normally fragmented operations of the criminal justice system. Moreover, the Program is unique in the range of dispositional alternatives available, geared to varying offender characteristics. (NILECJ, 1973, pp. 1-2).

Although the Department was evaluated in its early years by the National Council on Crime and Delinquency (NCDD, 1972, 1972a; Venezia, 1973; Venezia and Steggerda, 1973; Steggerda and Venezia, 1974), and although the programs of the DCS were evaluated by the State of Iowa as they were expanded throughout Iowa (Bureau of Correctional Evaluation, 1975, 1975a, 1976), one can make a valid case that the true impact of the Des Moines Project on the justice system of Polk County has never been tested. While the NCCD evaluations looked at the operation of specific DCS programs at specific points, they made no attempt to assess the impact of the entire DCS program as it developed.

Seeing the utility of a different type of assessment of what has been regarded as a model community-based corrections project, in the mid-1970s the author designed a study to analyze more broadly the impact of the DCS. Rather than examining only the offenders going through the four DCS programs (ROR release, supervised release, probation, and residential facilities), the study attempted to combine some of the attributes of prior community-based corrections (CBC) and juvenile diversion evaluations, making use of the goal-oriented approach of CBC evaluations while putting them in the system-oriented framework often used in evaluation of diversion programs.

In addition to studying, longitudinally, the impact of the DCS on offender case processing, the study also used interview data obtained from justice system practitioners in Polk County. Such a methodology not only provided an opportunity to determine what practitioners throughout the system actually thought about the Department, but also enabled a comparison of actual case processing data and the perceptions of practitioners about the impact of community-based corrections in Des Moines. Although a brief review of the results of the offender-tracking portion of the research is included here, the practitioner perceptions will be our major focus.

The research also involved a review of the issues most frequently arising in evaluation of community-based corrections and diversion projects. Since being acclaimed by the National Crime Commission (The President's Commission and Law Enforcement and Administration of Justice, 1967) as a promising alternative to the oft-criticized prison system, community-based corrections has been a frequent topic of debate. Although initially touted as a less punitive alternative to the fortress prison, community-based corrections has been attacked by some (e.g., Greenberg, 1975) as being more egregious than the prison system from which it was meant to divert clients. While it has been hailed as a vehicle to reduce societal intrusion on the lives of offenders, others have maintained that community-based corrections results in widening the "social net" (e.g., Klein, 1979). In reviewing the community-based corrections literature, it became evident that four basic issues occupied most of the discussion:

1) *diversion:* whether the program under assessment was successful in truly diverting its clients from more secure programming;

2) *net-widening:* whether establishment of the program drew more offenders into contact with the correctional system, or kept offenders in programming for longer periods of time;

3) *cost savings:* whether the program resulted in any reduction in the cost of correctional program operation;

4) *protection of the public:* whether the program showed any evidence of reducing recidivism among its clients.

These four areas of concern provided the backdrop against which the DCS programs were assessed. Three of these areas—diversion, net-widening, and protection of the public—are dealt with in some detail here.

Methodology

Two types of data were used in the study: archival data taken from four samples of cases tracked through the Polk County justice system from 1969 through 1973, and interview data collected from 195 Polk County justice system practitioners. Additional archival data were taken (for comparative purposes) from previous National Council on Crime and Delinquency and State of Iowa evaluations of the Department. Such a methodology provided an opportunity to compare and contrast three independent data sources.

Archival Data Collection

The programs of the Department of Court (now Correctional) Services developed over a span of years in a somewhat piecemeal fashion, enabling an assessment of the impact of individual programs as they developed. Had all four components of the DCS become operational within a short period of time, it would have been very difficult to determine the impact of any one program; with the four components beginning operation over a span of about nine years, however, it is possible to attempt an assessment of each of them.

In the case-processing portion of the research, offender samples were selected from among those interviewed by Pre-Trial Release (PTR) during four years:

1969, when only PTR was operational;

1970, when PTR was operational and Release-With-Services (RWS) was starting operation;

1972, when PTR and RWS were operational, probation had come under DCS administration, and Fort Des Moines (residential facility for men) was in an experimental stage;

1973, when all four major DCS programs were operational.[1]

Several modifications were made to the samples to ensure comparability. The final samples were comparable in the number of points scored on the PTR interview, and did not show significant differences in the types of crimes alleged, criminal history, or a number of demographic variables. Most analyses of the archival data used defendants' PTR points or offense severity as the independent variable. There was a slight tendency for the latter two samples (1972 and 1973) to be somewhat more "hard-core" than the earlier samples, but, as will be shown below, this did not confound the research results. Final samples ranged from 296 (in 1972) to 325 (in 1970).

A wide variety of data were collected in tracking alleged and convicted offenders through Polk County's justice system. Most data pertained to case processing and sentencing, permitting the tracking of cases through the pre- and post-trial periods. Included in the tracking data was information on service referrals, within-program rearrests, and recidivism. Sources of information included DCS files and records from District and Municipal court, the County Jail, the State Bureau of Adult Corrections, and the Bureau of Criminal Investigation. Before/after demographic data were also collected on sample members to attempt to discern any changes during the criminal justice process.

Interview Data Collection

Seven groups of criminal justice practitioners were interviewed as part of the research:

Des Moines Police Department
Polk County Sheriff's Office
Polk County Attorney's Office
Private Attorneys
Offender Advocate (public defender)
The Judiciary
Department of Court Services

Selection of interview candidates from each of these groups involved the use of quota sampling. In the Des Moines Police Department (DMPD), only divisions appearing to feel potential impact from DCS operation were sampled. Similarly, in the County Sheriff's office, only individuals with primary responsibility for criminal cases were interviewed. In the case of defense attorneys, selection was made only from those having current or recent routine involvement in criminal defense work in Polk County.

One problem faced in the interviewing portion of the research was that while the case processing data covered 1969 through 1973, practitioner interviews did not occur until 1980 and 1981. To try to identify practitioners' perceptions of the impact of the DCS during its development, an effort was made to interview personnel who had been active in Polk County's justice system between 1969 and 1973, the years during which the DCS was developing. These individuals were thought to have more direct knowledge of the potential impact of the DCS on their agencies and on offender case processing than more recently-hired personnel. Thus, one cannot necessarily say that the interview responses were representative of a given agency as a *whole;* rather, they should have been representative of the *senior personnel* in each agency.

Results

Diversion

Pre-Trial Programming

As a general rule, while analysis of the case-processing data showed positive effects from the development of the DCS, practitioners perceived the DCS as having even more impact on operation of the justice system than suggested by the archival data. All groups of practitioners saw the DCS as having considerable influence on case processing in Polk County. Some, obviously, were more pleased about that influence than others.

The primary aim of the DCS pre-trial programs was to reduce the incidence of pre-trial detention, effectively trying to reduce the disparity in detention among those who could afford to pay cash bond and those who could not. Analysis of release practices in Polk County between 1969 and 1973 showed that, indeed, there had been changes in the percentage of defendants detained during the pre-trial period. When analyzing results with reference to offense severity or PTR points, it was clear that the development of supervised release fostered the release of more alleged felons and defendants who did not score sufficient points to be released on recognizance. On the other hand, there was also a reduction in the use of Pre-Trial Release (recognizance release) among those apparently qualifying for such release. Due to this decrease, the percentage of defendants actually released through DCS programs changed only slightly during the four-year period.

These results can be juxtaposed against the interview data, which showed that practitioners throughout Polk County's justice system perceived increases both in the *numbers* of people released before trial and in the *severity* of the crimes alleged to have been committed by releases. None of the interview samples showed less than 70 percent saying that there had been increases in the numbers of defendants released before trial. Only one of the seven interview samples (the public defender's office) showed fewer than 75 percent reporting that more serious defendants were being released as the DCS developed.

Post-Trial Programming

The development of county probation and (particularly) the Fort Des Moines facility as alternatives to imprisonment occurred in Des Moines amid much fanfare and under close scrutiny. As the Facility was being planned, and as it went through growing pains during its first two years, it was clear that the intention of those designing and operating the Facility was to reduce Polk County's reliance on the state prison system as a sentencing alternative.

Evaluation reports published by the National Council on Crime and Delinquency covering the Facility's first two years of operation were glowing, and found that the program was being used as an alternative both to jail and prison. In assessing the cost of the Facility, the NCCD team concluded in its first evaluation that it was "...an extremely low-cost correctional effort when compared to ongoing state correctional programs on the basis of cost per client from commitment to release" (Venezia and Steggerda, 1973, p. x).

Although practitioners outside the DCS appeared to have little familiarity with the NCCD evaluations, many concluded, as did the evaluations, that one impact of the DCS programming was less use of the state prison system. Over 90 percent of the respondents in each agency perceived that the programs of the DCS reduced Polk

County's reliance on the prison system, and in two agencies—the County Attorney's Office and the Offender Advocate—a majority of respondents reported that the DCS had caused *much less* use.

Similar results were obtained when respondents were asked specifically if the Fort Des Moines Facility was used as an alternative to prison, as shown in Table 10.1.

Table 10.1

Survey Item: Is Fort Des Moines Used as an Alternative to Prison?
(in percent)

	N*	No	Yes
Des Moines Police	61	4.9	95.1
Sheriff's Office	26	3.8	96.2
Total Law Enf.	87	4.6	95.4
County Attorney	18	0.0	100.0
Offender Advocate	7	0.0	100.0
Private Attorneys	29	0.0	100.0
Judges	11	18.2	81.8
Total Legal Sys.	65	3.1	96.9
Dept. of Corr. Serv.	36	5.6	94.4

*Excludes don't know and not applicable

Comparisons of the results of these two questions yielded some interesting conclusions. Fourteen of the respondents (throughout the system) believed that DCS programming either had *no* impact on the use of the prison system, or had caused an *increase*. Only ten respondents, however, reported believing that Fort Des Moines was not used as an alternative to prison. Thus, there appeared to be at least four respondents who, while they perceived a diversionary impact from Fort Des Moines, did not think the entire Department reduced use of the prison system. This group, then, must have believed that DCS programs other than Fort Des Moines caused *increased* use of the prison system, rather than reduced commitments.

According to the archival data, practitioners were correct in perceiving that DCS development coincided with decreased prison commitments from Polk County but the actual reduction was not as great as would be suggested by the strength of the opinions in Table 10.1. One cannot be entirely certain that there *was* a long-lived decrease, as the decrease in prison commitments for felons occurred only in the final year of archival data, 1973 (in the four years sampled, the percentage of felons directly committed to prison was 27.9 percent, 34.5 percent, 34.1 percent, and 16.9 percent). While few indictable misdemeanants were sent to prison in any of the four sample years (with a high of 6.5 percent in 1969), none were committed in 1973. Including probation revocations as prison commitments increased the percentage of cases resulting in imprisonment (to 38.2 percent, 45.5 percent, 43.2 percent, and 25.4 percent, respectively), but the year-to-year pattern remained the same. Analysis of sentencing options by statistical risk showed that the offenders having the highest risk for recidivism were frequently being sent to the residential facilities rather than prison.

The strong feelings of practitioners about the diversionary aspects of the DCS were somewhat difficult to assess. While some were aware of the NCCD evaluations which found a high level of diversion from prison, such knowledge was not extensive, particularly outside the DCS. Others who had been supportive of DCS programming may simply have concluded that community-based corrections programming *should* be diversionary in nature, and thus the DCS must so qualify. Even law enforcement respondents showed some support for the DCS fostering diversion in the cases of minor or first-time offenders. Some police officers who were critical of the DCS may have also perceived significant diversion from the prison system, but diversion which they did not support.

Many of the opinions about the DCS seem to have been based on practitioners' experience with a small number of cases, occasionally combined with ignorance of judicial sentencing practices. In this scenario, the police may have remembered one or more specific cases which resulted in sentences to DCS programs, believing that prison sentences surely would have resulted in the absence of the DCS. Actual sentencing practices before DCS development, however, may have been such that the offender, in fact, would not have been incarcerated. Similar case-by-case experiences also may have influenced the opinions of other practitioners. In any event, it was clear in the interviewing that one segment of the justice system was not necessarily cognizant of the operation of another.

Net-Widening

One of the most frequently discussed, but least often analyzed, aspects of programs which purport to divert offenders from the justice system is net-widening: either bringing more minor offenders into contact with alternative programs, or keeping more major offenders in programs for longer periods of time. Norval Morris (1974) has provided some of the most colorful language on this topic, with his reference to "cream puff" clients entering alternative programs. Such clients, of course, appear very likely to succeed in these programs, as they also would have probably succeeded in the absence of such programs.

Pre-Trial Net-Widening

Net-widening was one of the topics addressed in the interview survey portion of this research, with most of the questions dealing with this topic centered on the development of Release-With-Services, the supervised pre-trial release program of the DCS. The conclusion one reaches after considering the practitioners' responses is that, while net-widening was mentioned by some as one of the effects of the DCS, net-widening did not appear to be a major issue in the minds of most Polk County justice system practitioners.

Release-With-Services could have functioned to widen the correctional net primarily by drawing defendants away from Pre-Trial Release—basically release on recognizance—and into Release-With-Services, a program involving supervision, or at least referral for services. While practitioners from all portions of the system reported that RWS did indeed siphon some defendants from PTR, such sentiments were voiced primarily by legal system respondents, particularly the public defenders, five of seven of whom reported this occurrence.

Because the public defenders serve the system's most serious clientele, it is not surprising that they were most likely to identify net-widening as an RWS impact. A high proportion of the public defender clients have been released through RWS in Des Moines, sometimes to the chagrin of attorneys who believed that their clients frequently could have been released safely on recognizance. Offender Advocate staff members sometimes also saw Release-

With-Services being filled with low-risk clients while their own high-risk clients remained in jail. Other pre-trial net-widening sentiments were not widespread, as only in the County Attorney's office did more than ten percent of those responding to this question mention siphoning clients from PTR as a Release-With-Services impact.

Despite those who perceived that RWS pulled clients away from Pre-Trial Release, there was still general consensus throughout the system that Release-With-Services released higher-risk clients than PTR. Even some of those who earlier had indicated that PTR lost some clients due to RWS supported this position, apparently thinking that it was only the "worst" of PTR clients who were siphoned off to RWS (see Table 10.2).

Table 10.2

Survey Item: Does Release-With-Services Have Higher-Risk Clients Than Pre-Trial-Release?
(in percent)

	*N**	*No*	*Yes*
Des Moines Police	54	24.1	75.9
Sheriff's Office	25	20.0	80.0
Total Law Enf.	79	22.8	77.2
County Attorney	15	0.0	100.0
Offender Advocate	7	28.6	71.4
Private Attorneys	29	24.1	75.9
Judges	10	0.0	100.0
Total Legal Sys.	61	14.8	85.2
Dept. of Corr. Serv.	37	11.4	88.6

Excludes don't know and not applicable

The archival data tended to support practitioners' perceptions that RWS released higher-risk defendants than PTR. Using both the Iowa Risk Assessment System and another Iowa Scale developed to predict judicial sentencing practices (an "offender attribute scale"), there was little change over the four years in the risk or severity of those released through PTR. RWS releasees' scores on both of these items, however, tended to resemble those of detainees, not PTR. The average "offender attribute rating" over the four years for PTR releasees was 10.4, for example, while scores for detainees and RWS clients were 29.3 and 29.6. Risk assessment results were similar, with an average four-year PTR score of 17.0, detainees 38.0, and Release-With-Services 44.1.

Another facet of net-widening involves the encouragement of plea bargaining, which some think accompanies the development of non-secure programming such as that in the DCS. The rationale here is that, with increasing use of probation and other alternatives to incarceration, defendants are more likely to plead guilty, facing less likelihood of imprisonment or jail.

In only two agencies—the County Attorney's Office and the Offender Advocate—did respondents *not* perceive increases in plea bargaining due to DCS development. Increases in plea bargaining were perceived most often by employees of the DCS, although there were few differences among the DCS, both law enforcement agencies, private attorneys, and judges.

There appeared to be differing reasons for the sentiments of the County Attorney and the Offender Advocate staffs. The County Attorney's staff most likely saw little increase in plea bargaining largely because of an office policy which discourages bargaining. The County Attorney himself, when responding to this question, indicated that his office did not plea bargain. While his staff did not dismiss plea bargaining so resolutely, a majority indicated that the development of community-based corrections did not influence plea bargaining.

Offender Advocate responses here must be attributed to the nature of that office's clientele. Representing more "hard core" clients who may be facing lengthy incarceration even after plea negotiation, OA attorneys often may not be in a position where their clients would greatly benefit by pleading guilty. Clients of private attorneys, on the other hand, are less likely to be faced with imprisonment, and may have less to lose by pleading guilty.

The archival data here tended to support those who perceived no increase in plea negotiation due to DCS development. While external factors such as a rising caseload may have had greater impact than DCS development, the tracking data showed no increase in convictions for any category of offender during the four years examined. Overall, the conviction rate for sample members dropped steadily through the period, declining from 72.4 percent in 1969 to 68.7 percent in 1973. As expected, conviction rates for felonies were lower than for either misdemeanor group.

Accounting for most convictions, guilty pleas also changed little over the four years. The only evidence that the DCS might have influenced bargaining was that there appeared to be less of a drop in guilty pleas for felons than misdemeanants, with the former more often referred to DCS programming.

General Perceptions on Net-Widening

In a specific attempt to determine perceptions about any net-widening impact of DCS development, respondents were asked if there were more minor offenders receiving correctional treatment than had previously been true. Responses to this question were uniform to the extent that a strong majority in each agency perceived more minor offenders entering correctional programs since DCS development, as shown in Table 10.3.

Table 10.3

Survey Item: Are there More Minor Offenders Receiving Correctional Services Now?
(in percent)

	N*	More	Same	Fewer
Des Moines Police	65	86.1	10.8	3.1
Sheriff's Office	26	96.2	3.8	0.0
Total Law Enf.	91	89.0	8.8	2.2
County Attorney	17	82.3	11.8	5.9
Offender Advocate	7	85.7	0.0	14.3
Private Attorneys	28	96.4	3.6	0.0
Judges	11	81.8	18.2	0.0
Total Legal Sys.	63	88.9	7.9	3.2
Dept. of Corr. Serv.	36	94.4	2.8	2.8

*Excludes don't know and not applicable

One clear perception of respondents was that there have been more minor offenders entering the corrections system since DCS development than before. Whether this increase was perceived as being due to the DCS or to increasing arrests, however, is another issue. It appears that most respondents perceived the latter as being the primary reason for increasing use of community programming. There were few respondents who indicated clearly that the existence of the DCS was responsible for this increase, although it could be maintained honestly that the existence of a local probation staff increased the likelihood of sentences of probation for drunken drivers in the late 1970s.

Respondents also suggested in a follow-up question that they perceived this increase in minor offenders in corrections programming as beneficial. As is evident from Table 10.4, a majority of respondents in each agency perceived that either *some* or *most* of the minor offenders they perceived entering the correctional system were actually in need of services or supervision. Thus, they voiced little concern about the increased loss of liberty for offenders. Most net-widening due to the development of the DCS was perceived by practitioners as positive because it resulted in the provision of services or supervision to individuals who could benefit from them.

Table 10.4

Survey Item: If More Minor Offenders Are Receiving Correctional Services Now, Do They Really Need Them?

(in percent)

	N*	Most Need Help	Some Need Help	Few Need Help	Other
Des Moines Police	56	41.1	21.4	23.2	14.3
Sheriff's Office	25	36.0	24.0	28.0	12.0
Total Law Enf.	81	39.5	22.2	24.7	13.6
County Attorney	14	85.7	0.0	14.3	0.0
Offender Advocate	6	33.3	50.0	16.7	0.0
Private Attorneys	27	18.5	40.7	37.0	3.7
Judges	9	11.1	88.9	0.0	0.0
Total Legal Sys.	56	35.7	39.2	23.2	1.8
Dept. of Corr. Serv.	34	38.2	28.2	17.6	5.9

*Excludes don't know and not applicable

Perhaps this is the nature of the "helping" professions: if an agency is providing services to individuals—regardless of whether they desire the services—the services are presumed by practitioners to be needed. Only rarely during the interviewing was there any concern voiced about the potentially damaging aspects of net-widening. Even when such concern was voiced—with, for example, the movement of drunken drivers toward probation instead of fines—it was not unusual for respondents to note that the overall impact of such a change was positive, despite its net-widening aspects.

Also of note is that most of those apparently concerned about net-widening were attorneys. Among that group, it is not surprising that those from the Offender Advocate office—who, to some degree, fit the stereotype of the "liberal public defender"—were more likely to identify the negative aspects of net-widening than any other group.

Protection of the Public

Protection of the public has long been one of the foremost goals of the corrections system, be it in the form of minimizing new offenses by program participants during the correctional process, or modifying offender behavior in such a way as to reduce criminal activity following discharge. The debate on the advantages and disadvantages of correctional programming frequently hinges on public protection, and evaluations of correctional programming, as underscored by Lipton, Martinson, and Wilks' (1975) review of correctional evaluations, almost always assess some measure of public protection.

There has been continuing debate about the degree to which correctional programming has been effective in reducing criminal activity by its clients. Critics of community-based programming note two particular problems in this regard: (1) that retaining offenders in the community typically involves little incapacitation, and may permit continued criminal activity during the correctional process; and (2) that there is a lack of deterrence involved in community-based corrections, because punishment is not necessarily a specific goal of such programs. Critics of more traditional programming counter these allegations with the contention that prisons, rather than punishing offenders for their behavior, are instead schools of crime which force offenders to associate with other offenders, reinforcing criminal values and facilitating an education in crime.

The archival data collected for this research included information both on within-program arrests and post-program recidivism. In examining these data, rates were developed for each correctional program to which offender sample members were sent, providing information not only on DCS clients, but also those of the State correctional system, the County Jail, and several other local alternatives.

Re-arrest rates were examined both in their raw form and with controls for statistical risk. Within-program rates were developed controlling for the length of program participation. Sample members were followed up to 12 years following exit from the justice system, with a usable follow-up period for the entire sample of five years.

The interview portion of the research also examined public protection in detail, inquiring about failure-to-appear rates, probation revocation rates, and re-arrest rates during the pre- and post-trial periods. In addition to asking respondents to estimate the percentage of clients re-arrested in a given program, the interview schedule also asked if re-arrest rates were "very high", "high", "about right", "low", or "very low", in an attempt to make respondents judge the acceptability of re-arrest rates. This series of questions resulted in some of the most interesting data in the research.

The archival data provided a backdrop against which to assess the interview results. In a nutshell, analyses showed that failure-to-appear rates were low among the offender samples, as were within-program re-arrest rates. Although more offenders entered the DCS programs during the last two years examined here, there did not appear to be any significant negative impact on community safety. Probationers showed a within-program re-arrest rate of about one per every 1,000 client-days, and the residential facilities, holding higher-risk offenders, showed one re-arrest for about every 850 client-days. Post-program recidivism rates were also low, particularly for new violent crimes, either using the raw recidivism data or when controlling for risk.

To some degree, the archival pre-trial re-arrest data were consistent with those in the early NCCD evaluations of the DCS, as a relatively high rate of re-arrest was found for Release-With-Services. The data here, however, suggested that these higher RWS arrest rates were due both to the length of the pre-trial period for

RWS clients, and to the generally high-risk nature of RWS clientele. When the length of the pre-trial period and risk were controlled, the RWS within-program re-arrest rate appeared comparable to the rates for bond and Pre-Trial Release. On the other hand, the data did not show that RWS was effective in *reducing* within-program re-arrests. In other words, the within-program re-arrest rate for RWS was about what one would expect, given the nature of the Program's clientele.

Pre-Trial Protection of the Public

As might have been expected, the law enforcement officers interviewed for the research tended to be somewhat more negative about the public protection aspects of community-based corrections than other respondents. This was true for both failure-to-appear rates and re-arrest rates, but not for revocation rates. Law enforcement officers were significantly more likely (p<.05) to report a failure-to-appear rate of 5 percent or higher.

Employment was not always a good predictor of responses, as there was some variation within specific divisions of agencies. While the median estimated failure-to-appears rate in the DCS was 3.75 percent, two divisions of the program reported rates of over 6 percent. Similarly, three divisions of the Des Moines Police Department reported medians which were lower than one would expect from the Department's overall median (5.15 percent).

Surprisingly, although the police had just reported higher overall rates of failure to appear than other respondents, they did not score significantly higher on a question about the acceptability of failure-to-appear rates. All agencies, with the exception of the judiciary, rated failure-to-appear rates as being between "about right" and "low". Judges, perhaps patting themselves on the back for wise decisions in approving release, were most impressed with the low rate of failure to appear, with a median score between "very low" and "low".

In combination, the results of these two questions suggested that law enforcement officers in Polk County were more likely than other justice system officials to perceive high rates of failure to appear (over 5 percent) as acceptable. Although 35 percent of the police samples believed the local rate of failure-to-appear to be ten percent or higher, only 10 percent perceived that rate to be either "high" or "very high." Less than two percent of the DCS sample perceived the FTA rate to be over 10 percent, on the other hand, but 14 percent perceived the rate to be too high.

Consistent with their perceiving relatively high rates of failure to appear, the law enforcement samples also reported significantly higher (p<.001) rates of pre-trial re-arrest than other samples. Respondents from the Des Moines Police Department reported a median 16.67 percent pre-trial re-arrest rate, and the Sheriff's Office median was 22.5 percent, while no other group reported a median above 10.83 percent.

The police also were significantly more likely (p<.001) to say that the pre-trial re-arrest rate was "high" or "very high." This was particularly true in the Sheriff's office, half of whom reported the re-arrest rate to be "high." Within the law enforcement samples, however, there were some puzzling differences, as those most likely to be "on the line" (Uniform Division in the DMPD and Patroland Detectives in the PCSO) were those most likely to report the re-arrest rate as being acceptable.

To conclude this section on the public safety aspects of pre-trial programming, it was evident from survey responses that law enforcement practitioners tended to be more negative about defendants' activities during the pre-trial period when those activities were most likely to be observed by the police. Officers tended to perceive higher rates of re-arrest during the pre-trial period than other respondents, and also were more likely to report that rates of re-arrest were unacceptably high. In the case of failure to appear for trial, however—an area less likely to involve law enforcement—officers tended to report higher rates than other practitioners, but less often perceived those rates as unacceptable.

Those perceiving the most favorable rates of arrest and failure to appear were those who bore the most responsibility in bail and pre-trial programming: typically judges and pre-trial employees of the DCS. In matters of pre-trial policy, then, there were clear differences among justice system practitioners which appeared to be based upon their location and responsibilities in the system.

Post-Trial Protection of the Public

Questions dealing with the post-trial public safety aspect of the DCS pertained to probation and the Fort Des Moines Facility. The probation questions dealt with revocation and re-arrest rates, and with the acceptability of those rates. In asking about revocation rates, the writer expected to find that law enforcement personnel would perceive higher rates than others, consistent with their previous view that rates of pre-trial re-arrest and failure to appear were higher than perceived by others. In fact, while the two jail staffs perceived high rates of revocation (22.5 percent median for DMPD and 20.0 percent for PCSO), the highest *agency* medians were found for judges and the public defender attorneys.

One of the apparent reasons for this finding was the law enforcement perception that many probationers were not receiving adequate supervision, and had to be arrested for very serious crimes before probation was likely to be revoked. A number of times during interviewing, law enforcement respondents indicated that the revocation rate was not as high as it ought to be because re-arrest frequently did not lead to revocation.

This law enforcement perception was underscored when respondents were queried about their assessment of the acceptability of the revocation rate. Contrary to what was found for pre-trial programs, law enforcement personnel perceived *lower* revocation rates than did other respondents. This was particularly so among Des Moines police, a somewhat surprising result because in other areas the Sheriff's staff tended to be the most critical of DCS programs. One explanation for this discrepancy is that with more DCS clients living in the City, the Des Moines police were probably more likely than Sheriff's deputies to arrest DCS clients.

When specifically asked about probation re-arrests, respondents followed the pattern seen previously for pre-trial programming. Both police agencies reported high median rates of re-arrest (25.2 percent for DMPD and 22.5 percent for PCSO). While respondents from the Offender Advocate also reported a high median (25 percent), their responses can be explained, in part, by the high-risk clientele they served.

These same three groups were the most likely to perceive the rate as being "high" when asked about the acceptability of probation re-arrests. While other attorneys and the judges generally thought the re-arrest rate was "about right," four of the seven Offender Advocate attorneys reported the re-arrest rate as high. In no other agency did more than half the respondents indicate that the rate was anything above "about right". Similar to what was found in several earlier questions, the jail staffs of the two law enforcement agencies indicated more concern about probation re-arrests than others in their departments.

The police also perceived re-arrests in the Fort Des Moines Facility as higher than others, and again the Offender Advocate attorneys also reported high rates. Respondents in each of these agencies, however, perceived the Fort Des Moines re-arrest rate to be lower than that of probation. Respondents throughout the system perceived the highest re-arrest rates in probation. Residential and pre-trial programs were typically identified as having the lowest overall rate of re-arrest.

In judging the acceptability of Fort Des Moines' re-arrest rate, respondents tended to believe that the facility protected the community well, as most (law enforcement included) reported that the re-arrest rate at Fort Des Moines was "about right." Throughout the system, respondents were more likely to find the Fort Des Moines re-arrest rate to be acceptable than either probation or pre-trial rates. The probation re-arrest rate was assessed as least acceptable by five of the seven groups of respondents, while the Des Moines police and judges perceived the pre-trial rate as least acceptable.

Among the questionnaire's final questions were two attempting to elicit respondents' assessments of the DCS as either helping or hurting community safety. Any corrections program, in order to be considered a success, must be seen as adequately ensuring public protection, regardless of any rehabilitative accomplishments. In other words, a program's accomplishments in other areas always will be balanced against any failures in protecting the public. While it is certainly possible to protect the public to such a degree that the other aims of corrections—rehabilitation, reintegration, or whatever—are subverted, public protection must be considered foremost.

Asked whether the DCS has affected community safety in Polk County, respondents voiced a wide variety of opinions that tended to reflect opinions on a number of other questions. Law enforcement officers responded with an anticipated answer most frequently: that community safety has been reduced because of the lack of incapacitation inherent in community corrections.

According to these respondents, because of the number of alleged and convicted offenders on the streets—on pre-trial release, probation, or in non-secure facilities —community safety has been reduced. The only other response of this type heard with any frequency was that community safety has fallen because criminals were not receiving adequate punishment, and deterrence has been reduced.

Within the legal system and DCS, the most frequent assessment was that community safety has been enhanced because offenders were receiving more assistance than was available before the DCS developed. Those voicing this sentiment apparently supported the idea that treatment can assist in modifying offender behavior, thus reducing the likelihood of further criminal involvement.

The second most-frequent response to this question—and the most frequent heard from private attorneys and the Offender Advocate staff—was that community corrections has not affected community safety either positively or negatively. Those expressing this opinion appeared to espouse a combination of beliefs based on the replies above—that, while there might be some greater danger due to more offenders being released, this danger was balanced by the rewards of successful treatment or supervision. Some legal system and DCS respondents also indicated that the structure and supervision received by DCS clients also improved community safety. Statistical tests performed on the table resulting from this question showed a significant difference ($p < .001$) between law enforcement responses and those of the other combined agencies.

Summary on Public Protection

It was clear from the responses of the practitioners interviewed for this study that there were wide differences of opinion about the degree to which community-based corrections in Des Moines had either reduced or enhanced public safety. As was true when diversion was examined, it appears that the law enforcement personnel were most critical of the DCS, and were most likely to perceive that community safety had been jeopardized by the development of community-based corrections. There were, however, some areas in which the opinions of law enforcement personnel did not differ significantly from others. Although they generally reported higher rates of re-arrest and failure to appear, the police did not report that these rates were any less *acceptable* than the other groups. In other words, while the police reported higher rates of re-arrest and failure to appear, they were just as likely as others to report that these rates were "about right" for programs of the DCS type.

Like other respondents, the police also tended to see the most jeopardy stemming from probation, rather than those released during the pre-trial period or residing at Fort Des Moines. As a rule, respondents reported the highest (and least acceptable) rates of re-arrest on probation, and the lowest coming from residents of Fort Des Moines.

The survey data thus suggested that protection of the community has not been a burning issue resulting from the establishment of community-based corrections in Des Moines. Respondents seemed generally satisfied with the performance of the DCS in protecting the public from criminal behavior of those under supervision of community-based programs in Des Moines.

Taken in combination with earlier results, the interview data suggest that the more negative opinions of law enforcement personnel toward the DCS were due to factors other than high rates of within-program recidivism. One question, in particular, provided a clue to some law enforcement sentiments, as a number of officers reported decreases in public protection stemming from a *lack of punishment* and deterrence in community-based corrections. Much less frequent were allegations that employees of the DCS were not doing their jobs by providing inadequate supervision of clients.

Thus, law enforcement opinions of the public protection aspect of community-based corrections appeared based more on the philosophical underpinnings of such programs than in any inadequacies of day-to-day operation of programs. Regardless of the success in maintaining low rates of within-program re-arrests and post-program recidivism, it appeared from these data that a number of officers would be critical of community-based programming simply based on the lack of incapacitation and punishment involved.

Conclusions

This study was an example of the type of evaluations or assessments that developed along with the emphasis on community treatment. In addition to assessing the impact of community treatment on individual subjects (i.e., did it *work*?), the study attempted to determine its effects both on the processing of offenders and on existing agencies in the system. In other words, the study not only attempted to examine changes in offender behavior, but also organizational changes in operating agencies.

Unlike Lerman's (1975) re-examination of the California Probation Subsidy and Community Treatment Program, this research provided some reason to be optimistic about the impact of community-based programming. Data presented here suggested that the development of the Polk County Department of Court Services facilitated diversion from prison and jail for some groups of offenders, showed little evidence of having increased control of the correctional system over more minor offenders, yielded recidivism rates no worse than more secure programming, and generally cost less to operate per client.

One of the more interesting discoveries in this research was the relative ignorance of justice system practitioners about the operation of portions of the system other than their own. A major problem faced in this research was the time elapsing between the archival data (1969-73) and interviewing of justice system practitioners (in 1980 and 1981), so it is conceivable that the discrepancies evident between archival data and practitioners' opinions may have been due to changes in system operation occurring in the mid- to late 1970s. The magnitude of many of the discrepancies here, however, would suggest practitioner misperception; system operation would have had to change dramatically in order to make their responses correct.

One example of practitioner misperception was illustrated in opinions pertaining to reductions in detention and imprisonment. While the archival data suggested very little reduction in detention stemming from the development of Release-With-Services, a majority of respondents perceived that program both having a significant impact on the use of detention and releasing higher-risk clientele than Pre-Trial Release. Archival data supported the latter belief, as the characteristics of RWS clients showed them to be high-risk, but also showed that Release-With-Services had a significant diversionary impact only on defendants scoring fewer than five PTR points, especially if they had been charged with felonies. Impact on prison population stemming from probation and the residential facilities was similar. While respondents tended to see a general diversion from prison, the archival data showed diversion to have occurred most frequently for those scoring fewer than five PTR points.

More recent Iowa data further suggest that system operation has not changed dramatically since the period examined here, and that the practitioners interviewed here were frequently misinformed. Analyses of statewide sentencing data from the late 1970s and mid-1980s (e.g., Fischer, 1979, Stageberg, 1986) have suggested that whatever diversion occurred during the early DCS years did not increase as time passed. The observations of the author would also suggest that the developmental years of the DCS were truly its most experimental years, with more risk-taking and dynamism than in later years, when the program matured and became more set in its ways. This particularly may have been the case for Release-With-Services; interviews with some of those involved in the development and early operation of that program suggested strongly that conservatism became more common in the late 1970s.

Practitioners' responses frequently appeared to be dependent upon their employment, and often there appeared to be widely-held beliefs in one portion of the system which were seldom mentioned in another. On occasion, these opinions were largely department- or division-based; opinions of Polk County Jail staff were frequently near-unanimous, but they very well may have been in opposition to opinions expressed among the Des Moines police and, on occasion, at odds with other Sheriff's staff.

These differences of opinions *within* individual segments of the justice system in Des Moines were largely unanticipated. While it was expected that disagreements would be evident between prosecutors and defense attorneys, for example, the sometimes prominent differences between agency opinions in law enforcement came as a surprise. Generally speaking, respondents in the Des Moines Police Department tended to be non-judgmental about community-based corrections in Des Moines, and tended to support (both in specific and general terms) the objectives of the DCS. While some of the Sheriff's staff supported the DCS in philosophic terms, they were much less supportive of specific DCS programming. Thus, it would be unfair to imply a "law enforcement attitude" about community-based corrections; responses could not always be predicted based upon the employment of respondents. In some areas, it even would be unfair to characterize an "agency attitude," as opinions from one division to another might differ substantially. Much of the reason for these discrepancies appeared due simply to the professional relationships between the DCS and the agencies employing respondents. Because employees in different divisions of a single agency may have different types of associations with DCS staff and clients, their opinions about the DCS may be different than those in other portions of their agencies. Jail employees, for example, have seen DCS program failures more frequently: those who are re-arrested, those who are brought to jail pending revocation, or those who create a disturbance in the residential facilities and have to be returned to jail. While other law enforcement personnel may come into occasional contact with problem DCS clients, the jailers probably see them daily. One apparent result was that the jail personnel appeared to harbor the most negative opinions about community-based corrections.

Even in the jail staffs, however, the Sheriff's Office tended to be more critical of the DCS than the Des Moines Police. Some of this difference may be accounted for by the history and location of Pre-Trial Release, the first of the DCS programs to emerge. This program has been the least controversial of the DCS programs, probably due to its historical concentration on low-risk defendants and those with less serious charges. Until 1984, PTR operated out of the Des Moines Municipal Courthouse, which also houses the Police Department. Due to its location, employees of PTR have come into regular contact with the Des Moines police during the program's 20-year history, providing ample opportunity for personal, as well as professional, relationships to develop. While one still may hear law enforcement comments that defendants "beat me out the door," there was little apparent resentment about this possibility among the municipal police, who appeared to recognize that their primary responsibility had been fulfilled prior to the decision to release on bail. Because the bail decision is beyond their control, they indicated relatively little concern about it.

Location and history also can explain partially some of the ill will about the DCS within the County Jail staff. Prior to 1984, PTR had little contact with County Jail personnel, as most defendants released through PTR were released prior to transfer to the County. Thus, the two programs having the greatest impact on the Jail have been Release-With-Services—which tends more often to accept high-risk defendants—and Fort Des Moines, another alternative for higher-risk clientele.

It also appeared that the opinions of program administrators tended to influence the opinions of their staffs. This, again, was more evident in the County Jail, where the chief administrator is an acerbic, long-time employee who holds very negative feelings about the DCS. As many of the opinions voiced by jail employees echoed the sentiments of this administrator, it was unusual to find jail staff who were complimentary about community-based corrections.

Opinions in the jail did not appear philosophically-based, for while there was criticism of some of the high-risk clients of Release-With-Services or Fort Des Moines, there was also resentment about the Department's failure to release some defendants perceived as low-risk by jailers. Jail staff, rightly or wrongly, perceived considerable inconsistency in DCS release practices, particularly in Release-With-Services. Criticism of Fort Des Moines, on the other hand, centered around transportation and a perceived lack of control at the Facility.

Another finding stemming from the interview data was supportive of one conclusion in Lerman's (1975) research on the California Probation Subsidy and Community Treatment Project (CTP). Lerman found that correctional practitioners in California's juvenile justice system tended to regard the increasing control resulting from CTP in the context of providing beneficial treatment rather than as a mechanism resulting in any widening of the justice system's span of control. In that context, the practitioners had little apparent concern about the potential over-reach of the justice system. The Polk County practitioners interviewed for this study were similar in their judgment about potential net-widening. Concern over net-widening was limited to few respondents, the largest portion of whom were attorneys serving the Offender Advocacy

Office (public defender). Many practitioners perceived net-widening as one result of DCS development, a notable contrast from the conclusion reached based upon the archival data. There was little apparent concern over this expansion of justice system activity; however, most respondents perceived *some* or *most* of the minor offenders drawn into contact with the correctional system as being in need of the correctional services or supervision provided by the DCS. As was true in Lerman's assessment, these practitioners viewed correctional system activity in the context of providing services to offenders, not in the context of expanding control of the justice system. One conclusion stemming from the interview data is that justice system practitioners sometimes tend to develop opinions about other components of the justice system based upon isolated incidents which may have been due either to personal experiences or those of colleagues. If this is true, a single incident may significantly shape practitioners' opinions about other segments of the justice system, and an isolated incident—which may have been a freak occurrence or a one-time event—may haunt a program for years. Some of these incidents, through re-telling, may become so embellished as to have little relationship to fact, resulting in opinions based largely on fiction. This may, in fact, account for some of the opinions practitioners voiced in the interviewing segment of this research.

Another intriguing finding stems from the re-arrest and follow-up data, both of which showed acceptably low rates of re-arrest among DCS clients. Justice system practitioners tended to report that re-arrests and recidivism were low in the DCS programs, although (not surprisingly) the police perceived the highest rates of re-arrest. Despite reporting higher rates of re-arrest than other respondents, officers interviewed for this study did *not* perceive re-arrest rates to be any less *acceptable* than other respondents. While one might have speculated that the police would be less tolerant of re-arrests than others, in fact the opposite was true. Do the police perhaps become inured to arrests because they participate in so many? Do they regard re-arrests philosophically, as it appears they do the decision to release on bail before trial? Whatever the answers to these questions, law enforcement respondents perceived DCS re-arrest and recidivism rates as being generally acceptable, despite reporting higher rates than other practitioners.

A majority of practitioners, system-wide, viewed the public protection aspects of the DCS as acceptable.

Another interesting point pertaining to within-program re-arrest rates has to do with a comparison between probation and the residential facilities. The archival data showed about one probation re-arrest for each 1,000 client-days, while the residential facilities, with considerable higher-risk clientele, had about one re-arrest for each 850 client-days. Asked which program had the highest rate of re-arrest, however, interview respondents generally reported that more problems were presented by probationers, not those in the facilities. While the initial reaction to this finding might be that the practitioners were incorrect about re-arrest rates, an intervening variable may have accounted for the discrepancy here. Although there is a finite limit to the number of clients residing in the residential facilities (about 65 men and 20 women), no such specific limit exists for probation. At the end of July, 1985, for example, the DCS caseload included 79 residential facility clients and 2,009 probationers. Projecting the re-arrest rates found here onto the current probation and residential facility populations yields two re-arrests of probationers each day, and one re-arrest of residential facility clients each 11 days. This result should also be taken in the context of residential facility lengths of stay of about six months, compared to two years for probationers. Thus, the practitioner assessment, in this case, appears to have some basis in fact.

The interview data suggested that much of the negative attitude of law enforcement toward the DCS was not necessarily due to any perceived weakness in DCS program (e.g., high re-arrest rates, lack of control over clients), but rather a perceived lack of punishment inherent in community programming. Certainly there were practitioner complaints about inadequate supervision and control in the DCS, but these were not widespread. When given the opportunity to pinpoint the reason for any dissatisfaction with the DCS, however, many police officers referred to a lack of punishment. A similar sentiment was expressed with regard to recognizance release versus cash bond; many thought that non-appearance and re-arrests should be lower on cash bond because defendants had something to lose, and were threatened with potential punishment. Many police apparently did not perceive adequate punishment in probation, as the loss of freedom accompanying probation was judged to be low. Some similar opinions were expressed about Fort Des Moines, even though clients' movement there is much more restricted than is true on probation. A number of officers, particularly in the Sheriff's Office, referred to Fort Des Moines as "a joke." Their attitude thus seems traditionally hard-line: "you do the crime, you do the time."

This research can be instructive to students of community-based corrections and to those who are either planning or operating community-based programs. It shows, among other things, the importance of communication between segments of the justice system, as the study suggests that opinions about programs can sometimes be based on something other than fact. The research also warns that opinions about justice system programming are not necessarily monolithic within any segment of the system; individual experiences and direct contacts between individuals working in the system can carry great weight in developing credibility for a program. Thus, the care administrators and employees take in ensuring an understanding of their programs within other segments of the system can play a vital role in a program's success or failure.

Notes

[1]The DCS Women's Facility in 1973 was just beginning operation, but it historically has handled only a small number of clients, and does not play a major role in providing an alternative to traditional handling of criminal justice clientele.

Discussion Questions

1. What implications would Stageburg's study have for the findings of Musheno et al. in Chapter 9?

2. What are some of the major reasons that official perceptions appear to be inaccurate? If you were a community corrections manager, what strategies might you use to overcome such misperceptions? Would doing away with these misperceptions necessarily be a good thing, if you were concerned with program support?

3. In the introduction to Part III, we suggested that Chapter 9 is descriptive of vertical relationships and Chapter 10 of horizontal relationships. Why? When are vertical relationships likely to be more important to the success of a program? When are horizontal relations likely to be more critical?

Chapter 11
The Community Field and the Future of Community Corrections

David E. Duffee and Edmund F. McGarrell

In this book, we have taken the position that community corrections can be productively understood as an aspect of community, rather than as a particular form of correctional activity. That is, we have proposed that many significant community corrections policy issues and research questions—and particularly those related to the formulation and implementation of programs—can be framed within a knowledge of community structure and dynamics. Simultaneously, although of less immediate concern in this volume, was the related assumption that attempts to set off community correction as distinct from other (institutional) types of corrections can set up misleading policy and research activity.

We are not claiming that the framework is new, but only that the attention to the community as an interactional field has been underemphasized relative to its impact on certain correctional outcomes. We are not proposing that the community field offers comprehensiveness. It certainly does not. The employment of community variables in the examination of corrections is essentially a political/economic and administrative approach to correctional issues. There are many correctional problems fruitfully investigated without reference to such variables. But we do think that the routine addition of the variables of concern here to the normal correctional lexicon would indeed increase our understanding of correctional problems.

We suspect that the employment of community field variables in the study of correctional organizations and programs would highlight powerful forces that always have been of great concern to, or at least always have been of great influence on, correctional administrators. This is not, of course, to suggest that research should follow practice. But if research should be able to describe practice, there may be considerable utility.

A recent conference offers one example of this greater attention to community in practice than in research. The School of Criminal Justice at the University at Albany recently assembled a number of its alumnae/i who work in policy and research positions in criminal justice agencies. The theme of this conference was "The Relationship Between the School of Criminal Justice and its Graduates Who Work in Criminal Justice." The first issue addressed at this event was the identification of problems faced at work for which the study of criminal justice had not supplied the relevant knowledge and skills. The answers—across participants from a wide array of agencies and official functions—were quite uniform. A graduate education in criminal justice received high marks for provision of generic skills such as policy analysis, critical thinking, and research methods, and was praised for promotion of knowledge acquisition in areas such as criminology, criminal law and procedure, and the interaction of criminal justice agencies. But, according to practitioners, this education had been deficient in its examination of budgeting, administration, and the politics of criminal justice organizations.

There are limits to what any educational institution can and should do. However, initial responses by several faculty to the identified areas of "deficiency" appeared overly defensive. One response was that the practitioners had identified competencies which were not related to "criminal justice" but were, instead, areas covered in fields such as public administration. Another was that the deficiencies were "practical" rather than "academic" or "research" issues.

But there may be quite legitimate ways of integrating the practitioners' concerns into the study of criminal justice without changing the field of inquiry. A great deal of criminal justice research has focused on individual offenders and decisions about individual offenders. The criminal justice academic community has, by and large, focused on cops and robbers, even when it has examined systemic interactions, such as the impact of the pretrial release decision on sentencing or the impact of inmate program participation on parole decisions. If administrators focus instead on distribution of public resources across agencies or the impact of agency image on its ability to mount programs, it is difficult to see why such concerns should be dismissed as "practical" rather than "academic."

What Have the Case Studies Shown?

The approach used in these case studies demonstrates one means of examining policy formulation and program implementation processes. These case studies have shared a common concern for the location of correctional organizations in a two-dimensional network: a vertical dimension connecting front-line operations to centers of power and resources and a horizontal dimension connecting organizational units to each other.

The three chapters in Part One were chosen not only to demonstrate the importance of these dimensions in descriptions of what happens in corrections but also to suggest the complex interplay between these dimensions within the interactional fields of particular programs. In Chapter 2, Duffee's history of one halfway house depicts the imprecision of the common notion of "community" resistance. The struggles of "Help House" in "Capital City" are a portrayal of simultaneous support and resistance and both local and state levels. The fragmentation at the state level permitted the organization to gain a foothold in the local service network, as resources from one state organization were used to overcome reluctance of another state organization. However, as the temporary funds from the state legislature gave out, growing dependence on the state executive agencies altered fundamentally the location and function of Help House in the community.

The chapter by Lilly and Ball on electronic monitoring demonstrates the varying relationship between state governments and recent developments in correctional programs. In Kentucky, electronic monitoring proceeded quickly in one county but did not receive strong or uniform endorsement from state policymakers. In Florida, the initiative was apparently from the state level outward and with considerably greater initial attention to purpose. While the impetus may be quite different for electronic monitoring and halfway houses, the location of both monitoring programs and halfway houses in community fields would appear critical to implementation.

Finally, in Chapter 3, Maher examines the development of the federal probation system as a dual-authority system. While federal probation has often been used as an example of a "centralized" system, Maher's review suggests the inaccuracy of this designation and more importantly, the incapacity of the federal probation system to meet the expectations often imposed upon its perceived centralized capacity. What we appear to have instead is a very complex organization in which some functions are centralized and others are quite localized. To miss this characteristic of the federal system might be to miss a critical source of its strength as well as to overlook critical constraints on its operations.

In Part Two, Jester, Harlow and Nelson, and Duffee and Wright examine several different types of correctional organization and several different facets of operation. Jester's examination of correctional technologies indicates considerable similarities both within groups of probation and parole organizations and between probation and parole. She also indicates that the horizontal integration of probation and parole agencies into local service networks is a key distinction between agencies which emphasize surveillance and those which emphasize shaping of the client's environment.

A critical follow-up question would concern the directionality of relationships among organizational goals, technology, and the constraints imposed on the organization by its location on the horizontal axis of the community field. Do agencies choose punitive or deterrence goals, then select a control technology, and then purposefully avoid interaction with service agencies? Or, is it possible that correctional organizations located in an inhospitable environment, or in settings with few services to offer, adapt to that situation by relying on goals and technologies which can be implemented with less external cooperation? We suspect that internal choices and external relationships are interactive over time and generally are mutually reinforcing.

For example, Thomson, McAnany, and Fogel (1982) have found that small, rural probation departments often cannot depend on a rich array of service agencies. As a consequence, rural probation departments are likely to engage in a greater proportion of direct officer-client interactions than is the case in urban departments. Certain urban departments may face the same dependence on internal resources because of a hostile rather than a meager environment. In either case, as an agency becomes inwardly focused and self-reliant, it may help to foster the conditions by which it remains isolated. The other two chapters in this section provide some evidence for the mutual causal chain between internal and community variables.

Harlow and Nelson review a number of different paths taken by probation administrators in the struggle to secure and husband resources. Some of these are internal strategies, such as implementation of classification systems, which often have external consequences. Classification systems, when hooked to supervision strategies, may increase the frequency or accuracy of service referrals, and may increase the effectiveness of budget presentations (Clear and O'Leary, 1983). Others are decidedly external "repositioning" strategies (Kimberly and Quinn, 1984), in which probation administrators realign their agency with different agencies and redesign services to accommodate these new coalitions.

In the last chapter in this section, Duffee and Wright argue that transition services are a function of changing organizational position in specific community fields. The relative weakness of transition services in Minnesota in the mid-1970s would appear to be strongly influenced by the weak position of privately contracted services in the correctional network. The state decision to place a moratorium on the development of such programs (that is, to halt the vertical resource flow) was related to the illegitimacy and ineffectiveness of the halfway houses as service providers. Similarly, the vertical positioning of halfway houses in Michigan and Pennsylvania was critical to the types of services developed in those two states. The significantly greater autonomy of the Pennsylvania centers from central control appears to have permitted the greater attention to local networking. Later, the strong position of the centers in their local networks appears to have reinforced their autonomy. A recent visit to the Pennsylvania centers in 1988 provided evidence that the centers have remained essentially unchanged since 1978, despite major changes in the prison system which surrounds them. As a result, the Community Services Division of the Department of Correction has expanded by adding private centers operated on contract rather than attempting to alter the size or function of the public centers.

Maher's observations on the federal probation service and the contrasts between Michigan and Pennsylvania state-run centers highlight one important aspect of the community interactional field. The identification of an organization as part of a state or federal bureaucracy can be a misleading indicator of an organization's position in a community field. The horizontal and vertical placement of an organization should always be directly measured, not assumed from its association with federal, state, or local government. Secondly, the cases described by Harlow and Nelson, and Duffee and Wright, stress the dynamic nature of community field position. The network position of these organizations changed over time. Some of these changes were unintended by the community correctional officials. Others were consciously adopted strategies to gain support or ward off enemies.

In Part Three, the cases examine policy change and program implementation. Following the theory developed by Miller and Ohlin (1985), McGarrell's study of New York's juvenile corrections system indicates that horizontal interconnections are important at the policy level as well as at the service delivery level. Enacted policy, particularly at points of policy shifts, often entails a change in the structure of policy coalitions. Such coalitional shifts are often associated with politicized scandals—that is, with known errors in operation which cannot be deflected or explained as the responsibility of an erring individual. The McGarrell and Harlow and Nelson chapters indicate that coalitional shifts may follow resource crises (such as the near bankruptcy of New York City or the tax revolt in California) in addition to scandals. In either case, major and sudden shifts in perceived legitimacy or available resources may be required to break up the mutually reinforcing tendencies of external field constraints and internal adjustments.

If, as Miller and Ohlin (1985) assert, the community field in corrections tends toward gridlock, executive policy choice is quite limited, although not absent. Timing becomes critical to strategic choice and to interagency rearrangements. The "practical" lesson for administrators is not to seize the day but to know which day to seize. If this is part of the practical wisdom which separates practitioners and academics, its essence is not a distinction between practical and theoretical interests. Instead, it indicates a distinction between theoretical knowledge and knowledge about the opportunities to apply theory. Correctional researchers may supply information on the efficacy of programs on the basis of outcomes at the individual level of analysis. Administrators may have to bank rather than ignore such information, until such time as an unfreezing of the community field permits the political use of empirical findings as a rationale for remobilization of resources. Political use could also be a field for theory development. To that end, we could use more studies of strategic and coalitional shifts in corrections. Studies of program operation and outcome are certainly important, but studies of how and when such information gets used in the alteration of the community field should also be important (Hagan, 1989).

The other two chapters in this section provide complementary views of developing community fields. The first, by Musheno and colleagues, examines community corrections acts in the 1980s. The second, by Stageberg, contrasts official perceptions and actual program effects of the first comprehensive local corrections department in the 1960s. Community Corrections Acts, or state subvention of local corrections activity, was pioneered in California with the Probation Subsidy and significantly improved by David Fogel and Ken Schoen in Minnesota. CCA's following the Minnesota design, are perhaps the best example of executive attempts to manipulate community fields. The design includes both a new vertical relationship and altered horizontal interactions at the local level. The Musheno evaluation suggests that the vertical dimension has been altered to varying degrees in different states, with significant implications for local commitments to program implementation. Apparently Colorado has provided greater participation to local correctional officials than is the case in Oregon and Connecticut. In other words, Colorado has gone further than Connecticut and Oregon in altering the vertical relationship between program operators and central policymakers.

In contrast, Stageberg focuses on horizontal interaction among the many different Des Moines agencies which have some stake in the formation of the Department of Correctional Services. His study provides evidence that agency position in the criminal justice process will provide the vantage points from which inter-agency evaluations are made. Additionally, he gives us the important reminder that what agency officials see is not necessarily what they get. Stageberg's evaluation would suggest that new correctional agencies do not always alter the horizontal flow of information across agencies. In the Des Moines case, at least in the formative years, the new programs appear to have followed the habits and patterns of interagency interaction and perception built into the prosecution and sentencing process. The new programs were included in this system, but did less to alter offender flow and outcome than initially supposed. In contrast, CCA states, especially those following the Minnesota lead, apparently require new kinds of interaction among the horizontally linked agencies at the local level. As the officials take on responsibility to make policy decisions as a group, their perceptions of each other, and their interactions, reportedly change. Whether these reported community field changes are institutionalized or deteriorate over time, and whether they have any major impacts on correctional outcomes, are issues that await further study.

New Elements in the Community Field

As we look towards the next century, a number of changes in typical community fields appear important. Among the most interesting for their potential impact are (1) variations in the state-local, or vertical, dimension; (2) developments in technology and associated influence of the technology industry on correctional policy; (3) the spread of user fees; (4) the continued development of privatization, or, perhaps more appropriately, the changing mix and functions of public and private networks.

The Vertical Dimension

Community corrections has rarely been a local business, because communities are not politically or economically self-contained. Community corrections has usually been a sharing of state authority and resources with local public and private authority and resources. Throughout the 20th century, the trend has been toward greater control at the state level. This trend has promoted greater uniformity and standardization in correctional programs across localities. This has been done in some states by the state assumption of previously local services. In other states, while local government agencies are still formally in charge, the services they render are increasingly regulated by the state, often in return for some reimbursement of expenses.

The apparent divergence from this trend introduced by CCA's following the Minnesota model is the decoupling, to some extent, of the state's interest in quality of services from the choice of content of services. This decoupling is only a matter of degree—as the CCA states have required a correctional policy at the local level which lessens use of state institutions. But what the localities do to achieve this reduction is left—apparently—to them, within broad limits. Whether these claims for increased local discretion will hold up over time is an interesting question.

Technology and the Technology Industry

Electronic monitoring is one of the few examples of a hard technology in an otherwise labor intensive, people-to-people enterprise. Some correctional administrators are very enthusiastic, others are quite cautious. Technology vendors are extravagantly hopeful. While massive amounts of research have examined the impact of technology on other aspects of social life, we have few precedents in corrections with which to gauge the potential influence of this new wave.

The electronic monitoring technology complicates the field of forces influencing corrections. It adds to the interest groups which may have some hand in shaping correctional policy and the distribution of resources, the private businesses which develop, manufacture, and market the equipment. How influential these new interests prove to be is an important question. Certainly one element of the answer will hinge on the dynamics of the technology market. Can a few large firms corner the technology and concentrate their power across a large number of correctional systems, or will there be a high degree of competition across a larger number of firms? If large, national firms gain a foothold, then they may have significant influence on policymaking at central levels. Once particular correctional agencies have invested in this technology, how will the investment influence their future policy and program decisions?

User Fees

Closely associated with, but not limited to, the employment of electronic monitoring is the apparent increase in the requirement that correctional clients pay for the cost of supervision. User fees for government services are certainly not unusual—tourists may be charged for use of public parks, travelers for use of some roads and bridges, golfers traversing government-owned courses. The demand that offenders pay for some portion of probation or parole supervision may be defended as just another of those practices. However, critics will assail the justification that offenders are just like other users of public services.

Is an offender truly a client or consumer who, in the absence of the public service, would either forego the service or seek more expensive private alternatives? If governments wish to argue that the service purchase analogy is apt, will the correctional department also have to demonstrate that the fee-paying client has indeed received a service of value equal to the fee paid? Should correctional services be available only to persons who can afford a particular fee? To what extent will user fees raise the same type of equity issues that have been inherent in the traditional cash bail system? Should user fees be imposed on an income-based sliding scale, similar to the European day fine? Will user fees emerge as the principal form of punishment for certain types of cases?

As is the case with the introduction of the technology industry, user fees for the consumption of punishments may change the position of the correctional agency in the community field. It would appear to change the source of and the availability of certain correctional options. To what extent is the increased use of user fees promoted by technology salesmen in the attempt to promote the adoption of their equipment?

Privatization

The final change in the community field which we will note here is an apparent trend toward privatization of some correctional services. There are numerous explanations of why privatization is occurring, including the greater flexibility and variety provided by private contractors and the reduced start-up time and lesser cost. Most of these claims are assertions rather than empirical findings. Moreover, it is difficult to make comparisons between private-public networks and purely public networks in operation, cost, and outcome.

It is likely that the impact of the increased utilization of private contractors will be highly variable, depending in part upon the emerging position of the private organizations in the vertical and horizontal community matrix. Reports from the Massachusetts juvenile deinstitutionalization program point to two extremes. On the one hand, the Massachusetts Department of Youth Services dominated and, at least in some early cases clearly exploited, small private organizations begun by ideologically driven, young service providers. One result was that the Department amassed a wide array of program types with which it could match the needs of various youngsters. Another result was that many young service workers were literally driven to exhaustion and out of business. At the other extreme, some Youth Services contractors were large and wealthy and sought to use their influence to dictate policy to the department (Miller and Ohlin, 1985). A different set of observations in the same state provided evidence that private community organizations were not necessarily more successful than state organizations in establishing group homes. The crucial variables influencing start-up had to do with how agency leaders approached community leaders about the rationale and operations of the proposed programs (Coates and Miller, 1974).

Such observations indicate that privatization is a variegated phenomenon. Private organizations vary in their placement in community fields, just as government organizations do. Hence, we need to ask what advantages and disadvantages different types of public and private agencies provide in different types of community fields.

The Impact of Technology, Fees, and Privatization on Correctional Populations and Correctional Fields

The emergence of electronic monitoring and related technologies, expansion of user fees, and re-emergence of privately run corrections also raise issues related to the size of the correctional population, the mix of institutional and non-institutional programs for different types of offenders, and the tension between state and local forces.

The fact that these programs and services are gaining popularity at a time during which correctional institutions have experienced two decades of unprecedented growth, raises concerns over the ultimate scope of the correctional system. Traditional concerns over alternatives to incarceration acting in a net-widening fashion are magnified by a new set of alternatives that allow surveillance without capital construction costs, that are being advocated by private entrepreneurs with clear self-interest in expansion, and whose costs may be offset by user fees.

A similar concern relates not only to the size of the correctional population but to the characteristics of clients involved in private versus public correctional programs. There is some evidence from the juvenile justice system that a two-tiered system is emerging with white youths going to privately-run programs and minority youths being confined in public institutions (Krisberg, et al., 1987). A similar observation has been made about the socioeconomic distribution of public and private policing services (Comment, 1988). An important issue thus arises over the extent to which these programmatic developments in community corrections lead to the emergence of a racially and socioeconomically based two-tiered system.

Beyond the fundamental justice and equity issues raised by these trends, these developments are also likely to raise issues that have been of prime interest throughout this book. That is, evidence of a two-tiered system is likely to be a source of state-local tension and conflict. One can easily imagine, in a relatively homogeneous community, the conflicting perspectives and interests of local criminal justice officials committed to electronic monitoring for predominantly white clients juxtaposed with a director of the department of corrections or an appellate court judge reviewing conditions in increasingly minority-filled state prisons. The point is that these trends, if continued, are likely to raise significant tensions over local concerns for autonomy and central concerns for system equity.

The Reemergence of Community as a Focal Concern

The organization of community in relation to crime and criminal justice was a major concern prior to World War II. As the states and the federal government asserted increasing control in the 1950s and 1960s, policy and research attention shifted away from community. Recently, community organization has reasserted itself as an issue in crime (Sampson, 1987, Sampson and Groves, 1989; Leighton, 1988); policing (Trojanowicz and Moore, 1988; Bayley and Skolnick, 1987); and neighborhood crime prevention (Wilson and Kelling, 1989; Skogan and Maxfield, 1981).

Correctional research has generally taken a less sophisticated approach to community, since it has often focused on the non-residential character of some programs rather than on the positioning and repositioning of correctional organizations in the community interactional field. Perhaps one reason for the slower development of community study in corrections is the complexity introduced in needing to consider simultaneously the structure and dynamics of communities and the structure and dynamics of large state correctional bureaucracies. Although community policing research also involves some large police organizations intersecting with various groups and organizations in metropolitan areas, the fact that municipal police policy appears more local than state-level correctional decisions may enhance the study of police as an important community institution. The development of community research in corrections may do well to follow leads in education or welfare, which are community functions carried out by a mixture of local, state, and federal agencies. To the extent that the cases in this collection demonstrate the potential for a community perspective across a wide variety of correctional programs and time periods, it is a contribution to that development.

REFERENCES

Aaronson, David E., B.H. Hoff, P. Jaszi, N. Kittrie, and D. Sarri (1977). *The New Justice: Alternatives to Conventional Criminal Adjudication.* Washington, DC: U.S. Government Printing Office.

Adams, Stuart (1977). *Evaluative Research in Corrections: A Practical Guide.* U.S. Department of Justice, Law Enforcement Assistance Administration, National Institute of Law Enforcement and Criminal Justice (March).

Administrative Office of the U.S. Courts (1975). *Division of Probation.* Probation Division, Washington, DC (April 1).

_____ (1979). *Guide to Judicial Policies and Procedures, Probation Manual.* Washington, DC, X-A (February).

_____ (1979). *1979 Annual Report of the Director.* Washington, DC.

_____ (1980). *Federal Probation Workload Statistics.* Statistical Analysis and Reports Division (February 5).

_____ (1984). *1984 Annual Report of the Director.* Washington, DC: Administrative Office of the U.S. Courts.

Allen, Harry E., Eric Carlson and Evalyn Park (1979). *Critical Issues in Adult Probation.* U.S. Department of Justice, Law Enforcement Assistance Administration, National Institute of Law Enforcement and Criminal Justice, Washington, DC.

Allen, Harry E. and Clifford E. Simonsen (1986). *Corrections in America.* NY: Macmillan.

Austin, James and Barry Krisberg (1981). "Wider, Stronger and Different Nets: The Dialectics of Criminal Justice Reform," *Journal of Research in Crime and Delinquency* 18(1):165-196.

_____ (1982). "The Unmet Promise of Alternatives to Community Corrections," *Crime and Delinquency* 28:396-411.

Bailey, Walter (1966). "Correctional Outcome: An Evaluation of 100 Reports," *Journal of Criminal Law, Criminology and Police Science* 57 (June) 153-160.

Ball, Richard A. and J. Robert Lilly (1983a) "Home Incarceration: An Alternative to Total Incarceration." IX International Congress on Criminology, Vienna, Austria.

_____ and J. Robert Lilly (1983b). "The Potential Use of Home Incarceration with Drunken Drivers." Presented at the Annual Meeting of the American Society of Criminology, Cincinnati.

—— and J. Robert Lilly (1985). "Home Incarceration: An International Alternative to Institutional Incarceration," *International Journal of Comparative and Applied Criminal Justice* 9:85-97.

—— and J. Robert Lilly (1986a). "The Potential Use of Home Incarceration with Drunken Drivers," *Crime and Delinquency* 32:187-196.

—— and J. Robert Lilly (1986b). "A Theoretical Rationale for Home Incarceration," *Federal Probation*, 50:17-24.

——, C. Ronald Huff, and J. Robert Lilly (1988). *House Arrest and Correctional Policy: Doing Time at Home.* Newbury Park, CA: Sage Publications.

Barry, Donald M. and Alexander Greer (1981). "Sentencing Versus Prosecutorial Discretion: The Application of a New Disparity Measure," *Journal of Research in Crime and Delinquency* 18(2):254-271.

Bates, Sanford (1950). "The Establishment and Early Years of the Federal Probation System," *Federal Probation* (June): 18.

Bayley, David and Jerome Skolnick (1987). *The New Blue Line.* NY: The Free Press.

Beaumont, Gustave and Alexis Toqueville (1964). *On the Penitentiary System in the United States and Its Application in France.* Carbondale, IL: University of Southern Illinois Press.

Beccaria, Cesare (1963). *On Crime and Punishments.* Indianapolis: Bobbs-Merrill. (originally published in 1764)

Becker, Howard S. (1963). *Outsiders.* NY: Free Press.

Beckley, Loren et al. (1981). " Presentence Investigation Report Program," Sacramento, CA: American Justice Institute.

Benson, J.K. (1975). "The Interorganizational Network as a Political Economy," *Administrative Science Quarterly* 20:229-249.

Bentham, Jeremy (1789) (1973). *An Introduction to the Principles of Morals and Legislation.* Garden City, NY: Anchor Books.

Berk, Richard A., Harold Brackman and Selma Lesser (1977). *A Measure of Justice: An Empirical Study of Changes in the California Penal Code, 1955-1971.* NY: Academic Press.

—— and Peter H. Rossi (1977). *Prison Reform and State Elites.* Cambridge, MA: Ballinger.

Blackmore, John (1978). "Minnesota's Community Corrections Act Takes Hold," *Corrections Magazine* 4(1):46-56.

Blumberg, A. (1970). *Criminal Justice.* Chicago: Quadrangle Books.

Brewer, G. (1974). "The Policy Sciences Emerge to Nurture and Structure a Discipline," *Policy Sciences* 8:239-44.

Briar, Scott (1973). "The Age of Accountability," *Social Work* 18 (January).

Bureau of Correctional Evaluation (1975). "Community Corrections in Iowa: An Alternative to Tradition," Des Moines, IA: State of Iowa Department of Social Services.

———— (1975). "Community Corrections in Iowa: Preliminary Findings," Des Moines, IA: State of Iowa Department of Social Services.

———— (1976). "Corrections in Iowa: A System of Growth and Change," Des Moines, IA: State of Iowa Department of Social Services.

Campbell, Donald T. (1979). "Degrees of Freedom and the Case Study," in Thomas D. Cook and Charles S. Reichardt (eds). *Qualitative and Quantitative Methods in Evaluation Research*. 49-67. Beverly Hills, CA: Sage.

Carlson, Eric and Evalyn Park (1979). "Issues in Probation Management," *Critical Issues in Adult Probation*. Law Enforcement Assistance Administration, Washington, DC (September).

Chambliss, William J. (1964). "Sociological Analysis of the Law of Vagrancy," *Social Problems* 12:67-77.

Chapman, Brian (1970). *The Police State*. London: Praeger.

Chappell, Richard (1950). "The Federal Probation System Today." *Federal Probation* (June): 30.

Clear, T.R. and Vincent O'Leary (1983). *Controlling the Offender in the Community*. Lexington, MA: D.C. Heath and Company.

Coates, Robert and Alden D. Miller (1974). "Neutralization of Community Resistance to Group Homes," in Y. Bakal (ed.) *Closing Correctional Institutions*. Lexington, MA: Lexington Books.

———— and Lloyd Ohlin (1978). *Diversity in a Youth Correctional System*. Cambridge, MA: Ballinger.

Cohen, Stanley (1985). *Visions of Social Control*. Cambridge, England: Polity Press.

Cole, George F. (1973). *Politics and the Administration of Justice*. Beverly Hills, CA: Sage.

Community Corrections Resource Programs, Inc. (1974). "State of Michigan Corrections Centers, Analysis and Recommendations," Ann Arbor, MI: Community Corrections Resource Programs, Inc.

Comment (1988). "Future Focus for Policing," *Liaison* (July-August) 16-20.

Comptroller General of the United States (1977). *Probation and Parole Activities Need to Be Better Managed.* Washington, DC: U.S. General Accounting Office.

Conrad, John (1973). "Reintegration: A Practice in Search of a Theory," in *Reintegrating the Offender into the Community: Criminal Justice Monograph.* Washington, DC: U.S. Department of Justice.

Correctional Services News (1981). Albany, NY: New York State Department of Correctional Services, January: 6.

_____ (1981). Albany, NY: New York State Department of Correctional Services, April: 2.

"Costs of Institutional Care for Delinquent Adolescents in New York State: Crises and Legislative Remedies" (1973). Albany, NY: A Report Prepared by the Assembly Ways and Means Committee.

Council of State Governments (1977). *Reorganization of State Corrections Agencies: A Decade of Experience,* Lexington, KY: Council of State Governments.

Critchley, T.A. (1967). *A History of Police in England and Wales 900-1966.* Great Britain: The Garden City Press.

Cruthirds, Thomas (1976). "Management Should Be Accountable Too," *Social Work* 20 (September): 417-419.

Cullen, Francis T. and Karen E. Gilbert (1982). *Reaffirming Rehabilitation.* Cincinnati, OH: Anderson Publishing Co.

Dell Apa, F. et al. (1976). "Advocacy, Brokerage, Community: The ABC's of Probation and Parole," *Federal Probation* 40(4):37-44.

Diana, L. (1960). "What is Probation?" *Federal Probation* 24 (December): 20-24.

Downs, George W. (1976). *Bureaucracy, Innovation, and Public Policy.* Lexington, MA: D.C. Heath and Company.

Dressler, D. (1969). *Practice and Theory of Probation and Parole.* NY: Columbia University Press.

Duffee, David E., K.N. Wright, T. Maher (1974). "Final Evaluation Report: Pennsylvania Bureau of Correction Community Treatment Centers," Harrisburg, PA: Governor's Justice Commission.

_____ Thomas Maher and Steve Lagoy (1977). "Administrative Due Process in Community Pre-parole Programs," *Criminal Law Bulletin* 13(5):383-400.

_____ and R. Richard Ritti (1977). "Correctional Policy and Public Values," *Criminology* 14(4):439-448.

———— Peter Meyer and Barbara Warner (1977). *Offender Needs, Parole Outcome, and Administrative Structure in the Pennsylvania Bureau of Corrections Division of Community Services.* Harrisburg, PA: Governor's Justice Commission.

———— (1980). *Explaining Criminal Justice.* Cambridge, MA: Oelgeschlager, Gunn and Hain.

———— and R. Richard Ritti (1980). "Public Opinion and the Formulation of Correctional Policy," in D.E. Duffee, *Correctional Management.* Englewood Cliffs, NJ: Prentice-Hall.

———— and Barbara D. Warner (1980). "Interorganizational Behavior and Correctional Programming," in D.E. Duffee, *Correctional Management,* Englewood Cliffs, NJ: Prentice Hall.

———— and John Klofas (1983). "Organizational Mandates and Client Careers: An Examination of Penal Policy," in Richard H. Hall and Robert E. Quinn (eds.), *Organizational Theory and Public Policy.* Beverly Hills, CA: Sage.

———— (1984). "Models of Probation Supervision," in P. McAnany, D. Thomson and D. Fogel (eds.), *Probation and Justice.* Cambridge, MA: Oelgeschlager, Gunn and Hain.

———— (1985). "The Interaction of Organizational and Political Constraints on Community Pre-release Program Development," in E. Fairchild and V. Webb (eds.) *The Politics of Crime and Criminal Justice.* Beverly Hills, CA: Sage..

————, and D. Clark (1985). "The Frequency and Classification of the Needs of Offenders in Community Settings," *Journal of Criminal Justice* 13:243-268.

Edwards, G.C. (1980). *Implementing Public Policy.* Washington, DC: Congressional Quarterly Press.

Evien, Victor (1975). "The Federal Probation System: The Struggle to Achieve It and Its First 25 Years," *Federal Probation* (June).

Fantini, M. and Gittell, M. (1973). *Decentralization: Achieving Reform.* NY: Praeger.

Federal Judicial Center (1973). *Probation Time Study.* Washington, DC: Federal Judicial Center.

———— (1976). *An Introduction to the Federal Probation System.* Washington, DC: Federal Judicial Center, 76-1.

Fischer, D.R. (1979). "Crime and Criminal Justice in Iowa, Vol. IX: Prison Population," Des Moines, IA: State of Iowa, Statistical Analysis Center.

Flynn, Leonard E. (1986). "House Arrest: Florida's Alternative Eases Crowding and Tight Budgets," *Corrections Today* (July): 64-68.

Fogel, David (1975). *"...We Are the Living Proof..."* Cincinnati, OH: Anderson Publishing Co.

Foucault, M. (1977). *Discipline and Punish* (A. Sheridan, trans.) NY: Random House.

General Accounting Office (1976). *State and County Probation Systems in Crisis.* Washington, DC: U.S. Government Printing Office.

Gerety, Pierce (1980). "A French Program to Reduce Pretrial Detention," *Crime and Delinquency* 26:22-34.

Gettinger, Stephen (1983). "Intensive Supervision: Can It Rehabilitate Probation?" *Corrections Magazine* 9(2):6-18.

Glaser, D. (1964). *The Effectiveness of a Prison and Parole System.* Indianapolis: Bobbs-Merrill.

_____ and A. Wohl (1970). "Pilot Time Study of the Federal Probation Officer's Job," in R. Carter and L. Wilkins (eds.), *Probation and Parole* (First Edition). NY: John Wiley.

Glisson, Charles (1975). "The Accountability Controversy," *Social Work* 20 (September): 417-419.

Gooch, H. Richard (1977). *Continuing Education Needs of U.S. Probation Officers.* Unpublished Ph.D. Dissertation. Ohio State University.

Gottfredson, Michael and Don Gottfredson (1980). *Decision-Making in Criminal Justice.* Cambridge, MA: Ballinger.

_____ (1979). "Treatment Destruction Techniques." *Journal of Research in Crime and Delinquency* 16(1):39-54.

Grant, Douglas and Marguerite Grant (1959). "A Group Dynamics Approach to Non-Conformity in the Navy," *Annals of the Academy of Political and Social Science* 322:126-155.

Greenberg, David F. (1975). "Problems in Community Corrections," *Issues in Criminology* 7:1-10.

Grupp, S. (1971). *Theories of Punishment.* Bloomington, IN: Indiana University Press.

Hagan, John (1989). "Why Is There So Little Criminal Justice Theory? Neglected Macro-and Micro-Level Links Between Organization and Power," *Journal of Research in Crime and Delinquency,* 26.

Hahn, Paul (1975). *Community-Based Corrections and the Criminal Justice System.* Santa Cruz, CA: Davis.

Hall, G. and S. Loucks (1977). "A Developmental Model for Determining Whether the Treatment is Actually Implemented," *American Educational Research Journal* 14:263-76.

Hall, Jerome (1952). *Theft, Law and Society*. Indianapolis: Bobbs-Merrill.

Handler, Joel F. and Julie Zatz, eds. (1982). *Neither Angels Nor Thieves: Studies in Deinstitutionalization of Status Offenders*. Washington, DC: National Academy Press.

Harland, A.T. (1982). "An Empirical Examination of Criminal Restitution in Law and Practice," Albany, NY: Unpublished doctoral dissertation, University at Albany, State University of New York.

Harlow, N. and E.K. Nelson (1982). *Management Strategies for Probation in an Era of Limits*. Washington, DC: National Institute of Corrections.

Heiland, R.E. and W. Richardson (1957). *Work Sampling*. NY: McGraw-Hill.

Heinz, John R., Robert W. Gettleman and Morris A. Seeskin (1969). "Legislative Politics and the Criminal Law," *Northwestern Law Review* 64:277-358.

Hylton, J.H. (1982). "Rhetoric and Reality: A Critical Appraisal of Community Correctional Programs," *Crime and Delinquency* 28:314-373.

Informatics, Inc. (1973). "Pennsylvania Community Treatment Services: An Evaluation and Proposed Evaluation Information System." Rockville, MD: Informatic, Inc.

Irwin, J. (1980). *Prisons in Turmoil*. Boston: Little, Brown and Co.

Jacobs, J. (1976). "The Politics of Corrections: Town/Prison Relations as a Determinant of Reform," *Social Service Review* 50(4) (December): 623-631.

Jenkins, W.O. et al. (1973). *A Longitudinal Follow-Up Investigation of the Post-Release Behavior of Paroled or Released Offenders*. Elmore, AL: Rehabilitation Research Foundation.

Johnson, P. and W. Kime (1975). "Performance Screening—A New Correctional Synthesis." Lansing, MI: Michigan Department of Corrections, mimeo.

Keenan, Michael (1980). Regional Administrator, Administrative Memorandum, Washington, DC (January).

Killinger, G., H. Kerper, and G. Cromwell (1976). *Probation and Parole in the Criminal Justice System*. St. Paul, MN: West Publishing Company.

Kimberly, John R. and Robert E. Quinn (eds.) (1984). *Managing Organizational Transitions*, Homewood, IL: Itwin.

Klein, Malcolm (1979). "Deinstitutionalization and Diversion of Juvenile Offenders: A Litany of Impediments," in N. Morris and T. Tonry (ed.), *Crime and Justice: An Annual Review of Research.* Chicago: University of Chicago Press.

Klofas, John and David E. Duffee (1981). "The Change Grid and the Active Client: Challenging the Assumptions of Change Assumptions of Change Agentry in the Penal Process, *Criminal Justice and Behavior* 8(1):95-118.

Krisberg, Barry, Ira M. Schwartz, Gideon Fishman, Zvi Eisikowits, Edna Guttman and Karen Joel (1987). "The Incarceration of Minority Youth," *Crime and Delinquency* 33:173-205.

Ku, Richard (1980). *American Prisons and Jails Volume IV: Supplemental Report Case Studies of New Legislation Governing Sentencing and Release.* Washington, DC: National Institute of Justice.

Langan, Patrick (1985). *The Prevalence of Punishment.* U.S. Department of Justice, Bureau of Justice Statistics. Washington, DC: U.S. Government Printing Office.

Langworthy, Robert (1986). *The Structure of Police Organizations.* NY: Praeger.

LeClair, Daniel P. (1979). "Community-Based Reintegration: Some Theoretical Implications of Positive Research Findings." Paper Prepared for Annual Meeting of the American Society of Criminology, Philadelphia.

Leighton, Barry (ed.) (1988). "The Concept of Community in Criminology: Four Papers from Canada," *Journal of Research in Crime and Delinquency* 25: entire issue.

Lemert, Edwin M. (1970). *Social Action and Legal Change.* Chicago: Aldine.

Lerman, Paul (1975). *Community Treatment and Social Control.* Chicago: University of Chicago Press.

Levine, J., M. Musheno, and D. Palumbo, (1980). *Criminal Justice: A Public Policy Approach.* NY: Harcourt, Brace and Jovanovich.

Levine, R.A. (1972). *Public Planning: Failure and Redirection.* NY: Basic Books.

Lichtman, O.M. and S.M. Smock (1981). "The Effects of Social Services on Probationer Recidivism: A Field Experiment," *Journal of Research in Crime and Delinquency* 18(1):81-100.

Lilly, J. Robert, Richard A. Ball and Jennifer Wright (1987). "Home Incarceration with Electronic Monitoring in Kenton County, KY: An Evaluation," in Belinda R. McCarthy (ed.), *Intermediate Punishments: Electronic Surveillance and Intensive Supervision.* Monsey, NY: Willowtree Publishers.

_____ and W. Robert Lotz (1986). "Electronic Jail Revisited," *Justice Quarterly* 3:353-61.

Lipsky, M. and M. Lounds (1976). "Citizen Participation in Health Care: Dilemmas of Government Induced Participation," *Journal of Health Politics, Policy and Law* 1: 85-111.

_____ (1980). *Street-Level Bureaucracy.* NY: Russell Sage Foundation.

Logan C. and S. Rausch (1985). "The Emergence of Private Enterprise Prisons," *Justice Quarterly* 2:303-318.

Majone, G. and A. Wildavsky (1977). "Implementation as Evolution," in Wildavsky, A. (ed.) *Implementation.* Berkeley, CA: University of California Press.

Martinson, Robert M. and J. Wilkes (1977). "Save Parole Supervision," *Federal Probation* 41:23-27.

_____ (1974). "What Works? Questions and Answers About Prison Reform," *The Public Interest* 35 (Spring): 22-54.

_____ (1971). *Treatment Evaluation Survey.* New York Division of Criminal Justice Services, unpublished study.

Marx, Gary (1981). "Ironies of Social Control: Authorities as Contributors to Deviance Through Escalation, Nonenforcement and Covert Facilitation," *Social Problems* 28:221-246.

Maynard-Moody, S., M. Musheno, D. Palumbo, and A. Oliverio (1987). "Street-Wise Social Policy: Resolving the Dilemma of Discretion and Successful Implementation." Unpublished Paper Presented at the Annual Meeting of the American Political Science Association. Chicago, IL.

McAnany, Patrick, Doug Thomson, and David Fogel (1984). *Probation and Justice: Reconsideration of Mission.* Cambridge, MA: Oelgeschlager, Gunn and Hain.

McCleary, Richard (1978). *Dangerous Men.* Beverly Hills, CA: Sage Publications.

McClintock, F.H., M.A. Walker, and N.C. Savill (1961). *Attendance Centres.* London: Macmillan.

McEwen, Craig (1978). *Designing Correctional Organizations for Youths.* Cambridge, MA: Ballinger.

McGarrell, Edmund F. (1988). *Juvenile Correctional Reform: Two Decades of Policy and Procedural Change:* Albany, NY: State University of New York Press.

McLaughlin, Chester (1975). "The Federal Probation System: An Inside View." *Federal Probation* (June): 32.

Mennel, Robert M. (1973). *Thorns and Thistles: Juvenile Delinquents in the United States, 1825-1940.* Hanover, NH: University Press of New England.

Menninger, Karl (1971). "Love and Hate," in S. Grupp (ed.), *Theories of Punishment.* Bloomington, IN: Indiana University Press.

Meyer, P.B. and B.L. Wayson (1976). "Final Report, Economic Study of Subcontracting for Correctional Services." Washington, DC: Correctional Economic Center, American Bar Foundation.

Michigan Department of Corrections (1977). *Annual Report.* Lansing, MI: Michigan Department of Corrections.

Miller, Alden D. and Lloyd E. Ohlin (1983). *Final Report of Research on Correctional Reforms in the Massachusetts Department of Youth Services.* Boston: Center for Criminal Justice, Harvard Law School.

―――― (1985). *Delinquency and Community.* Beverly Hills, CA: Sage.

――――, Robert B. Coates and Lloyd E. Ohlin (1980). "Evaluating Correctional Systems Under Normalcy and Change," in Malcolm W. Klein and Katherine S. Teilmann (eds.), *Handbook of Criminal Justice Evaluation.* Beverly Hills, CA: Sage.

―――― (1977). *A Theory of Social Reform: Correctional Change Processes in Two States.* Cambridge, MA: Ballinger.

Miller, T. (1984). "Conclusions: A Design Science Perspective," in Miller, T. (ed.) *Public Sector Performance: A Conceptual Turning Point.* Baltimore: Johns Hopkins University Press.

Minnesota Citizen's Council on Criminal Justice (1983). "Adult Incarceration: The Cost to the Minnesota Taxpayers." Minneapolis, MN: Minnesota Citizens' Council on Criminal Justice.

Minnesota Governor's Commission on Crime Prevention and Control (1976). *Residential Community Corrections Programs: A Final Evaluation Report.* St. Paul, MN: Minnesota Governor's Commission.

―――― (1975). *Residential Community Corrections Programs: A Preliminary Evaluation.* St. Paul, MN: Minnesota Governor's Commission (April).

Mitford, Jessica (1973). *Kind and Usual Punishment.* NY: Knopf.

Moore, Joel (1950). "Early Reminiscences," *Federal Probation* (June): 22.

Moos, Rudolph (1974). *Evaluating Correctional and Community Environments.* NY: John Wiley.

Morash, M. (1982). "Introduction: Understanding Criminal Justice Policy Implementation," in Morash, M. (ed.), *Implementing Criminal Justice Policies.* Beverly Hills, CA: Sage.

Morgenbesser, L. and J. Pollock (1980). *Survey of Services Provided by Pre-release Centers in the New York State Department of Correctional Services.* Albany: New York Department of Correctional Services.

Morris, N. (1974). *The Future of Imprisonment.* Chicago: University of Chicago Press.

Mullen, Joan (1980). *American Prisons and Jails Vol I.* Washington, DC: U.S. Government Printing Office.

Musheno, M., D. Palumbo and J. Levine (1976). "Evaluating Alternatives in Criminal Justice: A Public Policy Approach," *Crime and Delinquency* 22:265-83.

Musheno, M. (1982). "Criminal Diversion and Social Control: A Process Evaluation," *Social Science Quarterly* 63:280-292.

Nagel, Stuart, Erika Fairchild and Anthony Champagne (1983). *The Political Science of Criminal Justice.* Springfield, IL: Charles C Thomas.

Nagel, William (1973). *The New Red Barn.* NY: Walker & Co.

National Advisory Commission on Criminal Justice Standards and Goals (1973). *Corrections.* Washington, DC: U.S. Government Printing Office.

National Council on Crime and Delinquency (1972). "Des Moines Model Neighborhood Corrections Project Research Evaluation Report No. 1." Davis, CA: National Council on Crime and Delinquency.

National Institute of Law Enforcement and Criminal Justice (1973). "Community Based Corrections in Des Moines: A Coordinated Approach to The Improved Handling of Adult Offenders," Washington, DC: U.S. Department of Justice.

Nelson, Elmer K. and Nora Harlow (1980). *Responses to Diminishing Resources in Probation: The California Experience.* Los Angeles: University of Southern California School of Public Administration.

Nelson, Elmer, Howard Ohmart and Nora Harlow (1978). *Promising Strategies in Probation and Parole.* Washington DC: National Institute of Law Enforcement and Criminal Justice.

Newman, Graeme (1983). *Just and Painful: The Case for the Corporal Punishment of Criminals.* NY: Free Press/Harrow and Heston.

―――― (1978). *The Punishment Response.* Philadelphia: J.B. Lippincott.

New York Governor's Special Committee on Criminal Offenders (1968). *Preliminary Report.* Albany, NY: State of New York.

New York Times (1987). "3 of 100 Men in Corrections." Jan. 2:10.

New York Times (1987)." Department Priorities: Highlights of Budget." Jan. 6:9.

Office of Technology Assessment (1985). *Electronic Surveillance and Civil Liberties.* Washington, DC: U.S. Office of Technology Assessment.

Ohlin, Lloyd E. (1960). "Conflicting Interests in Correctional Objectives," in Richard A. Cloward et al., *Theoretical Studies in Social Organization of the Prison.* NY: Social Science Research Council.

―――――, Herman Piven and Donald Pappenfort (1956). "Major Dilemmas of the Social Worker in Probation and Parole," *National Probation and Parole Association Journal* 11:211-225.

O'Leary, V. and D. Duffee (1971). "Correctional Policy: A Classification of Goals Designed for Change," *Crime and Delinquency* 17(4):373-386.

Packer, Herbert (1968). *The Limits of the Criminal Sanction.* Stanford, CA: Stanford University Press.

Palumbo, D, M.C. Musheno and S.M. Maynard-Moody (1986). "Public Sector Entrepreneurs. The Shakers and Doers of Program Innovation," in T.S. Wholey, M.S. Abramson, and C. Bellanta (eds.), *Performance and Credibility.* Lexington, MA: Lexington Books.

―――― (1985). *Implementation of Community Corrections in Oregon, Colorado and Connecticut.* Washington, DC: National Institute of Justice.

Palumbo, D., S. Maynard-Moody, and P. Wright (1984). "Measuring Degrees of Successful Implementation," *Evaluation Review* 8:45-74.

Pease, K. (1985). "Community Service Orders," in M. Tonry and N. Morris (eds.), *Crime and Justice, An Annual Review of Research* Vol. 6. Chicago: University of Chicago Press.

Petersilia, J., S. Turner and J.E. Peterson (1986). "Prison Versus Probation in California: Implications for Crime and Offender Rehabilitation." Santa Monica, CA: Rand Corporation.

_____ (1985). *Granting Felons Probation: Public Risks and Alternatives.* Santa Monica, CA: Rand Corporation.

Petersilia, Joan (1985). "Community Supervision: Trends and Critical Issues," *Crime and Delinquency* 31:329-47.

Platt, Anthony M. (1969). *The Child Savers: The Invention of Delinquency.* Chicago: University of Chicago Press.

President's Commission on Law Enforcement and Administration of Justice (1967). *Task Force Report: Corrections.* Washington, DC: U.S. Government Printing Office.

_____ (1967). *Task Force Report: Juvenile Delinquency and Youth Crime.* Washington, DC: U.S. Government Printing Office.

Pressman, Jeffrey L. and Aaron B. Wildavsky (1973). *Implementation.* Berkeley, CA: University of California Press.

Pugh, D.S. (1984). "The Measurement of Organizational Structures: Does Context Determine Form?" in Pugh, D.S. (ed.), *Organization Theory.* NY: Penguin Books: 67-86.

Quinn, R. E. and D.F. Anderson (1984). "Formalization as Crises: Transition Planning for a Young Organization," in J.R. Kimberly and R.E. Quinn, *Managing Organizational Transitions.* Homewood, IL: Irvine.

Reintegration Program Planning Committee (1980). Eastern District of Pennsylvania, Probation Office Memorandum, Philadelphia, PA (March 17).

Roby, Pamela A. (1969). "Politics and Criminal Law: Revision of the New York State Penal Law on Prostitution," *Social Problems* 17:83-109.

Rose, Stephen (1972). *The Betrayal of the Poor.* Cambridge, MA: Schenkman.

Rossi, P., R. Berk, and K. Lenihan (1980). *Money, Work and Crime.* NY: Academic Press.

Rothschild, J. and J. Whitt (1986). *The Cooperative Workplace.* NY: Cambridge University Press.

Rothman, David J. (1980). *Conscience and Convenience: The Asylum and Its Alternatives in Progressive America.* Boston: Little, Brown, and Company.

Rubin, H. Ted (1985). *Juvenile Justice: Policy, Practice and Law* (2nd. ed.). NY: Random House.

Sabatier, P. and D. Mazmanian (1979). "The Conditions of Effective Implementation: A Guide to Accomplishing Policy Objectives," *Policy Analysis* 5:481-503.

Sampson, Robert J. (1987). " Communities and Crime," in M. Gottfredson and T. Hirschi (eds.), *Positive Criminology*. Newbury Park, CA: Sage.

Sampson, Robert J. and W. Byron Groves (1989). "Community Structure and Crime: Testing Social Disorganization Theory," *American Journal of Sociology* 94:774-803.

Schneider, Peter R., William R. Griffith, and Anne L. Schneider (1982). "Juvenile restitution as a sole sanction or condition of probation: An empirical analysis," *Journal of Research in Crime and Delinquency* 19(1):47-65.

Scull, A. (1982). "Community Corrections: Panacea, Progress, or Pretense?" in Abel, R.L. (ed.), *The Politics of Informal Justice*. 99-118. NY: Academic Press.

―――― (1977). *Decarceration: Community Treatment and the Deviant: A Radical View*. Englewood Cliffs, NJ: Prentice-Hall.

Selznick, Philip (1957). *Leadership in Administration: A Sociological Interpretation*. NY: Harper and Row.

Sherman, Michael and Gordon Hawkins (1981). *Imprisonment in America*. Chicago: University of Chicago Press.

Skogan, Wesley G. and Michael G. Maxfield (1981). *Coping with Crime: Individual and Neighborhood Reactions*. Newbury Park, CA: Sage.

Smith, Merrill (1975). "The Federal Probation System: An Organized Perspective," *Federal Probation* (June): 26.

Spergel, Irving A. (1976). "Interaction Between Community Structure, Delinquency, and Social Policy in the Inner City," in M. Klein (ed.), *The Juvenile Justice System*. Beverly Hills, CA: Sage.

Stageberg, P. (1986). "A Re-examination of the Impact of the Des Moines Project on Offender Case Processing and the Justice System in Polk County, Iowa." Albany, NY: Unpublished Doctoral Dissertation, University at Albany, State University of New York.

Stanley, David (1976). *Prisoners Among Us*. Washington, DC: Brookings Institute.

Steggerda R. and P.S. Venezia (1974). "Community-Based Alternatives to Traditional Corrections, The 1973 Evaluation of the Fifth Judicial District Department of Court Services—State of Iowa." Davis, CA: National Council on Crime and Delinquency.

Street, D., R. Vinter and C. Perrow (1966). *Organization for Treatment.* NY: Free Press.

Street, D., G. Martin, and L. Gordon (1979). *The Welfare Industry.* Beverly Hills, CA: Sage.

Studt, Eliot (1972). *Surveillance and Service in Parole.* Los Angeles, Institute of Public Affairs, University of California at Los Angeles.

———— (1973). "Reintegration From the Parolee's Perspective," in *Reintegrating the Offender in the Community, Criminal Justice Monograph.* Washington, DC: U.S. Department of Justice.

Thomson, Doug, Patrick McAnany and David Fogel (1982). *Probation Work in Small Agencies: A National Study of Training Provisions and Needs Volume I.* Chicago: University of Illinois at Chicago Center for Research in Criminal Justice.

Toch, Hans (1977). *Living in Prison: The Ecology of Survival.* NY: Free Press.

———— (1981). *Therapeutic Communities.* NY: Praeger.

Trojanowicz and Mark H. Moore (1988). *The Meaning of Community in Community Policing.* East Lansing, MI: National Neighborhood Foot Patrol Center, Michigan State University.

Tropp, Emanual (1974). "Expectation, Performance and Accountability," *Social Work* 19 (March): 139-148.

U.S. Code Title 18 (1949). Section 3654 (as amended August 2, 1949, C 383,2,63 Statute 491).

U.S. Department of Justice (1978). *State and Local Probation and Parole Systems.* Washington, DC: Law Enforcement Assistance Administration, National Criminal Justice Information and Statistical Service.

Van Buren, David P. (1984). "Rural Justice: A Study of the Prosecution, Adjudication, and Sentencing of Criminal Offenders in Selected Counties of Wisconsin." Albany, NY: Unpublished Doctoral Dissertation, University at Albany, State University of New York.

van den Haag, Ernest (1975). *Punishing Criminals: Concerning a Very Old and Painful Question.* NY: Basic Books.

Venezia, P.S. (1973). "Des Moines Community Corrections Project, Evaluation Project, No. 3." Davis, CA: National Council on Crime and Delinquency.

———— and R. Steggerda (1973)." Residential Corrections: Alternative to Incarceration." Davis, CA: National Council on Crime and Delinquency.

Vinter, R. (1965). "Analysis of Treatment Organizations," *Social Work* 8, 3 (July): 3-15.

———— G. Downs, and J. Hall (1975). "Juvenile Corrections in the States: Residential Programs and Deinstitutionalization: A Preliminary Report." Ann Arbor, MI: University of Michigan School of Social Work.

von Hirsch, Andrew (1976). *Doing Justice: The Choice of Punishments.* NY: Hill and Wang.

Wahl, Albert (1966). "Federal Probation Belongs With the Courts," *Crime and Delinquency* (October 12): 371.

Waller, I. (1979). *Men Released From Prison.* Toronto: University of Toronto Press.

Warren, Marguerite Q. (1967). "The Community Treatment Project: History and Prospects," *Law Enforcement Science and Technology* 1:191-200.

Warren, R., S. Rose, and A. Bergunder (1974). *The Structure of Urban Reform.* Lexington, MA: Lexington Books.

———— (1978). *Community in America.* Chicago: Rand McNally, 3rd edition.

Wilkins, Leslie (1965). *Social Deviance.* Englewood Cliffs, NJ: Prentice-Hall.

Williamson, O.E. (1981). "The Economics of Organization: The Transaction Cost Approach," *American Journal of Sociology* 87:548-577.

Wilson, James Q. and George Kelling (1989). "Making Neighborhoods Safe," *Atlantic Monthly* February: 46-52.

Winterfield, L.A. (1983). "Colorado Community Corrections: A Case of Not Widening the Net." Netherland, CO: Timberline Associates.

Wright, Kevin N. (1985). "Improving Correctional Classification Through A Study of the Placement of Inmates in Environmental Settings." Binghamton, NY: Center for Social Analysis, State University of New York at Binghamton.

———— (1981). "The Desirability of Goal Conflict Within the Criminal Justice System," *Journal of Criminal Justice* 9:209-218.

———— (1979). *An Organizational Approach To Correctional Effectiveness,* Jonesboro, TN: Pilgrimage Press.

Subject Index

Names Index

ABOUT THE AUTHORS

Richard A. Ball is Professor of Sociology at West Virginia University. He received his Ph.D. from the Ohio State University in 1965. He has authored several monographs and approximately 100 articles and book chapters. His research interests include home incarceration, criminological theory, social problems theory, sociology of law, and women inmates. He is co-author of *Criminological Theory: Its Context and Consequences* (1989), and *House Arrest and Correctional Policy*.

David E. Duffee is Professor of Criminal Justice and Dean of the School of Criminal Justice, University at Albany, State University of New York. He has held positions at the Pennsylvania State University and State University of New York at Binghamton. He is the author or co-author of seven books, including *Explaining Criminal Justice* and *Corrections: Practice and Policy*. He has conducted research in prisons, halfway houses, juvenile courts, and public schools.

Nora Harlow has written extensively on issues in criminal justice and corrections, with an emphasis on community-based alternatives to institutionalization. Formerly assistant director of the Information Center of the National Council on Crime and Delinquency and a research associate in NCCD's Research Center, she now works as a consultant on federal research projects, primarily in the field of probation and parole.

Jean Jester received her Ph.D. from the School of Criminal Justice, Nelson A. Rockefeller College of Public Affairs and Policy. She has served as a consultant to the Criminal Justice Institute in New York and was a mediator for the National Center for Correctional Mediation, and Associate Professor of Justice and Law Administration at the Ancell School at Western Connecticut State University. She is the author of numerous articles relating to business, organization and crime, and the monograph, *Legitimate Business and Organized Crime*. Dr. Jester is currently Senior Security Advisor for the International Business Machines Corporation.

James P. Levine is Professor of Political Science at Brooklyn College of the City University of New York, and he is on the Doctoral Faculty in Criminal Justice of John Jay College of Criminal Justice. He has co-authored *Criminal Justice: Law in Action* (New York, John Wiley, 1986) and *Criminal Justice: A Public Policy Approach* (New York, Harcourt, Brace, Jovanovich, 1980). His most recent work is a series of studies of jury decision-making appearing in *Judicature, Crime and Delinquency, Trial Lawyers Quarterly,* and the *American Bar Foundation Research Journal.*

J. Robert Lilly is Professor of Criminology and Adjunct Professor of Law at Northern Kentucky University. His research interests include juvenile delinquency, house arrest and electronic monitoring, criminal justice in the People's Republic of China, the sociology of law, and criminological theory. He has published articles in a variety of journals and is co-author of *Criminological Theory: Its Context and Consequences* (1989) and *House Arrest and Correctional Policy.* He is also the Treasurer of the American Society of Criminology, and has been Visiting Professor, School of Law, Leicester Polytechnic and a Visiting Fellow, (1988), Centre for Criminological Research, University of Oxford, Oxford, England.

Thomas R. Maher is the Program Development Coordinator of the U.S. Probation Office, Eastern District of Pennsylvania. He received his master's degree in Community Systems Planning and Development fromthe Pennsylvania State University, where he was previously engaged in the evaluation of community correctional programs in the Pennsylvania Bureau of Correction.

Steven Maynard-Moody is Associate Professor of Public Administration in the Division of Government and Director of the Policy Analysis Program in the Institute for Public Policy and Business Research at the University of Kansas. Recent publications have appeared in *Public Administration Review* and *Administration and Society.*

Edmund McGarrell is Assistant Professor of Criminal Justice, Indiana University at Bloomington. He received his Ph.D. in Criminal Justice from the University at Albany, where he was Project Coordinator of the Utilization of Criminal Justice Statistics Project at the Hindelang Criminal Justice Research Center and a co-editor of the *Sourcebook of Criminal Justice Statistics*. His research interests focus on the process of change in the juvenile and criminal justice systems and the politics of crime and justice. He is the author of *Juvenile Correctional Reform: Two Decades of Policy and Procedural Change*.

Michael C. Musheno is Professor of Justice Studies, Political Science and Public Affairs at Arizona State University. He has co-authored four books on organization and policy and recent writings have appeared in *Contemporary Crises, Justice Quarterly* and *Work and Occupations*. Currently, he is co-editor of *Policy Studies Review* and is interested in applying rules of distributive justice to study the implementation of inner city, school reform policies.

E. Kim Nelson, both a lawyer and psychologist, is Professor Emeritus at the University of Southern California School of Public Administration, and he previously served as its Dean. Before coming to USC in 1958, he headed the Criminology program, University of British Columbia and was the first warden of the Haney Correctional Institution. He headed the Corrections Task Force in the President's Commission on Law Enforcement and Administration of Justice and was elected to the National Academy of Public Administration in 1972. He is the author of numerous books and articles on bureaucracy and criminal justice.

Dennis J. Palumbo is Professor of Justice Studies and Director of the Interdisciplinary Ph.D. Program in Justice Studies. His publications include *Public Policy in America* (1968) and *The Politics of Program Evaluation* (1987). He is co-editor of *Policy Studies Review* and working currently on a critique of the theory-driven approach to validity and also the politics of privatization.

Paul Stageberg is the Executive Director of the Vermont Criminal Justice Center. He has been associated with state criminal justice statistical programs for more than ten years, having directed the Iowa Statistical Analysis Center (SAC) prior to assuming his present position in Vermont. While directing the Iowa SAC, he served as Chairperson of the Criminal Justice Statistics Association, serving on the Association's Executive Committee for four years. He received his undergraduate training at Dartmouth College, and M.A. and Ph.D. degrees were received from the School of Criminal Justice, State University of New York at Albany.

Kevin N. Wright is currently Associate Professor of Political Science and Career and Inter-disciplinary Studies, and Director of the Center for Education and Social Analysis, State University of New York at Binghamton. He received his doctorate in Community Systems Planning and Development from the Pennsylvania State University. He has been a Kellogg Fellow and is now a Visiting Fellow at the National Institute of Justice for which he recently completed a project on correctional classification. Among his books are *Crime and Criminal Justice in a Declining Economy* and *The Great American Crime Myth*.